Lecture Notes in Artificial Inte

Edited by R. Goebel, J. Siekmann, and W. Wahlster

Subseries of Lecture Notes in Computer Science

Nadeem Jamali   Paul Scerri
Toshiharu Sugawara (Eds.)

Massively Multi-Agent Technology

AAMAS Workshops,
MMAS 2006, LSMAS 2006, and CCMMS 2007
Hakodate, Japan, May 9, 2006
Honolulu, HI, USA, May 15, 2007
Selected and Revised Papers

 Springer

Series Editors

Randy Goebel, University of Alberta, Edmonton, Canada
Jörg Siekmann, University of Saarland, Saarbrücken, Germany
Wolfgang Wahlster, DFKI and University of Saarland, Saarbrücken, Germany

Volume Editors

Nadeem Jamali
University of Saskatchewan
Department of Computer Science
176 Thorvaldson Building, 110 Science Place, Saskatoon, SK S7N 5C9, Canada
E-mail: n.jamali@usask.ca

Paul Scerri
Carnegie Mellon University
Robotics Institute
5000 Forbes Avenue Pittsburgh, PA 15213, USA
E-mail: pscerri@cs.cmu.edu

Toshiharu Sugawara
Waseda University
Graduate School of Science and Engineering
Department of Computer Science and Engineering
3-4-1 Okubo, Shinjuku, Tokyo 169-8555, Japan
E-mail: sugawara@isl.cs.waseda.ac.jp

Library of Congress Control Number: Applied for

CR Subject Classification (1998): I.2.11, I.2, C.2, H.3.4-5, H.5.3, I.6, J.1

LNCS Sublibrary: SL 7 – Artificial Intelligence

ISSN   0302-9743
ISBN-10   3-540-85448-7 Springer Berlin Heidelberg New York
ISBN-13   978-3-540-85448-7 Springer Berlin Heidelberg New York

Springer is a part of Springer Science+Business Media

springer.com

© Springer-Verlag Berlin Heidelberg 2008
Printed in Germany

Typesetting: Camera-ready by author, data conversion by Scientific Publishing Services, Chennai, India
Printed on acid-free paper   SPIN: 12512935   06/3180   5 4 3 2 1 0

Preface

With the proliferation of consumer devices, computation is becoming truly ubiquitous. Multi-agent systems hold the promise to enable utilization of these computational resources for ground-breaking new applications. However, as the number of agents involved in multi-agent computations rises, traditional approaches of building multi-agent systems fail to scale. Massively multi-agent systems address this challenge of scale. Massive, in this context, is meant to capture the complexity of such systems, which precludes decision making to focus on individual agents. Agents making decisions have to reduce the complexity of the space in which they must decide. The focus, therefore, is on the approaches to manage the complexity, implications of this abstraction, as well as on identifying ways of applying the paradigm to problems.

Papers appearing in this volume have been selected from three international workshops held in conjunction with the International Conferences on Autonomous Agents and Multiagent Systems (AAMAS) held in 2006 and 2007: First International Workshop on Coordination and Control in Massively Multi-agent Systems (CCMMS 2007); and the jointly held Second International Workshop on Massively Multi-agent Systems (MMAS 2006) and the Third International Workshop on Challenges in the Coordination of Large-Scale Multi-agent Systems (LSMAS 2006).

The papers in this collection, authored by some of the leading researchers in massively multi-agent systems, fall into four broad categories, presenting a snapshot of current research. Included are implementation strategies addressing coordination in the space of spatial and temporal distributed systems; approaches to deal with complexity to make decisions such as task allocation and team formation efficiently, by creating implicit or explicit encapsulations; and finally, a diverse range of applications to which these approaches may be applied, from large-scale agent-based simulations to managing different types of networks to image segmentation. As may be expected, a number of the authors have drawn inspiration from human and animal organizations evolved through time to scale naturally.

One of the invited submissions is a comic strip depicting an artist's vision of a future with massively multi-agent systems. This admittedly unconventional inclusion is intended less for editorializing the volume or capturing the breadth of research in the field, and more to illustrate the need to shift from reasoning about the individual to reasoning about the less countable. We hope that readers will find this to be a valuable and interesting addition.

March 2008

Nadeem Jamali
Paul Scerri
Toshiharu Sugawara

Organization

First International Workshop on Coordination and Control in Massively Multi-agent Systems, 2007

Program Co-chairs

Nadeem Jamali   University of Saskatchewan, Canada
Zahia Guessoum   Laboratoire d'Informatique de Paris 6, France
Gaku Yamamoto   IBM Research, Tokyo Research Laboratory, Japan

Program Committee

Gul Agha   University of Illinois at Urbana-Champaign, USA
Francois Bousquet   CIRAD, France
Dan Corkill   University of Massachusetts, USA
Keith Decker   University of Delaware, USA
Tom Holvoet   Katholieke Universiteit Leuven, Belgium
Toru Ishida   Department of Social Informatics, Kyoto University, Japan
WooYoung Kim   Intel Inc., USA
Yasuhiko Kitamura   Kwansei Gakuin University, Japan
Mark Klein   Massachusetts Institute of Technology, USA
Satoshi Kurihara   Osaka University, Japan
Victor Lesser   University of Massachusetts, USA
Jiming Liu   Hong Kong Baptist University, Hong Kong
Simone Ludwig   University of Saskatchewan, Canada
Ren Mandiau   Université de Valenciennes et du Hainaut-Cambrésis, France
Hideyuki Nakashima   Future University – Hakodate, Japan
Akihiko Ohsuga   University of Electro-Communications, Toshiba Corporation, Japan
Azuma Ohuchi   Hokkaido University, Japan
Ei-ichi Osawa   Future University, Japan
Van Parunak   NewVectors LLC, USA
Juan Pavn   Universidad Complutense Madrid, Spain
Norman M. Sadeh   School of Computer Science, Carnegie Mellon University, USA
Ichiro Satoh   National Institute of Informatics, Japan

Paul Scerri   Robotics Institute, Carnegie Mellon University,
                                 USA
Toshiharu Sugawara   Waseda University, Japan
Walt Truszkowski   NASA Goddard Space Flight Center, USA
Carlos Varela   Rensselaer Polytechnic Institute, USA
Regis Vincent   SRI International, USA
Jung-Jin Yang   The Catholic University of Korea, Korea

Second International Workshop on Massively Multi-agent Systems, 2006

Program Co-chairs

Toshiharu Sugawara   NTT Communication Science Laboratory,
                                 Japan
Alexis Drogoul   Laboratoire d'Informatique de Paris 6, France
Nadeem Jamali   University of Saskatchewan, Canada

Program Committee

Gul Agha   University of Illinois at Urbana-Champaign,
                                 USA
Robert Axtell   The Brookings Institution, USA
Dan Corkill   University of Massachusetts at Amherst, USA
Satoru Fujita   NEC Corporation, Japan
Les Gasser   University of Illinois at Urbana-Champaign,
                                 USA
Zahia Guessoum   Laboratoire d'Informatique de Paris 6, France
Koiti Hasida   Information Technology Research Institute,
                                 AIST, Japan
Toru Ishida   Department of Social Informatics, Kyoto
                                 University, Japan
WooYoung Kim   Motorola Inc., USA
Yasuhiko Kitamura   Kwansei Gakuin University, Japan
Kazuhiro Kuwabara   ATR Intelligent Robotics and Communication
                                 Laboratories, Japan
Satoshi Kurihara   Osaka University, Japan
Koichi Kurumatani   Information Technology Research Institute,
                                 AIST, Japan
Victor Lesser   University of Massachusetts at Amherst, USA
Jiming Liu   Hong Kong Baptist University, Hong Kong
Hideyuki Nakashima   Future University - Hakodate, Japan
Akihiko Ohsuga   Toshiba Corporation, Japan
Ei-ichi Osawa   Future University - Hakodate, Japan
Van Parunak   ALTARUM, Japan
Jeffrey S. Rosenschein   Hebrew University, Israel

Larry Rudolph	Massachusetts Institute of Technology, USA
Norman M. Sadeh	Carnegie Mellon University, USA
Ichiro Satoh	National Institute of Informatics, USA
Paul Scerri	Carnegie Mellon University, USA
Olivier Simonin	University of Belfort, France
Walt Truszkowski	NASA Goddard Space Flight Center, USA
Tom Wagner	DARPA, USA
Gaku Yamamoto	IBM Research, Tokyo Research Laboratory, Japan
Jung-Jin Yang	The Catholic University of Korea, Korea
Makoto Yokoo	Kyushu University, Japan
Franco Zambonelli	Universita di Modena e Reggio Emilia, Italy

Third International Workshop on Challenges in the Coordination of Large-Scale Multi-agent Systems, 2006

Program Co-chairs

Paul Scerri	Carnegie Mellon University, USA
Roger Mailler	Cornell University, USA
Regis Vincent	SRI International, USA

Program Committee

Robin Glinton	Robotics Institute, Carnegie Mellon University, USA
Mark Klein	Massachusetts Institute of Technology, USA
Charlie Ortiz	SRI International, USA
Marian Nodine	MCC, USA
Victor Lesser	University of Massachusetts, USA
Soundar Kumara	Pennsylvania State University, USA
Keith Decker	University of Delaware, USA
Adele Howe	Colorado State University, USA
Stephen Smith	Carnegie Mellon University, USA
Tom Wagner	DARPA, USA
Yang Xu	University of Pittsburgh, USA

Table of Contents

A Platform for Massive Agent-Based Simulation and Its Evaluation

Gaku Yamamoto, Hideki Tai, and Hideyuki Mizuta

IBM Research, Tokyo Research Lab. 1623-14, Shimotsuruma, Yamato-shi,
Kanagawa, Japan
{yamamoto,hidekit,e28193}@jp.ibm.com

Abstract. Agent based simulation (ABS) is efficient for the simulation of objects whose mathematical modeling is not easy. There are many studies on ABS and several frameworks for ABS have already been published. However, there are few frameworks that can enable agent-based simulation using large numbers of agents. We have been developing a Java-based platform for Massive Agent-Based Simulation (MABS) called "Zillions of Agents-based Simulation Environment" or ZASE. The purpose of ZASE is to develop MABS applications on multiple general computers such as PCs or workstations where they are connected with a high performance but generally available network such as gigabit Ethernet. ZASE is designed to host over millions of agents. In this paper, we introduce ZASE and explain the fundamental capabilities for MABS provided by ZASE. We evaluated ZASE for the agent-based auction simulation where the number of agents varied from ten to a million. The results indicate that the number of agents affects the final bid prices and their distributions. Performance measurement results on both an SMP computer environment and a multiple-computer environment are shown. The results in the both cases were about 3.5 millions of times of that agents handle messages in a second. The scalability ratio on the SMP computer and the multiple-computers environment were 78% and 85% respectively. Those scalability ratios are such good values for the simulations.

Keywords: Agent-based Simulation, Massively Multi-Agent Systems.

1 Introduction

Agent based simulation (ABS) is efficient for the simulation of objects whose mathematical modeling is not easy. There are many studies on ABS and several frameworks for ABS have already been published [1, 2, 3, 4, 5, 6]. However, there are few frameworks that can enable agent-based simulation using large numbers of agents. MASON provides a runtime for managing a large number of agents in a single process. SOARS aims to support a PC grid. Takahashi proposed a framework for managing large numbers of agents on BlueGene/L, which is an IBM multi-nodes supercomputer [7]. A simulation platform for managing large numbers of agents (we call such a simulation a Massive Agent-Based Simulation (MABS) in this paper) has not matured. We have been developing a Java-based platform for MABS. We called

N. Jamali et al. (Eds.): CCMMS 2007, MMAS 2006, LSMAS 2006, LNAI 5043, pp. 1–12, 2008.

the platform "Zillions of Agents-based Simulation Environment" or ZASE in this paper. The purpose of ZASE is to develop MABS applications on multiple general computers such as PCs or workstations where they are connected with a high performance but generally available network such as gigabit Ethernet. ZASE is designed to host over millions of agents. ZASE provides not only basic functions for ABS but also capabilities for MABS, such as a thread control mechanism, a mechanism for dividing a simulation environment into multiple simulation runtimes and agent runtimes, a mechanism for controlling simulation cycles shared among runtimes, an effective mechanism for exchanging runtimes, and a mechanism for monitoring performance indexes.

In this paper, we introduce ZASE and explain the fundamental capabilities for MABS provided by ZASE. We evaluated ZASE for the agent-based auction simulation described in [8]. In the evaluation, we varied the number of agents from ten to a million. This paper presents the simulation results. The results indicate that the number of agents affects the final bid prices and their distribution. Performance measurement results on both an SMP computer environment and in a multiple-computer environment are also shown.

An overview of ZASE is introduced in Section 2. We explain fundamental capabilities for MABS in Section 3. An agent-based simulation as an application example and its simulation results are described in Section 4. Performance measurement results are shown in Section 5. Related Work and Conclusions are covered in Sections 6 and 7, respectively.

2   Overview of ZASE

ZASE is a scalable platform for multi-agent simulations potentially using billions of agents. On the ZASE platform, a simulation environment is divided into multiple runtimes, and they are executed either on a single computer or on multiple computers. Each agent runtime provides a management mechanism for hundreds of thousands or millions of agents. ZASE interconnects multiple distributed processes by means of message communication and integrates them into a single system. ZASE provides simulation developers not only with some basic features such as simulation cycle management and logging but also various essential capabilities required for simulations which use millions of agents. Figure 1 is an outline of the architecture of ZASE.

ZASE is based on the agent model of [9]. Each agent of ZASE has internal states, handles messages and updates its own states as needed. Messages are sent by a simulator or by other agents. When a message object is delivered to an agent, a callback method of the agent is called. A returned message object will be sent back to the sender. The ZASE framework provides functions to create and to delete agents. Developers can add service objects to an agent runtime. Agents can look up the reference to a service object and can directly invoke methods of a service object. A service object also has functions similar to those of agents.

Messages are exchanged among agents, simulation runtimes, and agent runtimes. ZASE provides point-to-point messaging and multicast messaging.

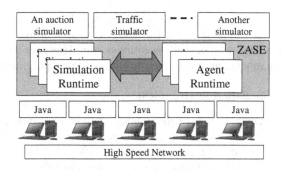

Fig. 1. Architectural overview of ZASE

3   Technologies for MABS

A MABS system requires a capability to manage large numbers of agents in a single runtime and a capability for linking multiple runtimes. Therefore, the following mechanisms are needed.

- A mechanism for managing many agents in a single runtime
- A mechanism for dividing an entire simulation system into multiple runtimes
- A messaging mechanism which can reduce the number of messages transferred among multiple runtimes
- A mechanism for load balancing

3.1   Runtime Technologies for Managing Large Numbers of Agents

The key issues of a runtime managing large numbers of agents are how to control memory and how to handle threads. We had already developed an agent swap in/out mechanism [9]. If a runtime does not have enough memory to load all of the agents, our mechanism will unload some agents when the mechanism tries to load other agents into memory. The mechanism is efficient for business applications such as Web applications. However, it is not efficient for simulation systems. Since agent loading and unloading invokes disk accesses, the system performance becomes bound to disk access speed. Since MABS applications require high performance, performance degradation from agent loading and unloading is not acceptable. ZASE is designed to use multiple computers without any need for loading and unloading of agents.

In contrast, the need for a thread control mechanism cannot be eliminated. A frequently used approach involves a thread pool mechanism [3, 9] and ZASE uses this approach, too. In a thread pool architecture, an agent does not own any threads. The threads are managed by a runtime and the runtime schedules a thread for an agent to use if the agent has messages that need processing. The number of threads is controlled by the runtime. Therefore, an agent in an environment based on the thread pool architecture must be "reactive." When a message is sent to an agent, the message is stored in a queue assigned to the destination agent. The runtime will assign a thread in the thread pool to the agent at an appropriate time. Then the agent will quickly handle the stored message, because the agent has to release the assigned thread as quickly as possible. It cannot wait for incoming message during message handling because that would cause deadlock of the entire system. However this is a restriction on the programming model, but it is not serious limitation for programmers.

3.2 Division of a Simulation Environment

A single runtime can manage tens of thousands or hundreds of thousands agents, but it cannot manage millions of agents. Therefore, we need a capability that allows dividing a simulation environment into multiple runtimes and communicating among them. Division of a simulation environment is designed to take into account the cost of communications between each simulation runtime and each agent runtime, the cost of communications among the simulation runtimes, the cost of communications among the agent runtimes, the load of each runtime, and the memory available to each runtime. Takahashi showed that communication cost especially affects on performance for an MABS [6]. In our pilot study of ZASE, the number of messages transferred between two Java virtual machines in a second averages 2,746.8 per CPU where the CPU is AMD Opteron^{TM} 2.19 GHz, so the average time for transferring a message is 364.1 microseconds. In contrast, the time for an agent to handle a message is only 1.16 microseconds described in later.

An efficient division depends on the application's characteristics. For the auction simulator described later in this paper, the full simulation environment can be divided into a single simulation runtime and multiple agent runtimes. The simulation runtime multicasts a bid request message to all of the agents in each simulation cycle. Each agent can reply with a message containing new bid price or zero if the agent does not bid. As described later, the bid request messages sent from the simulation runtime to the agents in an agent runtime can be aggregated into a single message. The reply messages from the agents in an agent runtime to the simulation runtime are aggregated. In contrast, Swarm-type simulations [2] are different from the auction simulation. The agents spread over a geographical environment. Each agent communicates with its neighbors. Since the communication pattern used in the simu-lation is not multicast messaging but point-to-point messaging, message aggregation is not possible. Therefore, the division approach used for the auction simulation is not suitable for Swarm-type simulations. However, a geographical environment can be divided into multiple cells. If the cells are not too small, then the amount of data transferred among the cells will not be too large. Therefore, an approach in which the entire simulation environment is divided geographically into multiple cells and each divided agent runtime is located with a divided part of the simulation runtime is appropriate.

The ZASE simulation environment consists of one or more simulation runtimes and one or more agent runtimes. ZASE provides a capability to divide an agent runtime into multiple agent runtimes and a capability to divide a simulation runtime. The divisions of an entire simulation environment can be configured in a configuration definition in ZASE. In order to support such division, the runtimes for the simulations and the agents are connected by message communication. A simulation runtime can send messages to agent runtimes as well as other simulation runtimes. ZASE also provides the capability which an agent moves between agent runtimes to support Swarm-type simulation.

3.3 Message Reduction Capability

Though the number of point-to-point messages cannot be reduced, multicast messages can be reduced. The *"MessageResolver"* and the *"Aggregator"* in ZASE reduce the number of messages transferred between a simulation runtime and an agent runtime.

A MessageResolver object determines the destination of a multicast message. It works in an agent runtime. When an agent runtime receives a multicast message, it calls a registered MessageResolver object. The object returns a collection which contains identifiers of destination agents.

When an agent handles a request-response multicast message, the agent will send a reply message. Therefore, many reply messages will be transferred from agent runtime to a simulation runtime. In an MABS, this causes substantial performance degradation. An application creates an Aggregator object in a simulation runtime and calls a method for sending a message with the Aggregator object. The Aggregator object will be sent to an agent runtime with a message. When an agent sends a reply message, the reply message will be handed to the Aggregator object prior to transferring the reply message to the simulation runtime. If the Aggregator object returns null, no reply message will be sent. If the Aggregator object returns an array of messages, the messages in the array will be transferred to the simulation runtime which sent the multicast request message.

For multicast messages, the number of messages transferred between a simulation runtime and an agent runtime can be reduced by using both MessageResolver and Aggregator.

3.4 Load Balancing

In general, there are two types of load balancing: static load balancing and dynamic load balancing. For the static approach, the load balancing strategy is determined according to statistical performance data and the system configuration is changed the next time the same simulation runs. The advantage of static load balancing is that the runtime mechanism is simple. For dynamic load balancing, the system configuration is dynamically changed to adapt to the changing load. This is very good for long running simulations, but the runtime mechanism for supporting dynamic load balancing will be complex. In ZASE, we used static load balancing because the mechanism is simple.

4 An Application Example: Agent-Based Auction Simulation

4.1 Application

We applied ZASE to the agent-based auction simulation described in [8]. In the simulation, there are two types of bidder agents: an EarlyBidder or a Sniper. An EarlyBidder starts bidding from when the auction opens and raises the bid price little by little. A Sniper bids at a high price once just before the auction closes. This is a Vickrey auction, so the auction model is that the agent bidding at the highest price wins, but only pays a price equal to the second highest bid. The auction simulator sends a bid request message as a request-response multicast to all EarlyBidders and

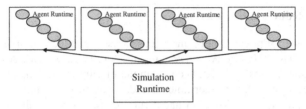

(a) An agent based auction simulation

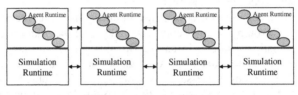

(b) Swarm-type simulation

Fig. 2. Examples of simulation environment divisions

Snipers in each simulation cycle. A bid request message contains the CitizenID of the bidder agent who bid at the highest price up to the current simulation cycle and the second highest bid. Each agent sends a reply message which contains a next bid price decided according to the agent's strategy. Algorithms to decide the next bid price for an EarlyBidder or a Sniper are included in [8].

In [8], the number of agents was fixed at ten. We ran six trials for 10^x agents, with x ranging from 1 to 6 (10 to 1,000,000 agents). The ratio of Snipers was set to 30%. We iterated the simulation for each number of agents one thousand times.

The simulation environment is divided into one simulation runtime and multiple agent runtimes as shown in Figure 2 (a). Each runtime runs on its own Java virtual machine. We used MessageResolver to send multicast messages from the simulation runtime to the agent runtimes. Therefore, only one message was sent from the simulation runtime to each of the agent runtimes in one simulation cycle. We also used an Aggregator object to aggregate reply messages from agents into a single message. There was one more internal message from an agent runtime to a simulation runtime. Therefore, there are two messages from an agent runtime to a simulation runtime in one simulation cycle.

4.2 Simulation Results

The graph of the final bid prices for each number of agents is shown in Figure 4. We can see that the final bid price increases as the number of agents increases and its incremental ratio gradually shrinks as the number of agents increases.

Figure 5 shows the distributions of the final bid prices. The distribution of the final bid price becomes more sharply peaked as the number of agents bidding increases.

In Figure 6, we see that even though the number of Snipers is always 30% of the total, the Snipers always have a better chance of winning than the EarlyBidders. The graph also shows that the gap between Snipers and EarlyBidders decreases as the number of bidders increases.

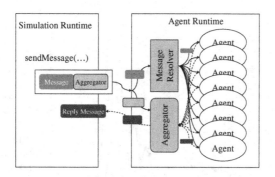

Fig. 3. MessageResolver and Aggregator

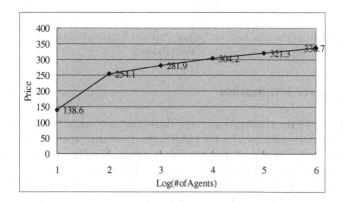

Fig. 4. Final bid prices

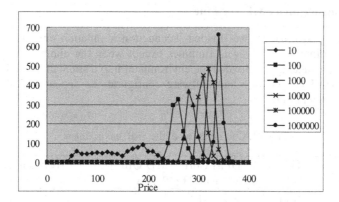

Fig. 5. Distribution of the final bid prices

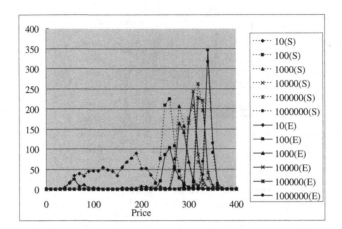

Fig. 6. Distributions of the final bids for Sniper wins and for EarlyBidder wins. The "(S)" after a number indicates Snipers, and "(E)" is for EarlyBidders.

5 Performance Evaluation

The performance of the simulations is significant for an MABS. However, there is no consensus on performance metrics for MABS. Here, we use "aps" (agents per second) which is the total number of times of that agents handle messages during the execution of a simulation divided by the total simulation time.

We measured the performance of the auction simulations for two system configurations: a symmetric multi-processor (SMP) machine (SMP) and a system with multiple computers.

5.1 Performance on a SMP Machine

To maximize performance, we divided the auction simulation environment into a simulation runtime and four agent runtimes except when the number of agents was only ten. For ten agents, we divided the environment into a simulation runtime and an agent runtime. The hardware and software configurations appear in Table 1. The results are shown in Figure 7.

Table 1. Configuration of the SMP environment

CPU	Dual Core AMD Opteron ™ Processor 275 2.19 GHz, 2-way
Memory	3.25 GB
OS	Microsoft Windows XP Professional Version 2002 SP2
Java	J2RE 1.4.2 IBM Windows 32 build cn142-20060421 (SR5)

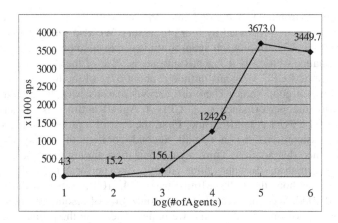

Fig. 7. Performance on the SMP environment

The performance for 100 agents is 15244 aps and peaks at 3,670,000 aps for 100,000 agents. The reason why performance is small when the number of agents is small is that the processing overhead for an agent processing a message is much smaller than the processing cost of the other processes such as message transfer. The processing cost of the other processes is constant and does not depend on the number of agents because we used MessageResolver and Aggregator. Therefore, the aps values are small as the number of agents is small.

Next, we measured effect of runtime division on the SMP computer. The result is shown in Figure 8.

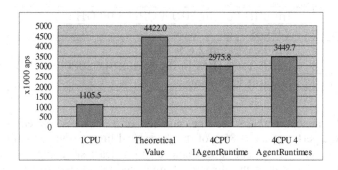

Fig. 8. Scalability on the SMP computer environment

The number of agents was fixed at one million. The reported value is the percent of aps compared to the "Theoretical Value" aps, which is four times of the value for "1 CPU." The label "1 CPU" means that the simulation environment would be divided into one simulation runtime and one agent runtime and both be processed by the same processor. The label "4 CPU 1 AgentRuntime" means that the simulation environment is divided into one simulation runtime and one agent runtimes and they were processed by four processors. The label "4 CPU 4 AgentRuntimes" means that the simulation environment is divided into one simulation runtime and four agent runtimes and they were processed by four processors. We also set the CPU affinity to each agent runtime. Therefore, each agent runtime is executed on a single CPU.

The performance of 4 CPU 4 AgentRuntimes is 78% of the theoretical value and the performance of 4 CPU 1 AgentRuntime is about 67% of the theoretical value. We think that 78% is a good value. There are various reasons why those values are not 100% and why the performance of 4 CPU 4 AgentRuntimes is higher than the performance of 4 CPU 1 AgentRuntime. First, the cost of a process in the simulation runtime and message transfer is not small. Second, conflicts of Java synchronization cause performance degradation. Third, synchronization among the processors' cache decreases performance. In our pilot study, the performance of 4 CPU 4 AgentRuntimes without the CPU affinity was 3,142,100 aps where the number of agents was 100,000. We can guess that synchronization of resources among multiple CPUs decreases performance. Although we believe these are the primary reasons, we need more investigation to confirm them.

5.2 Performance on Multiple Computers

In this section, we show the performance measurement results where the auction simulation is executed on multiple computers. The simulation environment is divided as described in the previous section. The configurations of hardware and software are shown in Table 2. All of the computers have the same configuration. The number of agents was set as one million. The number of computers varied from one to six. The measured results are shown in Figure 9.

Table 2. Configuration of each computer in the multiple-computer environment

CPU	Intel(R) Pentium(R) 4 CPU 3.00 GHz
Memory	2.0 GB
OS	Linux version 2.6.9-34.EL
Java	J2RE 1.4.2 IBM build cxia32142-20060824 (SR6)
Network	Gigabit Ethernet

The performance increases as the number of computers increases. For six computers, the performance is 85% of the theoretical limit (so the scalability ratio is 85%). We can say the system is scaleable up to at least six computers. However, performance is lower than the theoretical limit because there is overhead for the execution of the simulation runtime and for messaging. In addition, the time when an agent runtime finishes processing in a simulation cycle is not the same as when the other agent runtimes finish. Therefore, the total performance is somewhat lower than the theoretical limit.

This performance degradation might be serious on the environment where the number of computers is ten and above. If the number of agents is ten millions, the simulation time of the agent-based auction simulation described in this paper will be about 16 days. Although 3.5 millions aps is fast, we need more than ten computers to

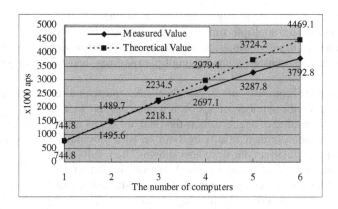

Fig. 9. Scalability on the multiple-computer environment

reduce the simulation time to a few days. Therefore, scalability will be significant if the number of computers is ten and above. We need more investigation on scalability in the multiple-computer environment.

6 Related Work

Many ABS simulation frameworks have been developed and shared among research communities, mainly for education and for shared research tools such as Swarm [2], AScape [5], and StarLogo [6]. Recent research trends along with practical applications for large scale simulations of the real economy and complex networks with power law distributions call for the development of new frameworks. For example, MASON (which can reproduce SugarScape social models on a lattice) provides a toolkit to execute high speed simulations with many agents in a single process. SOARS provides a common platform for education and realworld applications, and it is easy to develop simulation models with its GUI and also to visualize its simulation results. SOARS can utilize Grid computing and FPGAs for scalability and high speed execution. On the other hand, ZASE aims at performing even larger-scale simulations by managing many agents in each process and by combining the processes hierarchically.

Takahashi and Mizuta proposed an agent-based simulation framework on the supercomputer BlueGene/L [7]. In this framework, agents will be distributed on many nodes connected with a very high-speed network. Compared with these systems targeted for specific computing platforms, ZASE is a framework intended to construct a large-scale multiple-agent simulation system which can be executed on more general computing systems.

7 Conclusion

We described ZASE, is a platform for MABS, and described its fundamental capabilities for MABS applications. The capabilities are as follows: a mechanism for managing many agents in a single runtime, a mechanism for dividing an entire simulation system into multiple runtimes, a mechanism for controlling a simulation cycle spanning multiple runtimes, a messaging mechanism which can reduce the number of messages transferred among multiple runtimes, and a mechanism for load balancing.

To demonstrate the use of ZASE, we also presented agent-based auction simulations where the number of agents varied from ten to a million. The results indicate that the number of agents affects the final bid prices and their distributions.

Performance measurement results on both an SMP computer environment and a multiple-computer environment were also shown. The results were about 3.5 millions aps in the both cases. For the agent-based auction simulation, the scalability ratio is 78% on the SMP computer environment when a simulation environment is divided into one simulation runtime and four agent runtimes. The scalability ratio on the multiple-computer environment is 85% when six computers are used. Those scalability ratios are such good values for the simulations because ZASE has low costs for message transfers among runtimes, but we need more investigations into the reasons for the performance degradations in the multiple-computer environment.

Acknowledgments. This work was supported by "Strategic Information and Communications R&D Promotion Programme (SCOPE)" of the Ministry of Internal Affairs and Communications, Japan.

References

1. Repast, http://repast.sourceforge.net/
2. Minar, N., Burkhart, R., Langton, C., Askenazi, M.: The Swarm Simulation System: A Toolkit for Building Multi-Agent Simulations (1996), http://www.santafe.edu/projects/swarm/overview.ps
3. MASON, http://cs.gmu.edu/~eclab/projects/mason/
4. Deguchi, H., Tanuma, H., Shimizu, T.: SOARS: Spot Oriented Agent Role Simulator - Design and Agent Based Dynamical System. In: Proceedings of the Third International Workshop on Agent-based Approaches in Economic and Social Complex Systems, pp. 49–56 (2004)
5. Parker, M.T.: What is Ascape and why should you care? Journal of Artificial Societies and Social Simulation 4(1) (2001), http://www.soc.surrey.ac.uk/JASSS/4/1/5.html
6. StarLogo, http://education.mit.edu/starlogo/
7. Takahashi, T., Mizuta, H.: Efficient Agent-based Simulation Framework for Multi-Node Supercomputers. In: The proceedings of the 2006 Winter Simulation Conference (to appear, 2006)
8. Mizuta, H., Steiglitz, K.: Agent-Based Simulation of Dynamic On-Line Auctions. In: Proceedings of the 2000 Winter Simulation Conference, vol. 2, pp. 1772–1777 (2000)
9. Yamamoto, G.: Agent Server Technology for Managing Millions of Agents. In: International Workshop on Massively Multi-Agent Systems 2004, pp. 1–12. Springer, Heidelberg (2004)

Distributed Coordination of Massively Multi-Agent Systems

Nadeem Jamali and Xinghui Zhao

176 Thorvaldson Building, 110 Science Place
Department of Computer Science, University of Saskatchewan
Saskatoon, SK, S7N 5C9, Canada
{n.jamali,x.zhao}@agents.usask.ca

Abstract. Coordination is a key problem in massively multi-agent systems. As applications execute on distributed computer systems, coordination mechanisms must scalably bridge the network distance between where decisions are made and where they are to be enforced.

Our work on the CyberOrgs model[1] addresses this challenge by encapsulating distributed multi-agent computations along with computational and communication resources they require (for carrying out the application's functions as well as for coordinating actions of the agents) plus purchasing power represented by an amount of eCash for acquiring additional resources. Resources are defined in time and space, and are owned by cyberorgs. Resource ownership changes as a result of trade between cyberorgs.

Ownership of resources coupled with an effective and scalable control structure creates a predictable resource environment for multi-agent systems and their coordination mechanisms to execute in. Particularly, the coordination mechanism can reason about the possibility of successful coordinated action based on predictable communication and processing delays.

This paper presents our experience with hierarchical coordination of distributed processor resource for a system of cyberorgs internally distributed across a number of physical nodes. We demonstrate that encapsulation of network resources creates a scalable opportunity for reasoning about distributed coordinated action to support decision making.

Experimental results show that the CyberOrgs based resource-aware approach scalably increases opportunities for successful coordinated distributed actions involving up to 1500 agents (in much larger systems) by reducing the delay in determining their feasibility, as well as helps avoid attempts of infeasible actions.

1 Introduction

A multi-agent computation distributed over a network of computers faces a number of sources of uncertainty. When an agent's decision about the action to take next depends on actions taken by other agents, agents must contend with the uncertainty of other agents' actions. When agents are distributed across a number of physical nodes, both computational as well as resource uncertainties emerge.

---

[1] The model is referred to as *CyberOrgs*, and the entities are referred to as *cyberorgs*.

N. Jamali et al. (Eds.): CCMMS 2007, MMAS 2006, LSMAS 2006, LNAI 5043, pp. 13–27, 2008.
© Springer-Verlag Berlin Heidelberg 2008

Coordination between agents emerges as a key concern for achieving optimal results [5], especially when the computations are distributed [4]. It turns out that requirements of computation and coordination can be treated as separate and orthogonal dimensions of computing [6], leading to an opportunity for separating concerns and addressing coordination explicitly.

Coordination presents significant challenges when agents execute in a distributed environment with a number of processors connected by communication networks. Specifically, coordination mechanisms must bridge the network distance between the agents whose actions need coordination. This is a difficult problem because network delays are generally unpredictable, in large part because network performance goals are typically systemic, and applications are free to engage in virtually unrestricted competition for network resources, leading to resource dependencies. This is part of a more general problem. In *open systems* [7], when there are both *logical* and *resource* dependencies [5] between agents, resource dependencies sometimes lead to logical dependencies. Unrestricted competition for resources between agents collaborating to achieve a shared goal may hamper progress toward the goal. Coordinating resource access by agents is hence critical to reducing uncertainty and enabling agents to make control decisions for the best global performance [12].

In a bounded resource environment, if a computation can launch other computations as in a multi-agent system, it is difficult to control resource consumption reactively. If an erroneous or malicious agent begins creating other agents with similar characteristics, and if the only mechanism employed for identifying such agents is observation of their own threatening behavior, the rate of growth in the number of agents can be shown to be exponential. Intuitively, this means that irrespective of how conservatively the system purges misbehaving agents, so long as the mechanism relies solely on the observation of individuals' suspicious activity, by the time the system reacts, it may be too late: other agents have potentially been created about whose behavior the system will know nothing until it has observed them individually.

Our approach to controlling such behavior is by bounding resource consumption at the outset, and limiting resources available to a multi-agent computation. In this approach, each agent would receive a resource consumption allowance, which it could utilize or give a part of to other agents. Our work on the CyberOrgs model [9] uses this approach by encapsulating distributed multi-agent computations inside hierarchically organized resource encapsulations. [10] described scheduling strategies for efficiently controlling processor resource for a hierarchy of cyberorgs.

The difficulty of resource coordination is compounded by distribution of the resources. A number of approaches have been used to address the problem. [13] introduces a hierarchical scheduling scheme to apply a set of algorithms that enforce various processor usage constraints. Although the scheduling scheme is used for mobile programs, the interaction paradigm is client/server. Furthermore, network resource is not considered. [14] addresses network delay in the context of distributed scheduling, and provides approximation algorithms for distributed task scheduling problems. This approach focuses on specific global objectives of scheduling, such as minimizing the makespan, minimizing the average completion time, etc. Therefore, for a given network, they have specific ways to schedule the tasks, and no complex coordination is involved. Furthermore, the tasks are assumed to be unrelated, and there are no inter-actions or constraints between tasks. Coordination between distributed schedulers is considered in [3], for providing multimedia to multiple clients without conflict. Each scheduler is located on one computer and only has a partial view of the global schedule, requiring the schedulers to coordinate. Because the schedulers have the specific purpose of preventing access conflict, and the distributed clients do not interact with each other, coordination is simple.

Our approach is to carry out resource coordination within distributed resource encap-sulations provided by the CyberOrgs model. When a computation can rely on the avail-ability of computational and communication resources, its coordination mechanisms can be assisted by the knowledge in making decisions about coordinated distributed action. This improves overall efficiency by avoiding infeasible coordination attempts.

2   CyberOrgs

CyberOrgs [9] is a model for resource sharing in a network of self-interested peers, where application agents may migrate in order to avail themselves of remotely located peer-owned resources. CyberOrgs organize computational and communication resources as a market, and their control as a hierarchy. Specifically, each cyberorg encapsulates one or more multi-agent distributed computations (to be referred to as computations con-tained in the cyberorg), and an amount of *eCash* in a shared currency. Cyberorgs act as principals in a market of distributed resources, where they may use their *eCash* to buy or sell resources among themselves. A cyberorg may use the resources so acquired for carrying out its computations, or it may sell them to other cyberorgs.

CyberOrgs treat computational and communication resources as being defined in time and space. In other words, a resource is not available for use before or after the in-stant of time at which it exists. Sale of a resource is represented by a *contract* stipulating availability of resources to the buyer for a cost. Delivery of resources to cyberorgs is de-termined by a hierarchy of control decisions. In other words, cyberorg a makes control decisions required for delivery of resources purchased from it by cyberorg b; cyberorg b in turn makes control decisions determining how the resources purchased from it by cyberorg c are to be delivered. Cyberorgs may pre-pay to buy resources which will exist in the future. Cyberorg b may use the resources it owns only if the resources exist at a time when the cyberorg is being hosted by a. In other words, after signing a contract, a cyberorg must migrate to the prospective host cyberorg in order to avail itself of newly acquired resources. Additionally, if b migrates from a while it owns future resources through a contract with a, it cannot use those resources except if it eventually returns to a and if it possesses resources which have not yet expired.

The CyberOrgs model separates concerns of computations from those of the re-sources required to complete them.

We assume that computations are carried out by primitive agents called actors [1], and we represent the resource requirements of each computation by the sequence of resources required to complete it. *Ticks* serve as the unit of a consumable resource such as processor time. Every computation requires a certain number of ticks to complete.

Progress is represented by transitions occurring with introduction of ticks into the system. When a tick is inserted into a cyberorg, it may pass the tick on to a client cyberorg, use it for progressing on its system operations (such as for carrying out primitives) or on its actor computations. Whether a tick is passed on to a client or used locally depends on the contracts that the cyberorg has with its clients.

As illustrated in Figure 1, a new cyberorg is created by using the `isolate` primitive, which collects a set of actors, messages, and electronic cash, and creates a new cyberorg hosted locally.[2]

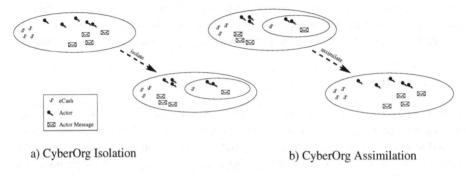

a) CyberOrg Isolation   b) CyberOrg Assimilation

Fig. 1. Creation and Absorption

A cyberorg disappears by assimilating into its host cyberorg using the `assimilate` primitive, relinquishing control of its contents to its host.

A cyberorg may realize that its resource requirements have exceeded what is available by its contract with the host cyberorg. This triggers its attempt to migrate. The tasks required for a cyberorg to migrate are: search (for a potential host), negotiate (a contract with potential hosts), and migrate (to a selected host).

A more formal treatment of the operational semantics may be found in [9].

3   Distributed Coordination

The way cyberorgs encapsulate computational and communication resources creates unique opportunities for scalable distributed coordination. Because delivery of network and processor resources to computations is controlled at a fine grain, idle resources are known precisely. As a result, communication and processing delays in carrying out fixed length system communications required for coordination become predictable. This - in turn - allows the distributed coordination components to reason about the feasibility of coordinated action based on good estimates of delays, and attempt only promising coordinated actions.

We use coordination of distributed processor resource delivery as an example of a distributed coordination problem. A single cyberorg may be internally distributed in that it may own computational resources at a number of physical nodes, on which its

---

[2] These primitives bear some similarity to those of the Interaction Abstract Machines (IAM) [2].

agents reside. Network resources would be additionally required by the cyberorg to enable communication between its distributed agents. Coordination decisions for the cyberorg may be local to a processor, or they may involve multiple processors. In cyberorg implementations, meta-agents called *facilitators* are responsible for making resource decisions for cyberorgs and interacting with the the processor scheduler to secure those resources. Facilitators, being agents, also require resources for executing. For a distributed cyberorg, there are as many facilitators as the number of processors on which parts of the cyberorg are located. One way of organizing these facilitators is to designate one of them as the *master* facilitator. The master facilitator maintains information required for global scheduling decisions; other *(slave)* facilitators maintain sufficient information for making local scheduling decisions autonomously. Coordinated global scheduling actions implementing cyberorg primitives offer a significant challenge in the context of unpredictable communication delays. However, cyberorgs allow communication as well as computation delays to be locally known based on knowledge of idle resources. If a master facilitator knows the global state of network and remote processor resource availability, it can use that information to predict delays in communicating with other facilitators, based on which it can determine whether a certain primitive operation can in fact be carried out. Particularly, assessment of feasibility of a coordinated action to implement a distributed cyberorg primitive can be made before actual communication with other facilitators regarding the specific operation.

3.1   Coordination Among Distributed Schedulers

Coordinated action involving a number of nodes hosting parts of a cyberorg requires prior agreement between the nodes. Therefore, there is a minimum delay between when the action is conceived and when it can actually be carried out at each of the nodes. If this delay can somehow be estimated, actions requested for sooner than this delay can be summarily dismissed. Given the benefit of knowledge of resource availability in a system of cyberorgs, here we attempt to calculate this delay.

Consider a 2-node (N_1, N_2) request for a coordinated primitive operation (Figure 2) to be carried out across the nodes hosting a cyberorg. The delay Δ in reaching agreement consists of several parts: D_1, the time delay from when the request is generated by the master facilitator on N_1 (or received from a slave) to when the request is scheduled to be processed on N_1; $P(a)$, the computational cost of analyzing the request and creating distributed tasks (where a is the total number of agents involved in the request); $C(N_1, N_2)$, the network delay in sending a message from N_1 to N_2[3]; D_2, the delay from when the request is received on N_2 to when the request is scheduled to be processed on N_2; $P(a_2)$, the computational cost of interpreting the request, and evaluating its feasibility on N_2 (where a_2 is the number of agents on node N_2 involved in the primitive); $C(N_2, N_1)$, the network delay of sending an acknowledgment back from N_2 to N_1; D_3, the delay from receipt of the acknowledgment to when the message is processed on N_1. Therefore, the coordination cost should be:

$$\Delta = D_1 + P(a) + (C(N_1, N_2) + D_2 + P(a_2) + C(N_2, N_1)) + D_3 \qquad (1)$$

---

[3] We assume that clocks are synchronized within some epsilon.

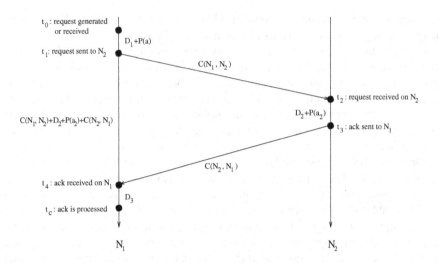

Fig. 2. Cost of coordination between distributed schedulers

The time delays D_1, D_2, and D_3 can be estimated from details of CPU scheduling. Figure 3 shows a scheduler cycle of length of l, where s is the time slice allocated to the facilitator responsible for processing the primitive request. If the primitive request arrives during the time interval $[T_0, T_s]$, probability of which is $p = \frac{s}{l}$, the delay would be 0; if the request arrives during $[T_s, T_l]$, probability of which is $1 - p$, the delay would be non-zero. In the latter case, we can take an average delay as an approximation: $\frac{l-s}{2}$. Therefore, the approximation of time delay between when a request is received on a node and when the request is scheduled is $(p \times 0) + (1 - p) \times \frac{l-s}{2}$, which is:

$$D = \frac{(l - s)^2}{2 \times l} \tag{2}$$

The communication costs $C(N_1, N_2)$ and $C(N_2, N_1)$ can be estimated from details of network resource control. In the current implementation, network control is message based, and the unit of control is a cyberorg. If r is the network flow rate (messages per second) that a cyberorg receives, the time delay of sending a message from an agent in this cyberorg would be $\frac{1}{r}$. Because a cyberorg processes its messages based on a first come first serve rule, the actual time delay of sending the specific primitive request would be $\frac{m+1}{r}$, where m is the number of messages to be processed before the message carrying the primitive request. After the message in question is processed, it

Fig. 3. A scheduler cycle

goes through the network link between N_1 and N_2, and the delay is determined by the bandwidth (b) of the network route and the size of the message (z).

$$C = \frac{m+1}{r} + \frac{z}{b} \tag{3}$$

For convenience, we use a function $f_{N_1,N_2}(r_{12}, m_{12}, z_{12}, b_{12})$ to refer to this network communication cost, where N_1, N_2 are names of nodes.

Using equations 1, 2, and 3, we obtain the approximation cost of achieving group agreement for a coordinated distributed action, which is:

$$\Delta = \frac{(l_1-s_1)^2}{l_1} + P(a) + f_{N_1,N_2}(r_{12}, m_{12}, z_{12}, b_{12}) + \frac{(l_2-s_2)^2}{2\times l_2} + P(a_2) \\ + f_{N_2,N_1}(r_{21}, m_{21}, z_{21}, b_{21}) \tag{4}$$

Although estimating $P(a)$ for a general purpose computation would be difficult, because we are dealing with special purpose computations for assessing feasibility of local actions, it is possible to obtain good estimates, so long as local resource availability is known, which is in this case.

Equation 4 illustrates the coordination cost of a 2-node distributed primitive. This can be generalized to the n-node case as follows:

$$\Delta = \frac{(l_1-s_1)^2}{l_1} + P(a) + max(f_{N_1,N_i}(r_{1i}, m_{1i}, z_{1i}, b_{1i}) + \frac{(l_i-s_i)^2}{2\times l_i} + P(a_i) \\ + f_{N_i,N_1}(r_{i1}, m_{i1}, z_{i1}, b_{i1})) \tag{5}$$

for i in $[2, n]$, where N_1 is the node with the master facilitator of the cyberorg. l_i is the length of scheduler cycle on node N_i, s_i is the time slice for which the facilitator agent on node N_i is scheduled, and $f_{N_i,N_j}()$ is the network communication cost of sending a message from N_i to N_j, which depends on network flow rate the cyberorg receives, number of messages to be processed before the specific message, the size of message to be sent, and the network bandwidth between the two nodes, for the path from N_i to N_j.

Optimistic Waits. The master facilitator of an internally distributed cyberorg is responsible for making global decisions for the cyberorg, while slave facilitators of the cyberorg are free to make local decisions involving agents on their own nodes.

A global decision of a master facilitator may require modifying resources available to agents spread across multiple nodes. In order to guarantee that the corresponding actions associated with an n-node global decision will be performed successfully by time t on all involved nodes, a master facilitator must generate the decision by time t', so that $t' < t - \Delta$. However, some savings can be obtained by eliminating some communication. Particularly, if the master facilitator can calculate Δ without explicitly communicating with the slave facilitators, it can send requests to the slave facilitators to carry out their parts of the global action, with the knowledge that all actions will indeed succeed. Although this is not possible in general, if the the master facilitator receives periodic updates from the slaves about their locally available resources, along with promises to maintain those availabilities for certain time intervals, the master may be able to assess feasibility of remote actions so long as the actions can be completed before expiration of the resource availability promises received from the slaves. Specifically, the master may send requests for coordinated actions, wait for the Δ it has independently calculated, and then assume that the actions successfully took place.

If the coordinated action itself is required in the future, the master facilitator may estimate the delay required for agreement on feasibility of the coordinated action in a similar manner. In this case, instead of waiting for each slave facilitator to acknowledge agreement, the master facilitator may be optimistic. In other words, the slave facilitators no longer have to send acknowledgments; they only report back if they find the action infeasible. The master facilitator, in turn, waits for Δ time for possible infeasibility reports, rather than wait for each slave to acknowledge. The master would be able to calculate this Δ if the promises of resource availability received from the slaves do not expire before the slaves finish assessing local feasibilities. Additionally, instead of waiting to be informed by the master of global agreement, the slaves too optimistically wait long enough to give the master a chance to inform them about possible cancellation of the coordinated action. Because the master facilitator calculates Δ prior to communication with the slaves, it can advise the slaves in the initial communication to wait for a period $\Delta + T_r$, where T_r is the time the master would take to report cancellation to them after it has received an infeasibility report from some slave. As a result, in the case when global agreement is achieved, all parties are ready for coordinated action after a delay of $\Delta + T_r$, without any need for communication after the initial requests from the master facilitator. Furthermore, any cancellations too are known by all parties by $\Delta + T_r$.

4   Implementing CyberOrgs

Our implementation of CyberOrgs is developed by extending Actor Architecture [11], which is a Java library and run-time system for supporting primitive agents. We extend Actor Architecture by adding two key components: *CyberOrg Manager* and *Scheduler Manager*.

A CyberOrgs platform is an instance of the system running on a single node, and CyberOrg Manager is the central component of each CyberOrgs platform. All resource control operations on a platform are carried out by the CyberOrg Manager. The results of such operations are sent to Scheduler Manager, which schedules all agents in the platform according to these results.

Algorithm 1 illustrates the algorithm of the Scheduler Manager. It schedules all agents in a loop, and each agent is executed for an amount of time which is allocated to it. After each scheduling cycle, the Scheduler Manager instructs the CyberOrg Manager to update the availability of resources for every cyberorg.

Network resources can be viewed as virtual links between two computers (or nodes) through which the connected computers may communicate with each other by exchanging data. Therefore, a cyberorg which owns network resources must be distributed between multiple nodes, which makes the cyberorg internally distributed.

An internally distributed cyberorg may own CPU resources on multiple nodes. The CPU resource on a single node can be represented using a tuple, (address, ticks, ticksRate). Here, address is the IP address of corresponding node, ticks is

Algorithm 1. Scheduling Algorithm

```
1:  while true do
2:     if the length of the thread queue > 1 then
3:        get the first element from the front of queue;
4:        if the first element is the start flag then
5:           tell CyberOrg Manager to refresh resource records for every cyberorg;
6:        else
7:           schedule the thread for required time slice;
8:           if the thread is alive then
9:              insert it at the end of the queue;
10:          end if
11:       end if
12:    else
13:       sleep for some time;
14:    end if
15: end while
```

the total processor time (in milliseconds) the cyberorg can receive, and `ticksRate` stipulates the rate at which CPU resources can be received (e.g., in milliseconds per second).

In this prototype implementation, communication is abstracted as exchange of asynchronous messages.[4] Accordingly, network resource availability is abstracted as fixed-sized messages that can be sent within a unit of time. Therefore, network resources can be represented by (`link`, `flow`, `flowRate`), where `link` identifies the the source and destination of the link, `flow` is the total number of messages that the cyberorg can send through the link, and `flowRate` specifies the number of messages that the cyberorg can send within a unit of time (e.g., per second), which indicates the rate of message flow.

To acquire these resources, a cyberorg negotiates contracts with other cyberorgs who own the resources. In addition to specifying the type of resource, a contract also stipulates the real-time interval (`time`) when the contract is in effect as well as the amount of eCash that the cyberorg must pay for the resources (`Price`). The price may be payable in full in advance (`type: 0`) or at regular intervals (`type: 1`).

Figure 4 shows an example contract. It applies to an internally distributed cyberorg with agents located on two nodes: N_1 with address "128.233.109.163" and N_2 with address "128.233.109.164". The cyberorg is to receive 1000 milliseconds of processor time on N_1, at the rate of 10 milliseconds per second, as well as 2000 milliseconds on N_2, at the rate of 5 milliseconds per second. In every second, the cyberorg is allowed to send 1 message from N_1 to N_2, and 2 messages from N_2 to N_1, as long as the total numbers of messages being sent in the two directions are less than 10 and 15 respectively. The contract takes effect at time 11:00:00 and expires at 17:05:30, and the

---

[4] Although we abstract over actual network bandwidth here by only accounting for messages, we have independently studied the effectiveness of fine-grained network resource control for cyberorgs. Preliminary results in this work show promise for effective fine grained control of network resource delivery [8].

CPU Resource
("128.233.109.163", 1000, 10)
("128.233.109.164", 2000, 5)
Network Resource
(("128.233.109.163", "128.233.109.164"), 10, 1)
(("128.233.109.164", "128.233.109.163"), 15, 2)
Time
11:00:00
17:05:30
Price
1
5

Fig. 4. An Example Contract: CPU resources on two nodes; network resources connecting the processors in both directions; start and end time for when the contract is in effect; price (1 is the type of payment and 5 is the price in units of eCash)

cyberorg receiving the resources must pay 5 units of eCash per second, and the payment is to be made in installments.

Network resource accounting and control are achieved by cooperation between the CyberOrg Manager and the Scheduler Manager. Before sending out a message, the platform checks with the CyberOrg Manager, which checks for availability of network resources for the cyberorg requiring it. If there is enough resource, the message is sent out, and the remaining amount of corresponding type of network resource (the specific link) in the cyberorg is decremented. Otherwise, if enough network resource is not available to the cyberorg, the message is blocked until the required network resource becomes available.

As shown in Figure 5, an internally distributed cyberorg has agents located on different nodes, representing distributed parts of the cyberorg. Each part has its own local facilitator agent, which is responsible for making local decisions and receiving requests for primitive operations involving local agents. The master facilitator maintains global information of the cyberorg, and it alone is responsible for enforcing global decisions of the cyberorg by coordinating its actions with those of other (slave) facilitators. By default, the master facilitator is the facilitator located at the node on which the cyberorg's creation is originally requested requested. Slave facilitators, by themselves, only possess the resource knowledge of their own parts of the cyberorg, and a slave facilitator can autonomously make local decisions involving agents in its own part of the cyberorg.

At an internally distributed cyberorg's creation time, an initial contract is generated by the creating cyberorg. This contract contains information about resources available to the new cyberorg and the terms of their availability. The runtime system can examine the contract to obtain IP addresses of involved nodes. The main part of cyberorg – which holds the master facilitator – is created first on the node where the creation is invoked. Afterwards, "create partial cyberorg" requests are sent to other involved nodes, where parts of the cyberorg with slave facilitators are created asynchronously. When the creation is completed on the slave nodes, "creation done" messages are sent to the master facilitator, completing the creation when all replies have been received.

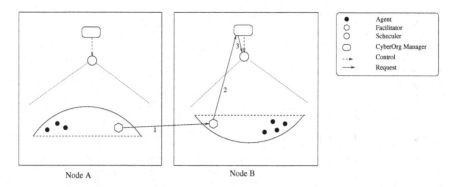

Fig. 5. Internally Distributed Cyberorg: master facilitator performs a primitive request on a remote node (1: master facilitator sends a primitive request to an involved slave facilitator on Node B; 2: slave facilitator tells CyberOrg Manager the requested primitive; 3: CyberOrg Manager controls Scheduler Manager to make changes on resource allocation)

A distributed primitive operation invoked by an internally distributed cyberorg is implemented through coordination between master and slave facilitators. The master facilitator is responsible for analyzing the primitive request, identifying the nodes involved, and sending instructions to relevant slave facilitators to carry out local actions. On completion of their actions, the slave facilitators send reply messages to the master facilitator, indicating success. When the last reply message reaches the master facilitator, the distributed primitive operation is completed.

5   Experimental Results

A number of experiments were carried out to assess the effectiveness and scalability of this approach. We collected results on delays in completing distributed schedule update tasks involving up to 1500 agents distributed over networks of two and three processors, representing systems with 10^4 or more total number of agents. Specifically, we compared the delay in achieving group agreement on feasibility of success or failure of global updates to distributed processor schedules, when using and not using our approach of exploiting predictability of resource availability in cyberorgs.

We applied the approach to an implementation of CyberOrgs. In the first set of experiments – in the absence of resource availability information – we used the pessimistic approach of requiring a series of acknowledgments confirming that the requested updates can indeed be carried out at the required time. In the second set, we relied on knowledge of available resources to (optimistically) assume that the requests have been satisfied unless a failure message is received by a deadline. The two alternatives are depicted in Figure 6. Note that this is not a fair comparison because in the resource unaware case, there is no guarantee of success of coordinated action until after the distributed actions have actually been attempted; nor is there a determination of failure, in which case a backtrack is required wherever the actions did happen to succeed. However, short of indicating that no comparison is possible, this appears to be a reasonable compromise.

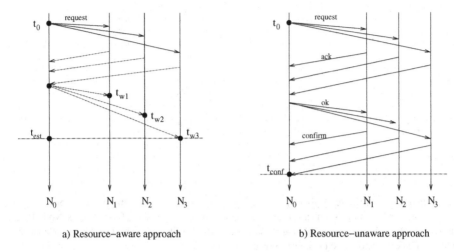

a) Resource–aware approach   b) Resource–unaware approach

Fig. 6. Resource-aware approach vs. resource-unaware approach. (a) Dotted lines represent possible infeasibility reports only received when some slave finds coordination action to be infeasible; otherwise, no communication is required. t_{est} is the time by which the master as well as all slaves can assume global agreement on coordinated action. (b) t_{conf} is the time by which master facilitator knows that all slaves received knowledge of global agreement in time to attempt coordinated action.

The distributed task in our experiments involved coordinated update of the distributed schedule being enforced for delivering processor resources to up to 1500 agents of a cyberorg distributed across three physical processors. Each processor hosted up to 500 agents, scheduled by a local scheduler. Global update requests were received by the cyberorg's master facilitator. We carried out experiments to see the delay between when a request is received by the master facilitator, and when all parties are ready for coordinated action to be carried.

In the resource-unaware approach, the master facilitator sends requests for local updates to the remote (slave) facilitators, which report to the master about likely success or failure based on information of local resource availability. Note that without access to this information about local resource availability and ability to assess feasibility of local action given such constraints, it would be meaningless to plan on coordination action short of actually attempting the action; therefore, we chose to allow the competing approach with this knowledge. Another alternative would have been to allow the slave facilitators to construct an updated schedule and then report their ability or inability to replace the active schedule at the requested time. In either case, if the master received positive reports from all slaves in good time, it could then instruct each slave to go ahead and carry out the actions. However, without knowledge of available network bandwidth, there is no way of ensuring that all slaves receive instructions to proceed with enough time remaining before the deadline to successfully carry them out. The last step, therefore, has to be each slave reporting back to the master, and the master sending instructions for backtracking in case the coordinated action has failed. We treat the point when the master knows of success or failure (not after backtracks have been completed) as the point when all parties are ready proceed. To summarize, despite significant communication, there is no way of predicting success of a coordinated action, short of actually attempting it, even when the distributed parties have the benefit of local resource information.

In comparison, in the resource-aware approach, slave facilitators periodically inform the master about their resource availability with promise of no change before an expiration time.[5] On receiving a new request for coordinated update, the master assesses its feasibility based on information about the updates as well as the slaves involved. Specifically, if some slaves will not have sufficient resources to carry out their parts of the coordinated action at the required time, the master summarily declines the request without ever communicating with the slaves; and if each slave will have sufficient resources to carry out the coordinated action at the required time, the master simply sends the requests, and prepares to carry out its part of the coordinated action at the required time. If, however, the master cannot make a summary determination – because the promises from slaves are expiring sooner than their resources would be required – the master assesses whether the slaves have enough resources to make local assessments of feasibility and report back by expirations of their promises. If so, the master sends the requests, and if no slave reports infeasibility by the time they should be able to (knowing their resources), the master assumes that all requests would be successful. If it does receive an infeasibility report, the action is cancelled. Of course, the slaves now have to be informed ahead of the time of coordinated action whether all slaves are ready to proceed. This too is handled optimistically. In the initial request, slaves are informed by the master about the time by which they would be informed if the coordinated action were not feasible for some of the slaves. The master calculates this time by adding to the time by which it would receive any infeasibility reports from the slaves, the time its own final report would take in arriving at the slaves, which in turn depends on the master's locally known network resource availability. The slaves too, in turn, guarantee that they will have enough processor resources to process the incoming final report from the master at the time when they were instructed to expect the report. If the slaves do not hear from the master by that time, they assume that all are ready for coordinated action, and proceed at the time, without requiring any information. In other words, if the coordinated action can be carried out by all parties at the required time, the only actual communication required is the requests sent by the master to all the slaves, following which, at specific times, each party knows that it is safe to proceed with the coordinated action at the required time. If the resource availability promises held by the master are not sufficient to know if the slaves can report infeasibility of their local actions reliably, the master simply waits for the next resource updates from the slaves.

Figure 7 compares the delays described above for the two approaches for coordinated update of schedules for up to 1500 agents distributed across two and three physical nodes. Note that the number of agents effected by an update would typically be a fraction of the total number of agents in the system, meaning that the results apply to systems of at least 10^4 agents. The graph shows that significant savings in the delay for global agreement on coordinated action are achieved using the CyberOrgs based

---

[5] It is assumed that the clocks are synchronized within some epsilon, which can be compensated by making conservative estimates.

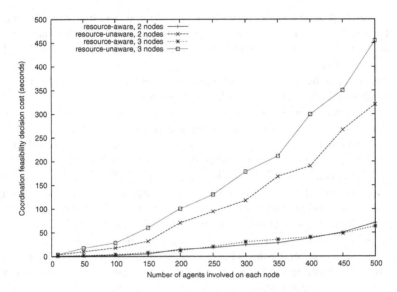

Fig. 7. Comparison of delay in achieving agreement on coordinated distributed schedule update

resource-aware approach. These savings are in addition to the savings achieve by avoiding attempting infeasible actions, which cannot be avoided in the resource-unaware approach, even when local resource information is available. Furthermore, the penalty of increasing number of agents linearly with the number of nodes is insignificant.

6   Conclusion

Coordinating distributed multi-agent systems is a difficult problem because of unpredictability of network and processor resource availability. Our approach of encapsulating computational and communication resources in cyberorgs creates execution environments for distributed multi-agent systems with predictable resource availability. Coordination mechanisms can exploit this predictability by computing expected delays and using the information in decision making.

In this paper, we have presented a prototype implementation of cyberorgs distributed over multiple processors. We have shared our experience with coordinating distributed scheduling of processor resources, where a number of local schedulers coordinate to enforce a global schedule for scheduling distributed processor resources.

Given the predictability of communication and processing delays in a system of cyberorgs, it is possible for the coordination mechanism to reason about whether or not a global scheduling change is feasible to enforce and to efficiently achieve global agreement on coordinated action. This achieves benefits in avoiding attempts of infeasible global actions. This approach also reduces communication overhead, which reduces the amount of time required in establishing that a coordinated distributed action is feasible, which in turn leads to enabling actions which would otherwise be infeasible. Experimental results show that the approach is effective and scalable.

Work is ongoing to extend these results to physical networks using approaches we have developed for reifying network resource control for systems of cyberorgs [8]. We are also examining the efficiency and effectiveness of this approach to support a wider class of coordination problems.

References

1. Agha, G.: Actors: A Model of Concurrent Computation in Distributed Systems. MIT Press, Cambridge (1986)
2. Andreoli, J.-M., Ciancarini, P., Pareschi, R.: Research Directions in Concurrent Object-Oriented Programming. In: Interaction Abstract Machines, pp. 257–280. MIT, Cambridge (1993)
3. Bolosky, W.J., Fitzgerald, R.P., Douceur, J.R.: Distributed schedule management in the tiger video fileserver. In: Symposium on Operating Systems Principles, pp. 212–223 (1997)
4. Bond, A., Gasser, L. (eds.): Readings in Distributed Artificial Intelligence. Morgan Kaufman Publishers, San Mateo, California (1988)
5. Gasser, L.: DAI approaches to coordination. In: Avouris, N.M., Gasser, L. (eds.) Distributed Artificial Intelligence: Theory and Praxis, pp. 31–51. Kluwer Academic, Dordrecht (1992)
6. Gelernter, D., Carriero, N.: Coordination languages and their significance. Communications of the ACM 35(2), 97–107 (1992)
7. Hewitt, C., de Jong, P.: Open systems. In: Mylopoulos, J., Schmidt, J.W., Brodie, M.L. (eds.) On Conceptual Modeling, ch. 6, pp. 147–164. Springer, Heidelberg (1984)
8. Jamali, N., Liu, C.: Reifying control of multi-owned network resources. In: Proc. of the IPDPS Intl Workshop on High-Level Parallel Programming Models and Supportive Environments (March 2007)
9. Jamali, N., Zhao, X.: Hierarchical resource usage coordination for large-scale multi-agent systems. In: Ishida, T., Gasser, L., Nakashima, H. (eds.) MMAS 2005. LNCS (LNAI), vol. 3446, pp. 40–54. Springer, Heidelberg (2005)
10. Jamali, N., Zhao, X.: A scalable approach to multi-agent resource acquisition and control. In: Proc. of the Fourth Intl. Joint Conf. on Autonomous Agents and Multi-Agent Systems (AAMAS 2005), Utrecht, pp. 868–875. ACM, New York (2005)
11. Jang, M., Agha, G.: On efficient communication and service agent discovery in multi-agent systems. In: Proc. of the International Workshop on Software Engineering for Large-Scale Multi-Agent Systems (SELMAS 2004), Edinburgh, pp. 27–33 (May 2004)
12. Jennings, N.R.: Commitments and conventions: The foundation of coordination in multi-agent systems. The Knowledge Engineering Review 8(3), 223–250 (1993)
13. Lal, M., Pandey, R.: A scheduling scheme for controlling allocation of CPU resources for mobile programs. J. AAMAS 5(1), 7–43 (2002)
14. Phillips, C., Stein, C., Wein, J.: Task scheduling in networks. SIAM Journal on Discrete Mathematics 10(4), 573–598 (1997)

Community-Based Load Balancing for Massively Multi-Agent Systems

Naoki Miyata and Toru Ishida

Department of Social Informatics
Kyoto University
Kyoto, 606-8501, Japan
miyata@ai.soc.i.kyoto-u.ac.jp, ishida@i.kyoto-u.ac.jp
http://www.ai.soc.i.kyoto-u.ac.jp

Abstract. Recently, large-scale distributed multiagent systems consisting of one million of agents have been developed. When agents are distributed among multiple servers, both the computational and interaction cost of servers must be considered when optimizing the performance of the entire system. Multiagent systems reflect the structure of social communities and artificial networks such as the Internet. Since the networks possess characteristics common to the 'small world' phenomenon, networks of agents on the systems can be considered as small worlds. In that case, communities, which are the sets of agents that frequently interact with each other, exist in the network. Most previous works evaluate agents one by one to select the most appropriate agent to be moved to a different server. If the networks of agents are highly clustered, previous works divide the communities when moving agents. Since agents in the same community often interact with each other, this division of communities increases the interaction cost among servers. We propose community-based load balancing (CLB), which evaluates the communities to select the most appropriate set of agents to be moved. We conducted simulations to evaluate our proposed method according to the network of agents. Our simulations show that when the clustering coefficient is close to 1.0, the interaction cost with CLB can be approximately 30% lower than that with previous works.

Keywords: mobile agents, scalability and performance issues: robustness, fault tolerance and dependability.

1   Introduction

Large-scale multiagent systems consisting of a million of agents are being researched and developed [1] [2]. For example, [3] proposed middleware for building large-scale multiagent systems and developed a multiagent system, the name of which is 'Goopas'. Multiagent simulations of large-scale traffic have been also conducted [4]. These systems lend themselves to the analogy that agents in the systems are equivalent to actors in reality such as humans or cars, and the

N. Jamali et al. (Eds.): CCMMS 2007, MMAS 2006, LSMAS 2006, LNAI 5043, pp. 28–42, 2008.

systems directly reflect structures of societies including networks of human relationships and artificial networks such as power grids.

For handling a massive number of agents, distributed multiagent systems consisting of multiple multiagent servers have been developed [5]. Distributed systems like this have been implemented on distributed OSs and workstation clusters, and their effectiveness has been proved [6]. Unfortunately, current methods of load balancing for distributed systems are inadequate when applied to multiagent systems. This is because the allocation of agents in a distributed multiagent system should be based on both the computation loads and the interaction costs of agents. In multiagent systems, agents interact with each other according to their needs. The interaction between agents residing on the same server (intra-server interaction) has lower cost than inter-server interaction. Interactions between agents residing on the same server (intra-server interaction) have lower cost than inter-server interactions. System performance can deteriorate if the amount of inter-server interaction increases.

One characteristic shared by the structures of human communities is the 'small world' phenomenon. 'Small world' networks are highly clustered and have small characteristic path lengths. For example, communities of people and artificial networks such as power grids and Internet have been described as being 'small worlds' [7]. The same could be said of multiagent systems since they reflect the features of the 'small worlds' seen in societies.

When networks of agents on multiagent systems exhibit the 'small world' phenomenon, communities, which are the sets of agents frequently interacting with each other, exist in the system. When a multiagent system has a community spread over different servers, previous approaches have high interaction costs. For example, when the server to which agents move doesn't have enough capacity to accept the community to which the agent belong, the community is split up. Since the agents which belong to the same community frequently interact with each other, dividing a community increase the interaction cost.

A goods distribution system developed as a multiagent system, manages a fleet of trucks carrying commodities. The agents correspond to trucks and delivery centers. Information regarding the estimated time of arrival and goods is exchanged between the agents. Since the interaction of agents reflects artificial networks such as the road network and delivery path, the network of agent interaction is a small world. The requirement for this system is to provide services to trucks and delivery centers with sufficient performance. When the time it takes for trucks to get through a path increases due to accidents or traffic jams, agents near the path have to recalculate the path or estimated time of arrival. It may overload some servers. For that reason, agents on an overloaded server should be moved to light loaded servers based on the computation and interaction cost.

This paper introduces the Community-based Load Balancing (CLB) algorithm, which allocates agents based on an evaluation of communities. Since allocating agents according to communities prevents their division, it can suppress the rise in the interaction cost.

2   Related Works

Some works in the mobile agent and multiagent areas describe techniques that allocate agents in a distributed environment. These techniques allocate agents based on the computation and interaction costs so as to optimize the performance of the system.

Several papers in the mobile agent area used techniques which decide agent migration so as to minimize the interaction cost incurred by the agent when doing a set of tasks. The techniques provided by Chia et al. [8] and Kawamura et al. [9] determine whether it is cheaper for an agent to either move to the server to eliminate inter-server message passing or remain with its original server and use inter-server message passing. Braun et al. [10] provided the technique of having agents forecast the message sizes and the computational load of the remote agent server based on historical information. They solve the migration decision problem at run-time to improve the performance of the entire system. Unfortunately, in multiagent systems where agents interact with each other according to their needs, moving an agent impacts the interaction cost of other agents. Therefore, we have to take into account the interaction cost of multiple agents in allocating agents.

Some works in the multiagent area allocate agents based on the computational and interaction costs among agents. The approach used in these works is to evaluate each agent. For example, Endo et al. [11] describes the technique of monitoring the interaction cost of agents and moving the agent whose interaction cost exceeds a threshold to the server with which the agent interacts most often. Comet [12] moves the agent with the lowest evaluation measure as calculated from both its computational and interaction costs from overloaded servers to light loaded servers. It repeats the procedure until the computation cost of the overloaded server falls under a threshold. Adaptive Actor Architecture (AAA) [13] evaluates agents based on the interaction cost to determine the server to which it should be moved. AAA creates group of agents, the determinate server of which is the same, and decides which group should be moved based on the evaluation of each group. These techniques decide which server agents should be moved to based on the evaluation of each agent. As described below, allocating sets of agents yields lower interaction costs that allocating them individually.

3   Agent Placement Problem

This section explains and formulates the agent placement problem.

3.1   Explanation of the Agent Placement Problem

In the multi-agent system assumed in this paper, n agents are distributed across a distributed multi-agent system composed of m agent servers connected via a network. We assume that all servers have identical capacity as do all connections among the servers. In this multi-agent system, agents interact with each other as demanded by the execution scenario. When an agent on one server interacts with another agent on another server, the servers exchange messages to achieve the interaction. We have to achieve the following two objectives to improve the efficiency of the system.

- Distribute the computational load of agents among servers
- Suppress the interaction cost among servers

First, it is necessary to distribute the computation load of agents among servers. Agents consume the calculation resources of the agent server that they reside on. Because an agent server has only limited resources, the performance of the server declines as the loads increase beyond the nominal capacity of the server. For that reason, if many agents are concentrated on one agent server, the server may become the bottleneck and system performance may decline.

Just as important, we have to suppress the interaction cost among agent servers. When an agent interacts with another agent on a different agent server, the agent servers have to exchange messages. Inter-agent interactions have higher costs than intra-agent interactions. To minimize the interaction cost, we have to place agents that frequently interact with each other on the same server.

3.2 Formulation of the Agent Placement Problem

In this section, we formulate the agent placement problem using the definitions of the notations given in Table 1. First, we define w_i as the computation cost incurred by the agents in providing service. w_i is the same whether the agents are executed on one server or distributed among multiple servers.

Next, we define $p(a_i, a_j)$ as the interaction cost incurred by an agent in exchanging messages with another agent. That is, when a_i and a_j residing on the same server exchange messages, $p(a_i, a_j) = 0$. $p(a_i, a_j)$ is the cost occured by distributing agents and depends on the allocation of agents.

The computation load of agent server m_i is defined as sum of the computational loads of agents residing on the server ($a_j \in A_i$), see Equation (1).

$$W(A_i) = \sum_{a_j \in A_i} w_j \tag{1}$$

To make the description simple, we define $P(A_i, A_j)$ in equation (2).

$$P(A_i, A_j) = \sum_{a_k \in A_i} \sum_{a_l \in A_j} p(a_k, a_l) \tag{2}$$

Assume that when agent server m_1 becomes overloaded, m_1 can move agents residing in m_1. We also assume that m_1 can acquire the following bits of information.

- computation load $W(A_i)(i = 1, 2, ..., m)$
- load $w_i(a_i \in A_1)$ of agents retained by m_1

Table 1. Notations

a_i	agent $i(i = 1, 2, ..., n)$
s_i	size of a_i (byte)
m_i	machine $i(i = 1, 2, ..., m)$
w_i	computation load of a_i (cycle/sec)
$W(A)$	computation load of agents A (cycle/sec)
$p(a_i, a_j)$	interaction cost between a_i and a_j (byte/sec)
$P(A_i, A_j)$	interaction cost between A_i and A_j (byte/sec)
A_i	set of agents residing on m_i before move
M_i	set of agents moving from m_1 to m_i
A'_i	set of agents residing on m_i after move
T_h	threshold of the computational cost of servers
t	interval of gathering computation cost

- interaction frequency $p(a_i, a_j)(a_i, a_j \in A_1)$ between the agents retained by m_1
- interaction frequency between the agent residing in m_1 and other servers

First, the overloaded server selects the destination servers $m_i(i = 2, ..., m)$ to which agents are moved. The overloaded server sends synchronizing requests to $m_i(i = 2, ..., m)$. This prevents multiple overloaded servers from moving agents to the same lightly loaded server at the same time. Even if there are many servers in the system, only the servers involved in the migration are synchronized. A similar process is used in Ishida at el. [14]. The destination servers $m_i(i = 2, ..., m)$ are the servers with which agents on m_1 interact. If a server included in $m_i(i = 2, ..., m)$ has been already synchronized, m_1 waits for termination of the synchronization state. When the sum of the capacity of the destination servers is larger than the excess computation cost of m_1. m_1 sends a synchronizing request to a new server which isn't synchronized by another overloaded server and has the largest capacities. That is, equations (3), (4) and (5) are satisfied as the initial condition.

$$W(A_1) > T_h \tag{3}$$

$$W(A_i) < T_h(i = 2, 3, ..., m) \tag{4}$$

$$\sum_{1 \leq i \leq m} W(A_i) < mT_h \tag{5}$$

Consider the movement of a set of agents from heavy loaded server m_1 to lightly loaded server $m_i(i = 2, 3, ..., m)$ to distribute the computation load among the servers. Note that M_i represents the set of agents moving from m_1 to m_i, A'_i represents the agents in m_i after the move as determined by equation (6).

$$A'_i = \begin{cases} A_1 \setminus \{\cup_{2 \leq j \leq m} M_j\} & (i = 1) \\ A_i \cup M_i & (i = 2, 3, ..., m) \end{cases} \tag{6}$$

Consequently, the object of distributing the loads of agents among agent servers and suppressing the amount of interaction among agent servers can be formulated as equation (7).

$$\min \sum_{1 \leq i < j \leq m} P(A'_i, A'_j) \ s.t. \ W(A'_i) < T_h \quad (i = 1, 2, ..., m) \quad (7)$$

When $|A_1|$ is large, it is difficult to find the set of agents that satisfies equation (7). This is because when the number of agents on s_1 is $|A_1|$, the number of combinations possible in a set is $m^{|A_1|}$. Our solution, an approximate algorithm, is introduced in Section 4.2.

4   Approximate Algorithms for Agent Placement Problem

This section describes Sequentially Load Balancing Algorithm (SLB), which allocates agents based on the evaluation of each agent, and Community-based Load Balancing Algorithm (CLB), which allocates agents based on the evaluation of each community.

4.1   Sequentially Load Balancing

SLB evaluates agents based on equation (8). The evaluation of an agent is the change in interaction cost achieved by moving the agent to the server that interacts with the agent the most among the servers that have enough spare capacity to accept the agent. In particular, the evaluation represents the change created by moving the agent to the appropriate server times t, which is the interval of gathering the computation cost, plus the interaction cost to exchange the agent between servers.

$$gain(a_i) = t \left\{ P(\{a_i\}, A_1) - \max_{\{m_k | w_i + W(A_k) < T_h\}} P(\{a_i\}, A_k) \right\} + s_i \quad (8)$$

The pseudo-code of SLB is shown in Algorithm1. SLB evaluates agents on a overloaded server one by one and then selects the agents with the least evaluation. SLB moves the agent to the server which the agent interacts most frequently. It repeats the above procedure until the load of the overloaded server becomes below the threshold and no agent can decrease the interaction cost by moving to another server.

4.2   Community-Based Load Balancing

In this subsection, we describe our algorithm to tackle the agent placement problem, Community-based Load Balancing (CLB), and the specifications of CLB.

Procedure of CLB. The evaluation metric of the set of agents A is $C(A)$, see equation (9). $C(A)$ is the change in interaction costs associated with moving A to the server that interacts with A the most among all servers that can accept A. In particular, $C(A)$ equals plus the change in interaction cost occurs with moving A to the appropriate server times t, interval of gathering computation

---

Algorithm 1. Sequentially Load Balancing

Require: $W(A_1) > T_h$, $W(A_i) < T_h (i = 2, 3, ..., p)$, $\sum W(A_i) < mT_h$

   loop
      $mingain \leftarrow \infty$
      for $a_i \in A_1$ **do**
         if $mingain > gain(a_i)$ **then**
            $mina \leftarrow a_i$
         end if
      end for
      if $W(A_1) < T_h$ and $mingain > 0$ **then**
         end loop
      end if
      move $mina$ to m_j $\left(P(a_i, A_j) = \max\limits_{\{m_k | w_i + W(A_k) < T_h\}} P(a_i, A_k) \right)$
   end loop

---

cost, plus the interaction cost invoked in exchanging A between servers. When no server can accept A, the evaluation of A is ∞.

$$
C(A) = \begin{cases} t\left\{ P(A, A_1 \setminus A) - \max\limits_{\{m_k | W(A_k \cup A) < T_h\}} P(A_k, A) \right\} + \sum\limits_{a_i \in A} s_i \\ \qquad (\exists m_i | W(A_i \cup A) < T_h) \\ \infty \qquad (\forall m_i | W(A_i \cup A) > T_h) \end{cases} \tag{9}
$$

The pseudo-code of CLB is shown in Algorithm2. Before explaining the CLB procedure, we define the procedure of OptimalSet. OptimalSet gets an agent as an argument and returns the optimal set of agents that should move with the agent and the destination server. CLB applies OptimalSet to each agent in the over-loaded server and moves the set of agents that has the lowest evaluation score, based on equation (9), to the server identified by OptimalSet. CLB repeats this procedure until the computation load of the server becomes smaller than the threshold and no community can decrease the interaction cost by moving to another server.

An agent is passed to OptimalSet and returns the optimal set of agents that should be moved with the agent and the destination server. It is, of course, computationally difficult to find the optimal set of agents given just the initial agent. Therefore, in this paper, we propose ApproximateOptimalSet to find an approximate solution of OptimalSet. The pseudo-code of ApproximateOptimalSet is shown in Algorithm 3. First, the set of agents to move, *Move* and the set of candidate agents to move, *Candidate* are defined. In the initial state, *Move* is an empty set and *Candidate* is a set consisting of the initial agent given as an argument. ApproximateOptimalSet repeats the below procedure until $W(Move)$ exceeds the capacity of any server. It selects the agent that has the lowest evaluation score as determined in (10) and adds it to *Move*.

$$
c(a_i) = C(Move \cup \{a_i\}) - C(Move) \tag{10}
$$

Algorithm 2. Community-based Load Balancing

Require: $W(A_1) > T_h$, $W(A_i) < T_h(i = 2, 3, ..., p)$, $\sum_{1 \le i \le m} W(A_i) < mT_h$

  loop
    $mincost \leftarrow \infty$
    $minM \leftarrow \phi$
    for $a_i \in A_1$ **do**
      $M, m \leftarrow OptimalSet(a_i)$
      if $mincost > C(M)$ **then**
        $mincost \leftarrow C(M)$
        $minM \leftarrow M$
        $tomachine \leftarrow m$
      end if
    end for
    if $W(A_1) \le T_h$ and $mincost \ge 0$ **then**
      end loop
    end if
    move $minM$ to $tomachine$
  end loop

Next, it adds agents that reside on the same server as a_i resides, that interact with a_i and that don't belong to *Candidate* or *Move*, to *Candidate*. Through this process, it selects the agent set that has the lowest $C(Move)$ and moves it to the server that interacts with *Move* the most among the servers that have enough capacity to accept *Move*.

Characteristic of CLB. This technique moves sets of agents rather than single agents. Moving sets of agents can decrease the interaction cost more than is possible by moving just single agents.

We give here an example based on Figure 1 and Figure 2: the change in the interaction cost for each agent is shown. Circles are agents and edges between circles are interaction costs between agents and their cost is 1.0. To make it simple, agents are so small that the interaction cost of exchanging agents between servers can be ignored. Here, server 'O' is over-loaded by three agents and server 'L' has capacity for four additional agents.

Figure 1 shows the case of allocating agents based on the evaluation of each agent. First, agents on Server 'O' are individually evaluated based on the computation and interaction costs. Next, 'O' moves agents 'a', 'b' and 'c' in the order corresponding to their evaluation. It leads to the right in the figure. The interaction cost after moving the agents increases from 4 to 6. Although moving agent 'a' triggers the movement of agents 'b' and 'c', the size of the community with which agent 'a' is actively interacting is larger than the spare capacity of the destination server. That is not all members of the community can move to the destination server. As the result, the divide of the community increases the interaction cost.

Figure 2 shows the case of allocating sets of agents. Here, communities 'A', 'B' and 'C' are identified. Moving community 'C' which has the least evaluation cost

---

Algorithm 3. ApproximateOptimalSet (a)

$Move \leftarrow \phi$
$Candidate \leftarrow \{a\}$
$minC \leftarrow \infty$
$minM \leftarrow Move$
repeat
    Select $a_i \in Candidate$ which has the least $c(a_i)$
    $Move \leftarrow Move \cup \{a_i\}$
    $Candidate \leftarrow Candidate \setminus \{a_i\}$
    if $minC > C(Move)$ **then**
        $minM \leftarrow Move$
        $minC \leftarrow C(Move)$
    end if
    Add $\{\ a_j | p(a_i, a_j) > 0 \wedge a_j \in A_1 \wedge a_j \notin Candidate \wedge a_j \notin Move\}$ to $Candidate$
until $W(Move \cup A_i) > T_h (i = 2, 3, ..., p)$
return $minM$ and $m_i \left(P(minM, A_i) = \max_{\{m_j | W(minM \cup A_j) < T_h\}} P(minM, A_j) \right)$

---

decreases the interaction cost from 4 to 2. Hence, the interaction cost reduction is maximized by considering/ moving sets of agents rather than individual agents.

Computation Time of CLB. Although CLB yields a larger decrease in the interaction cost than Comet, CLB has higher computational costs than SLB. c is the average number of agents which an agent interacts with. N is the number of agents moved to make the computation load of m_1 smaller than a threshold. In SLB, the computational effort of the evaluation of each agent is proportional to c and that of calculating the evaluation of all agents on over-loaded server is $O(c|A1|)$. Moving the agent that has the lowest evaluation score is repeated until the computation load of sm_1 is smaller than a threshold. Therefore, the computational effort of SLB is $O(Nc|A_i|)$.

Next, we estimate the computational effort of CLB. S represents the computational effort of OptimalSet. CLB applies OptimalSet to each agent and moves the set that has the minimum cost, so the computational effort of CLB is $O(NS|A_1|)$. Next, we estimate the computational effort of ApproximateOptimalSet which is an approximate algorithm of OptimalSet. The computational effort of evaluating an agent in $Candidate$ is $O(c)$. The procedure is repeated for each agent in $Candidate$. Assuming that the clustering coefficient is very large, the number of agents in $Candidate$ is $O(c)$, The computational effort of selecting the agent to be added to $Move$ is $O(c^2)$. The procedure is repeated until there is no server that can accept the community. Assuming that the procedure is iterated $O(N)$ times, the computational effort of ApproximateOptimalSet is $O(Nc^2)$. Therefore, the total computation cost of CLB is $O(N^2 c^2 |A_1|)$. Since $|A_i|$ and N increase with the number of agents, the computation cost of CLB increases exponentially.

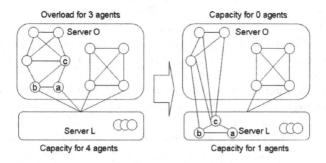

Fig. 1. Move agents based on evaluations of each agent

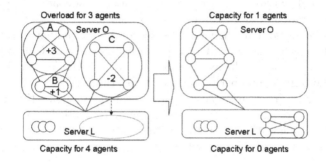

Fig. 2. Move agents based on evaluations of each community

5   Simulation of Placing Agents

This section describes a simulation conducted to test our technique. In this simulation, we apply two techniques to a distributed multi-agent system and record the change in interaction cost.

5.1   Simulation Settings

This simulation assumes a massively multi-agent system composed of multiple servers on a network. The interaction among agents on multiagent systems reflects the relationship among the people and something corresponding to agents. For example, in the goods distribution system, the interaction among truck agents and delivery center agents reflects the delivery paths and road network of the system. The artificial networks such as the delivery paths and road network are highly clustered and have small path lengths to make the system efficient. Therefore, we use the small world network [7] as the model of agent interaction.

In this simulation, each agent has 6 neighbors. That is, a_i interacts with $\{a_j | j = i \pm 3, i \pm 2, i \pm 1\}$. In building 'small world', we re-wired each edge at random with probability p. The interaction cost between agents is set to 0.1 KB/sec. There are no correlation between the computation cost and the interaction cost. That is, in the goods distribution system, agents don't interact every time a path or plan changes. They interact at fixed intervals to keep tab on each other. The agent size is set to a random number from 0KB to 1KB. During the simulation, agent size does not change. The interval of gathering computation cost, t, is set to 100 seconds.

The initial allocation of agents is based on the index of agents. The number of agents on a server, $l = n/m$, is set to the number of agents in the system divided by the number of servers. The agents on $s_i(i = 1, 2, ..., m)$ are $\{a_j|(i-1)l+1 \leq j \leq il\}$. In particular, agents are divided to allocate agents who interact with each other to the same server as much as possible. When the interaction network is 'regular', this allocation has the lowest interaction costs. This allocation is common to all algorithms used to move agents and the probability p used in building the 'small world'. After the simulation starts, the load w_i of each agent is updated by a random number in every iteration.

Because there are so many agents, if we set a random number as the load for each agent, there would not be any change in the server's load. Our solution was to set a random number as the average load for each server. We set the load for an agent to the random number from 0 to 1 times the average load of the server retaining the agent. The threshold of computation load equals the sum of the computation loads of agents times a constant number divided by the number of servers. In this simulation, the constant number was set at 1.1. Next, we applied each technique to the agent server whose load exceeded threshold T_h.

$$t \sum_{1 \leq i < j \leq n} p(a_i, a_j) + \sum_{a_i \text{ is moved}} s_i \qquad (11)$$

This simulation updates the computation load of agents iteratively, moves agents from over-loaded server to light-loaded server with each algorithm, and records the change in the total interaction cost in the system.

5.2   Interaction Cost Comparison

We compared the interaction cost of the system using CLB to one that used SLB. In this simulation, the number of agents, n, was set to 1,000. The number of servers, m, was set to 10. Figure 3 shows the results of this simulation when the probability, p, in building 'small world' was 0.001. The vertical axis is the sum of interaction costs among agent servers, defined in (11). The horizontal axis is the number of agents moved. To compare the interaction costs of stable systems, we plot the interaction cost between 150Ksec to 200Ksec. This graph shows the interaction cost in the simulation when applying SLB or CLB at every iteration.

As shown in Figure 3, CLB yields smaller interaction cost than SLB. The average interaction cost is 793.00 with CLB and 1077.36 with SLB.

Next, we changed the probability, p, used in building the 'small world' network from 0.0 to 1.0. The results are shown in Table 2. $Improve(p)$ is defined by

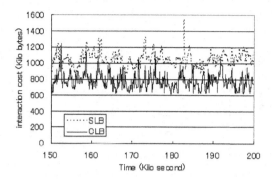

Fig. 3. The change of the interaction cost

Table 2. The average interaction cost and improvement

probability p	SLB	CLB	$Improve(p)$
0	1064.47	772.55	0.27423
0.0001	1075.23	768.86	0.28493
0.001	1077.36	793.00	0.26394
0.01	1280.87	1042.83	0.18583
0.1	3202.28	2924.78	0.08665
1.0	13884.98	13668.43	0.01559

Equation (12). It is the ratio of CLB to SLB in building the 'small world' with probability p.

$$Improve(p) = 1 - \frac{\text{Average interaction cost in CLB}}{\text{Average interaction cost in SLB}} \quad (12)$$

As shown in Table 2, the smaller p is, the larger the improvement in interaction costs is. Specifically, the interaction cost with CLB is about 18-28% smaller than that with SLB.

Figure 4 shows the relation between the clustering coefficient and the superiority of CLB over SLB. The horizontal axis plots p. The vertical axis is the ratio of CLB to SLB as defined by equation (12). As described in this graph, the larger the clustering coefficient of the network is, the larger the improvement is. As the clustering coefficient approaches 1.0, the superiority of CLB strengthens. This is attributed to the fact that since the number of communities on the source server increases with the clustering coefficient, the advantage of CLB becomes more obvious.

5.3 Computation Time Comparison

We compared the computation time of CLB to SLB while changing the number of servers and the number of agents per server. This simulation was implemented in Java and executed on a machine with 1.7GHz CPU and 512MB of memory.

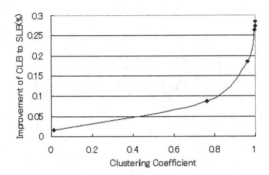

Fig. 4. Relation between clustering coefficient and improvement ratio

Table 3. The average computation time in changing the number of agents in a server

the number of servers	10	20	50	100
SLB (second)	0.01	0.03	0.08	0.21
CLB (second)	1.10	1.17	1.96	4.40

Table 4. Computation cost versus the number of agents per server

m/n	100	200	500	1000
SLB (second)	0.01	0.03	0.11	0.42
CLB (second)	1.10	9.77	343.56	7018.2

Table 3 shows the average computation time of the simulation in which the number of agents per server was set to 100 and the number of servers was set to 10, 20, 50, and 100. When the number of agents per server is constant, the computation time of CLB doesn't increase so much. This is because the computation cost mainly depends on the number of agents per server. As the number of servers increases, the computation time increases because CLB considers more destination servers when allocating agents.

Table 4 shows the average computation time of the simulation in which the number of servers was set to 10 and the number of agents per server was set to 100, 200, 500, and 1,000. As the number of agents per server increases, the computation time increases significantly; the computation cost of CLB increases because it depends on the cube of the number of agents per server.

6   Conclusion and Future Works

In this paper, we introduced a technique that allocates agents based on an assessment of both computation and interaction costs in massively multiagent systems. The main contributions of our research are as follows.

- provide Community-based Load Balancing, which allocates agents based on agent communities
- estimate the value of Sequential Load Balancing (SLB) and CLB following the behavior of networks constructed by agent interaction

Human communities and artificial networks replicate the small world phenomenon. The networks of agents on the multiagent systems that reflect the networks also evidence the small world phenomenon. Communities, which are sets of agents that frequently interact with each other, exist in the network because the interaction network is highly clustered. Allocating agents based on the evaluation of each agent causes the division of communities which increases the interaction cost of the entire system. CLB allocates agents based on evaluations of each community, and so can allocate agents with lower interaction costs.

We conducted simulations to estimate the impact of SLB and CLB. When the clustering coefficient of the agent network is large, a preliminary simulation result showed that CLB yields smaller interaction costs (about 30% smaller) than SLB. This is attributed to the fact that more communities exists on the source servers as the clustering coefficient becomes large.

One of the problems with CLB is its computation cost. As the number of agents per server increases, the computation cost of CLB strongly increases. Therefore, we have to improve CLB to decide the allocation in practical time.

Acknowledgments

This research was partially supported by Global COE Program "Informatics Education and Research Center for Knowledge-Circulating Society" and a Grant-in-Aid for Scientific Research (A) (18200009, 2006-2008) from Japan Society for the Promotion of Science (JSPS).

References

1. Gasser, L., Kakugawa, K.: Mace3j: fast flexible distributed simulation of large, large-grain multi-agent systems. In: AAMAS 2002: Proceedings of the first international joint conference on Autonomous agents and multiagent systems, pp. 745–752. ACM Press, New York (2002)
2. Ishida, T., Gasser, L., Nakashima, H. (eds.): MMAS 2005. LNCS (LNAI), vol. 3446. Springer, Heidelberg (2005)
3. Koyanagi, T., Kobayashi, Y., Miyagi, S., Yamamoto, G.: Agent server for a location-aware personalized notification service. In: [2], pp. 224–238
4. Balmer, M., Cetin, N., Nagel, K., Raney, B.: Towards truly agent-based traffic and mobility simulations. In: AAMAS 2004: Proceedings of the Third International Joint Conference on Autonomous Agents and Multiagent Systems, pp. 60–67. IEEE Computer Society, Washington, DC, USA (2004)
5. Yamamoto, G., Tai, H., Mizuta, H.: A platform for massive agent-based simulation and its evaluation. In: AAMAS 2007: Proceedings of the sixth international joint conference on Autonomous agents and multiagent systems, pp. 900–902. ACM Press, New York (2007)

6. Ahmad, I., Ghafoor, A.: Semi-distributed load balancing for massively parallel multicomputer systems. IEEE Transactions on Software Engineering 17(10), 987–1004 (1991)
7. Watts, D.J., Strogatz, S.H.: Collective dynamics of 'small-world' networks. Nature 393(6684), 440–442 (1998)
8. Chia, T.H., Kannapan, S.: Strategically mobile agents. In: Rothermel, K., Popescu-Zeletin, R. (eds.) MA 1997. LNCS, vol. 1219, pp. 149–161. Springer, Heidelberg (1997)
9. Kawamura, T., Joseph, S., Ohsuya, A., Honiden, S.: Quantitative evaluation of pairwise interactions between agents. In: Kotz, D., Mattern, F. (eds.) MA 2000, ASA/MA 2000, and ASA 2000. LNCS, vol. 1882, pp. 192–205. Springer, Heidelberg (2000)
10. Schlegel, T., Braun, P., Kowalczyk, R.: Towards autonomous mobile agents with emergent migration behaviour. In: AAMAS 2006: Proceedings of the fifth international joint conference on Autonomous agents and multiagent systems, pp. 585–592. ACM Press, New York (2006)
11. Endo, H., Noto, M., Toyoshima, H.: Quantitative evaluation of communication traffic of mobile agents in distributed constraint satisfaction model. In: SMC (4), pp. 3852–3857. IEEE, Los Alamitos (2004)
12. Chow, K.P., Kwok, Y.K.: On load balancing for distributed multiagent computing. IEEE Transactions on Parallel and Distributed Systems 13(8), 787–801 (2002)
13. Jang, M.W., Agha, G.: Agent framework services to reduce agent communication overhead in large-scale agent-based simulations. In: Simulation Modelling Practice and Theory (October, 2005)
14. Ishida, T., Gasser, L., Yokoo, M.: Organization self-design of distributed production systems. IEEE Transactions on Knowledge and Data Engineering 4(2), 123–134 (1992)

A Study of Coordinated Dynamic Market-Based Task Assignment in Massively Multi-Agent Systems[*]

MyungJoo Ham and Gul Agha

Open Systems Laboratory
University of Illinois at Urbana-Champaign, Urbana IL 61801, USA
{ham1,agha}@cs.uiuc.edu

Abstract. This paper studies market-based mechanisms for *coordinated dynamic task assignment* in large-scale agent systems carrying out *search and rescue missions*. Specifically, the effect of different auction mechanisms and swapping are studied. The paper describes results from a large number of simulations. The information available to agents and their bidding strategies are used as simulation parameters. The simulations provide insight about the interaction between the strategy of individual agents and the market mechanism. Performance is evaluated using several metrics. Some of the results include: limiting information may improve performance, different utility functions may affect the performance in non-uniform ways, and swapping may help improve the efficiency of assignments in dynamic environments.

1 Introduction

A number of physical agents are being developed such as robots, small unmanned aerial vehicles (micro-UAVs), and unmanned underwater vehicles (UUVs). Such mobile physical agents will be useful for many applications including surveillance, search and rescue, and mine sweeping. This paper focuses on a two dimensional search and rescue (SR) problem involving pursuer robots and mobile targets. In SR, we assume that the number of tasks generally exceeds the number of agents; there may be possible targets in an uncovered area, and the area can be large, allowing for many targets. This assumption requires each robot agent to serve multiple tasks. Moreover, we assume that each task requires a different number of multiple robot agents; this simplifies heterogenous aspects of target requirements–different types and load of services may be required–and robot agent capabilities. Thus, efficient methods, which enable coordination between the robot agents, are required. Note that the SR problem is computationally intractable. Even a simplified version of the SR problem, namely, the vehicle routing problem (VRP or truck dispatching problem) is NP-hard [2]. For example, we experiment a case, called "Dense", that has more than 10^{500} possible assignments for initial tasks. Thus, a centralized computation of the global optimum is not feasible.

To address the SR problem, *auctions* and *swapping*–both fully *distributed* and *asynchronous*–are investigated. Asynchronous auctions have a reasonable computational and message complexity. By using concurrent and asynchronous auctions, each with

---

[*] This is a revision and extension of [1].

N. Jamali et al. (Eds.): CCMMS 2007, MMAS 2006, LSMAS 2006, LNAI 5043, pp. 43–63, 2008.
© Springer-Verlag Berlin Heidelberg 2008

a limited number of participants, we can reduce the complexity. The computation and message complexity of each auction grows linearly in the number of the participating robot agents and tasks. If communication and sensing ranges are bounded, the mechanisms require constant time for each round of auctions. If the ranges are not bounded, $O(n)$ computation time is required, where n is the number of target and robot agents combined. However, note that such auctions yield sub-optimal assignments [3].

Our previous work [4, 5], and other similar work [6, 7, 8, 9] experimented the multi-agent coordination problem in small-scale. However, small-scale experiments, regardless of whether using software simulations or physical simulations, can be easily biased by specific experimental parameters. In small-scale simulations, only a few auctions are executed and each auction result is affected significantly by the initial positions of robot agents and tasks, not the mechanisms. On the other hand, in large-scale simulations, a large number of auctions are executed and the effects of initial positions are reduced. Besides, smaller-scale simulations have larger variance in the experimental results. Another limitation is that the scalability of mechanisms is not established.

These limitations motivate us to run large-scale simulations in which the strategies and experimental parameters, such as the density of agents, positions of agents, and utility and requirements of target agents, are varied. Different auction mechanisms (*forward, reverse, forward and reverse, forward and reverse with sealed bids*), *non-cooperative heuristic method* (N/C), which resembles *swarm intelligence* [10], as a control, and swapping are experimented. Different bidding strategies, which weigh the utility, cost, and popularity of a target, are used. The simulator will be available on our research group's web site: http://osl.cs.uiuc.edu.

Experimental parameters such as the robot density, sensing and communication ranges, and initial positions of robots are varied in order to test the robustness and characteristics of the mechanisms in different environments. Varying robot density and initial positions can show the adaptability and the generality of the mechanisms. Obviously, limiting sensing and communication ranges can provide more scalability in real applications because the cost of broadcasting to all the agents can be high. Perhaps more surprisingly, the results suggest that limiting sensing and communication ranges improves the performance.

In theory, assuming a fixed order of synchronized auctions and static utilities, different auction mechanisms (forward, reverse, and forward/reverse) would yield the same results. However, in this paper, these simplifying assumptions are not met and it is easy to see how different auction mechanisms may produce different results. The results suggest that sealed-bid auctions based on forward/reverse auctions perform better than the others (except for the number of messages). Forward/reverse auctions perform better than the rest of the auctions and result in a lower number of messages. The results also suggest that reverse auctions do not have any merit over forward auctions, if reverse auctions are used exclusively.

Two robots may swap tasks in order to reduce the costs for each of them–the side payments are not considered. Dynamicity of the environment and asynchrony of auctions create the need for swapping. The results suggest that swapping can improve performance although swapping causes additional costs.

The rest of this paper is organized as follows. Section 2 describes previous research on multi-agent coordinations. Section 3 describes the coordination methods studied. Section 4 describes the simulation results. Section 5 analyzes these results. Finally, Section 6 discusses the conclusions and directions for future research.

2   Related Work

A number of distributed approaches have been proposed although, in principle, a centralized approach can provide results that are equal to or better than those of a distributed approach. However, a centralized approach has a number of drawbacks: a single point of failure and the need for connected networks. More critically, a centralized approach is not scalable. Some of distributed approaches use non-market based mechanisms; i.e., swarm intelligence [10], which does not involve negotiations and communication, thus, being extremely scalable. However, it lacks knowledge about the other agents, which makes it very difficult to accomplish a task that needs multiple agents.

To address this problem, many distributed market based multi-robot coordination mechanisms have been proposed. Some of these are offline algorithms; i.e., [6]. Obviously, offline algorithms cannot adapt to dynamic environments. Other research has studied online mechanisms [7, 8].

Prior work has used different degrees of dynamicity of the environment; tasks may be static, passive, or dynamic. *Static tasks* do not change their utility or cost: [7, 11, 6]. *Passive tasks* are modified only by the action of robot agents: [8]. *Dynamic tasks* change their utilities or costs by themselves; i.e., tasks are mobile [4]. When tasks are dynamic, *preemption* (to change an agent's attention) and *adaptation* in real-time become important in order to let agents respond to the change of a dynamic environment. In this paper, as in our previous work [4], we focus on a dynamic environment.

A number of studies have assumed that a task requires only one agent [7, 8, 6]. In this case, coordination of multiple robot agents for each task is not required. However, coordination for each task is required if a task needs multiple agents. Some researchers have studied cases where coordination between agents for each task is beneficial, but not mandatory and synchronization between agents is not required; i.e., [9]. On the other hand, in [8], synchronization is required although the system serves only a single task. Our problem requires both assignment of multiple tasks to agents and synchronized coordination between several agents to complete any given single task. Distributed multi-robot coordination research related to robot agents that roam a geographic area has been based on small scale experiments: single task [8], less than 10 agents [9, 7, 4], and around 10 robot agents [6, 5].

The previous work [4] proposed forward/reverse auctions and swapping for task allocation with physical agents in dynamic environment. However, the main weakness is that the experiments were not sufficient–only one execution was carried out for each coordination method in small-scale experiments. Moreover, the effect of bidding strategies was not examined. In this paper, the problem size is extended to show the scalability of the algorithm (up to 250 robots and 750 targets), develop and test various mechanisms, and experiment more concretely with more performance metrics and various experimental parameters. For parameters of the algorithms, the values similar to those in [5], which are in turn based on [4], and partly on other analysis and estimates, are used.

3   Methods

This paper makes a number of simplifying assumptions for robot agents. All agents are located and move unobstructed on a bounded rectangular Euclidean plane. It is further assumed that the robot agents in a given simulation are homogeneous–i.e., all the robot agents use the same strategy. Robot agents can observe every target within its sensing range, and robots notify other robots in their communication range about the observed targets. However, robot agents do not relay information from other agents. Targets move around with some predefined patterns. However, robots do not try to predict the patterns; instead they use the current heading and speed of a target to track it. Although other algorithms–better roaming algorithms, optimal serving positions for targets, better collision/obstruction avoidance algorithms, and prediction of other agents' movement–may improve performance, they are not studied, as their benefits are likely to be marginal and our purpose is to focus on the effect of global mechanisms for coordination.

The following assumptions about targets are made to simulate the S/R problem, where each mobile rescuee needs multiple rescuers to be located near the rescuee at the same time to rescue the rescuee and the rescuee will stop moving once a rescuer approaches to the rescuee. Thus, in order to be served, a target t requires multiple dedicated robots ($\geq req_t > 1$) to be present nearby ($\leq 0.2m$) at the same time, where req_t is the requirement of t. t distributes its utility $util_t$ evenly to the robots that serve it, i.e., it provides $util_t/req_t$ to each robot, where $util_t$ is the utility of t. If the number of robots exceeds req_t, only the first req_t robot agents receive the payoff.

Each instance of the problem is defined as a *mission*; a mission is complete when 90% of the target agents have been served. In the previous work [4, 5], a mission is complete when every target agent has been served. However, in large-scale experiments, it may take too much time to search the last few targets and distort results if the sensing and communication ranges are bounded; the search for the last few targets, which takes completely random length of time, has often dominated the mission time with preliminary experiments. Therefore, in order to compare bounded sensing and communication ranges and unbounded ranges, we use the 90% metric for every experiment. The number of targets is assumed to be large enough for each robot to serve multiple times. Thus, a robot may participate in several auctions in the course of a mission.

3.1   Coordination Methods

Several methods for coordination between agents, including non-interactive methods, auctions, and swapping, are studied. The first two methods, N/C and forward auction, which are used as controls in the experiments, are the basic methods of non-market-based and market-based coordination mechanisms. N/C is a straight-forward approach without communication. Forward auction is the basic form of auction and it is the most frequently used auction in the problem domain. Thus, we use N/C and forward auction as controls. Reverse auction is the opposite approach to forward auction. Forward/reverse auction is supposed to accelerate the auction process by converging prices in both ways: forward and reverse. Then, sealed-bid is added to forward/reverse auction in order to see the effect of price considerations in agent systems where agents do not pay the price.

Non-cooperative Heuristic Method (N/C). With N/C, a robot agent chooses the target agent that has the largest expected benefit for the robot. The expected profit of N/C is $util_t/req_t - cost_{NC}(r,t)$, where $cost_{NC}(r,t)$ is the cost for robot agent r to serve target t. The cost is the distance and pivoting cost from r to the target t in N/C. Robot agent changes its target if another target agent becomes more attractive than the current target.

Forward Auction. A robot agent r bids for the target agent that has the largest expected profit, where the expected profit is $f_{util}(r,t) - cost(r,t) - price_t$. $cost(r,t)$ is a cost function, which is described in Section 3.2 and $f_{util}(t)$ is a utility function, which is described in Section 3.3. A bidder retracts its bid if the bidder finds another target to be more attractive, which incurs an additional retract bid cost in the cost function ($cost(r,t)$, which is described later) in order to prevent excessive bid retractions. Each auction is managed by its corresponding auctioneer. For simplicity, the simulation is implemented to choose one of the bidders as an auctioneer. However, conceptually, the corresponding target can be assumed to be the auctioneer because each auction represents a target. An auction for target t is finished if t has enough bidders ($\geq req_t$) after *round_time* and the bidders have confirmed their bids at the end of the auction.

$$price_t = \begin{cases} min\,(min\_bid, max\_rej\_bid)\,, & asn_t > 0; \\ max\_rej\_bid, & \text{otherwise.} \end{cases} \tag{1}$$

When an auction for a target agent t is started, the auctioneer accepts bids higher than $price_t$ of Eq. (1). asn_t is the number of bidders assigned to target t, min_bid is the lowest bid price among the bidders, and max_rej_bid is the larger value of the highest rejected bids and the initial price of t. If $asn_t > req_t$, an assigned robot agent with bid price min_bid is rejected. min_bid is then recalculated, and the rejection procedure is repeated until $asn_t = req_t$. When a bidder is outbid and rejected, it tries to bid for the current target with the updated conditions if it can bid again. Otherwise, the agent that has been outbid searches for other targets to bid on.

An auction is stopped after *round_time*, a specified time period from the beginning of the auction. If the auction does not result in a sufficient number of confirmed bidders, the bidders are released and the auction is paused for a random interval. The pause interval is a uniform random distribution $random(0.1, 1.0) \times round\_time$ in the experiments. After the pause, the auction restarts. This delay allows the environment to evolve (e.g. more robots to become free).

Reverse Auction. In contrast to a forward auction, where buyers (robots) increase price to attract sellers (targets), in reverse auctions sellers (targets) decrease prices to attract buyers (robots). A reverse auction is implemented by having the auctioneer cut its target price, assuming that the auctioneer has not received a sufficient number of bidders during the auction pause. An auctioneer also cuts the target price if a bid is retracted so that the auctioneer no longer has a sufficient number of bidders. Robot agent r bids for target t providing the highest expected profit $f_{util}(r,t) - price_t - cost(r,t)$. Unlike a forward auction, higher bids do not raise target prices. Eq. (2) shows how target price is discounted. In the experiments, $rate_{rev} = 0.5$ is used as it performs better than other values tested [4].

$$price_t = price_t \times rate_{rev} \tag{2}$$

Forward/Reverse Auction (F/R). Using both a forward auction and a reverse auction in order to reduce auction delay with equivalent auction results has been proposed by [11, 4]. A forward/reverse auction is implemented by running a forward auction during normal operations and a reverse auction when the auction is paused or a bid is retracted.

Sealed-Bid F/R Auction (S/B). Unlike auctions with actual fund transactions, robot agents do not actually pay anything to win auctions. Because bidders do not pay anything to win an auction, target price may not be a cost factor. Given this, a sealed-bid mechanism is implemented based on a forward/reverse auction. Using a S/B auction, expected profit of target t for robot agent r is $f_{util}(r,t) - cost(r,t)$; the target price is no more considered. However, a robot agent bids for a target with a price, which is the expected profit for serving the target, and an auctioneer determines which bids are to be rejected based on the bid price. As with other auction methods, the final cut-off price is the kth highest price for a target agent t, where k agents are required to serve t ($req_t = k$).

3.2 Cost Function

As we mentioned for the auction methods in Section 3.1, a cost function $cost(r,t)$ is required to calculate the expected profit of given targets. The cost function calculates the expected costs that are required for the robot agent to serve the given target. It includes direct costs such as the cost to move in order to approach the target and indirect costs such as a penalty for serving a target that already has pursuers in order to avoid duplicated service.

Eq. (3) shows an abstraction of the cost function, which represents the cost of target t for robot r. The estimated distance cost for r to pursue t including t's current velocity vector is $estimated\_distance(r,t)$. It also includes A* trajectory planner for collision avoidance and pivoting cost–robots in the experiments need to stop for turning. Unless t is r's current bidding target or pursuing target, $cost\_to\_assign(r,t)$ assigns additional cost. If t already has an auction result, in order to give penalty for redundant auctions, $cost\_redundant\_auction(t)$ assigns additional cost. If t is still mobile, $cost\_mobile(t)$ assigns additional cost. If t requires most additional pursuers other than those already assigned, $cost\_additional\_pursuers(t)$ assigns more cost; it is more difficult to coordinate synchronously if more pursuing robots are required. Specific values for the sub-functions of cost function are discussed in [5].

$$
\begin{aligned}
cost(r,t) = {} & estimated\_distance(r,t) \\
& + cost\_to\_assign(r,t) \\
& + cost\_redundant\_auction(t) \\
& + cost\_mobile(t) \\
& + cost\_additional\_pursuers(t)
\end{aligned} \tag{3}
$$

3.3 Utility Functions

Various utility functions, which determines the utility value of a given target, are experimented. Essentially, utility functions determine the bidding strategy of robots; i.e., these functions calculate the value of the given target. We examine various utility functions in order to see the effects of different bidding strategies.

The *default (static)* utility function directly addresses the pay-off that a robot agent will receive if the robot agent serves the given target. However, it may be more efficient if we consider a target that has more bidders to be more valuable in order to assign higher priorities for auctions that will probably end soon. The other five *'dynamic'* utility functions use the number of bidders and the requirement in order to consider the auction status. The previous work [4] used the *Division* utility function, which is the first dynamic utility function. However, the Division utility function sometimes attracts too many bidders, thus, we try to mitigate the problem with modified utility functions. *Division-Restricted* restricts assigning higher priorities for targets that already have enough bidders. *Division-Small* restricts the amount of a maximum utility increase. We also merged the two modified division utility functions by implementing *Division-Restricted and Small*. *Linear* shows another approach by addressing the mechanism of assigning priorities on auctions.

Default (Static). The default utility function for a robot agent r serving a target agent t is Eq. (4), which is the payoff that each robot receives after serving t. It is also called the *Static* utility function because the value never changes; other utility functions are called the *Dynamic* utility functions because the values change according to the status of corresponding auctions.

$$f_{util}(t) = util_t / req_t \qquad (4)$$

Division. Although the default utility function reflects the exact payoff value of a target when the target is served and the cost function calculates the cost to serve the target, it may be not sufficient because the status of an auction is not included. For example, let's assume that there are two targets t_1 and t_2 with $req_{t_1} = req_{t_2} = 5$, $asn_{t_1} = 4$, and $asn_{t_2} = 1$ and a robot agent r needs to choose either t_1 or t_2. Then, r may want to prioritize t_1 because t_1 needs only one more bidder while t_2 needs four more; t_2 will probably require more time to settle its auction.

$$f_{util}(t) = \frac{util_t}{req_t - min(asn_t, req_t - 1)} \qquad (5)$$

The division utility function, Eq. (5), is designed to increase $f_{util}(t)$ as asn_t increases and to increase more if asn_t is near req_t by dividing $req_t - asn_t$ into $util_t$.

Division-Restricted. The division utility function results in a hoarding problem. Even if target t already has enough bidders ($asn_t \geq req_t$), t's utility, $f_{util}(t)$, is still boosted so that t can attract more bidders. This over attraction can increase auction cost because a target can attract too many bidders; neighbor target agents may suffer from starvation. In order to mitigate this problem, the utility function, $f_{util}(t)$, uses the default utility function (boost deactivated) when the bidder is not yet assigned to t and the target t has enough bidders ($asn_t \geq req_t$).

Division-Small. When targets t_1 and t_2 ($req_{t_1} = 5$, $asn_{t_1} = 4$, $req_{t_2} = 2$, $asn_{t_2} = 1$, $\forall t : util_t / req_t = 10$) are close to a robot agent r, the utility values of t_1 and t_2 should be same because both t_1 and t_2 need only one more robot agent and the two targets provide the same utility for each serving robot agent (*util/req*). However, division and division-restricted utility functions give the utility values differently; $f_{util}(t_1) = 50$ and $f_{util}(t_2) = 20$. With *Division-Small* utility function, a maximum possible boost ratio is the same regardless of req_t: Eq. (6).

$$f_{util}(t) = \frac{util_t}{req_t} \cdot \left(1 + \frac{1}{req_t - min(asn_t, req_t - 1)}\right) \qquad (6)$$

Division-Restricted and Small. Division-restricted and division-small are combined.

Linear. In the four division methods, the utility value for a target t is boosted more when asn_t is closer to req_t. However, with *Linear* utility function Eq. (7), the utility boost per bidder is constant.

$$f_{util}(t) = util_t/req_t \cdot (1 + min(asn_t, req_t)/req_t) \qquad (7)$$

3.4 Swapping

The assignments between robot agents and target agents may become obsolete because there are a series of asynchronous auctions and the targets are moving. Thus, reassignment mechanisms may be beneficial. We may address this problem by executing auctions repeatedly after the initial assignment. However, auction mechanism is an expensive operation to execute repeatedly because the auction mechanism requires synchronization between asynchronous robot agents and heavy communication costs. On the other hand, the swapping mechanism, which is a one-to-one negotiation between robot agents, is a less expensive operation: there are less communication and computation costs. The swapping mechanism is executed after the auction is complete and both swapping robot agents have their dedicated targets.

Fig. 1 is an example when the asynchrony of auctions makes swapping attractive. In Fig. 1, $req_{t1} = 2$, $req_{t2} = 3$, and $req_{t3} = 1$). After $r1$ and $r2$ serving $t1$, $r1$ and $r2$ are assigned to $t2$ along with $r3$. $r4$ is assigned to $t3$ before $t1$ is served. $r4$ could not be assigned to $t2$ because there were not a sufficient number of robot agents nearby $t2$ at that time; $r1$ and $r2$ were serving $t1$. However, it is obvious that a swap between $r2$ and $r4$ can reduce costs.

Fig. 2 is an example where the dynamicity causes the need for swapping. Here $r1$ was pursuing $t1$ and $r2$ was pursuing $t2$. However, as $t1$ and $t2$ move, the best targets of $r1$ and $r2$ change. If $r1$ and $r2$ swap tasks then, the two robot agents can serve targets with less time and movement distance (fuel consumption).

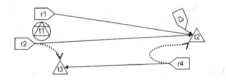   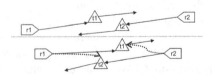

Fig. 1. Swap by auction asynchrony   **Fig. 2.** Swap by dynamicity

The robot agent that requests a swap becomes a swapper, which chooses a swappee that is estimated to maximize the benefit of the swap. A swap should be beneficial for both swapper and swappee, whose targets are different, to be accepted by the swappee. A swapper r_1 with target t_1 sends a swap request to swappee r_s with target t_s when the expected benefit $EB(r_1, r_s) > 0$ and $\forall i : EB(r_1, r_s) \geq EB(r_1, r_i)$. In Eq. (8), t_i is r_i's target before the swap, and TH_{swap} is the swap threshold. The cost function for swapping, which corresponds to the distance and azimuth difference between r and t, is $cost_s(r,t)$.

$$EB(r_1, r_i) = cost_s(r_1, t_1) + cost_s(r_i, t_i) \\ - cost_s(r_1, t_i) - cost_s(r_i, t_1) - TH_{swap} \tag{8}$$

4 Experiments

We have done physical robot experiments in the previous research [4]. Physical experiments enable a more realistic experimental environment, which can be ignored by software simulations. However, it is too difficult to setup large-scale physical experiments. Experiments with a thousand mobile robots require too much time and effort especially on jobs that are not directly related to the research; i.e., charging and replacing batteries, fixing and replacing damaged parts, reserving and maintaining a large and appropriate location, setting a massive number of cameras, and other logistical problems. Thus, we have implemented a software simulation for large-scale experiments and simulated the physical robot experiments by importing experimental parameters from the results of the previous physical experiments.

Fig. 3 shows the user interface of the agent simulator. The simulator shows the movement of robot and target agents, the intention of each robot agent, the status (roaming, chasing, bidding, serving, and others) of robot and target agents, and the progress of the system. With the GUI of the simulator, we can see how the mechanisms and the agents interact in run-time. Mission files (csv-formatted text files) describing initial positions, utility values, requirements, movement patterns, and coordination mechanisms are required to run the simulator. The simulator writes log files, which have detailed experimental results for each mission and can be parsed for statistical analysis.

The simulation is a discrete event simulation with a global clock. Fig. 4 shows the overview of the simulation architecture. Fig. 5 shows the state diagrams of the major component agents shown in Fig. 4. The simulator is implemented in C++ and MC++ using Repast.NET and executed on Pentium 4 3.2GHz Prescott with 2GB RAM running Windows XP Pro. Agents are programmed to behave similarly with the physical robots (Acroname Garcia/PPRK robots) by importing values from [4]. For example, robots are programmed to have maximum movement speed of 10cm/sec, maximum rotational speed of 20°/sec, communication delay of 100ms, service range of 20cm. Each simulation step represents 50ms; a longer step will not support the communication delay and a shorter step will increase the execution cost of the simulator. We configure $util_t$ according to the field size so that the expected benefit is positive when a target is found and $util_t/req_t$ to be constant so that each target has the same utility per serving robot.

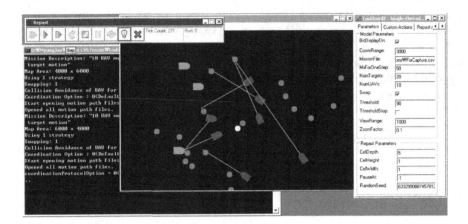

Fig. 3. The simulator user interface

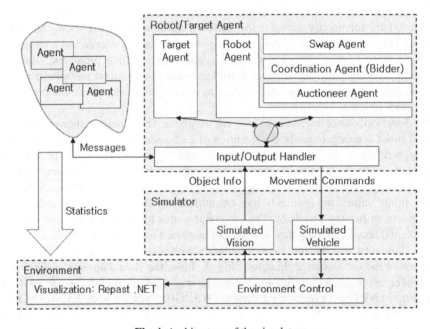

Fig. 4. Architecture of the simulator

4.1 Experimental Data

Several data sets are experimented with in order to vary simulation parameters as shown in Table 1. The data set *Dense* represents a field where each target agent almost always has enough robot agents nearby so that virtually no coordination between robot agents is required. Target agents are scattered on the field when a mission starts, and robot agents are scattered around the center (in about 25% surface of the field). In data set *Corner*

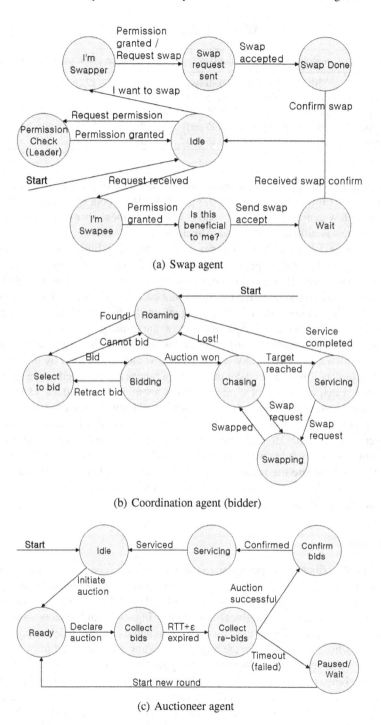

(a) Swap agent

(b) Coordination agent (bidder)

(c) Auctioneer agent

Fig. 5. State diagrams of component agents in a robot agent

Table 1. Simulation data set

Name	# Robot	# Target	Field size	Sensing range	Communication range
Dense	250	750	40x40 (*m*)	3 (*m*)	12 (*m*)
Corner	50	500	45x45 (*m*)	3 (*m*)	12 (*m*)
Scatter	50	500	45x45 (*m*)	3 (*m*)	12 (*m*)
G.Corner	50	500	45x45 (*m*)	Global	Global
G.Scatter	50	500	45x45 (*m*)	Global	Global

and *G.Corner*, robot agents start from a single corner area of the field and the density of robot agents is lower. In data set *Scatter* and *G.Scatter*, robot agents are scattered on the field with low density as in *Corner* and *G.Corner*. In these four lower density cases, servicing targets is difficult without coordination.

The first three data sets, Dense, Corner, and Scatter, have limited sensing and communication ranges and robot agents can coordinate with other robot agents within their communication ranges. In the other two data sets, *G.Corner* and *G.Sparse*, robots have global sensing and communication ranges so that each robot has the global knowledge and the capability to coordinate with any agent on the field. G.Corner has the same initial positions as Corner and G.Sparse has the same initial positions as Sparse.

A mission (single simulation run) is finished when 90% of the targets are served. We use the 90% metric because otherwise the results would be distorted by the search for the last few targets if sensing and communication ranges are bounded as we mentioned in Section 3. Each execution of a mission takes about 3 hours in data set Dense and about 1 hour in other data sets with our machines. In simulation time, each mission takes about 15 minutes in data set Dense and about 30 minutes in other data sets. We experiment with 15 times of simulation for every combination of 5 coordination methods, 6 utility functions, and swapping enabled/disabled for each data set. Mission time (time spent to complete the mission), movement distance (distance covered by robot agents, which implies the fuel consumption), auction delay, number of messages, and load imbalance ($\sigma/mean$ of movement distance) are measured.

4.2 Results

This section describes the experimental results in order to compare various coordination methods to the controls, such as N/C or forward auction with static(default) utility functions, swapping versus non-swapping, and local knowledge (bounded sensing and communication ranges) versus global knowledge. Fig. 6, 7, and 8 show performance comparisons to controls. Fig. 6 uses forward auction and default(static) utility function as a control, whose value is 1.0 in the figure, and swapping is disabled in every case of Fig. 6. Fig. 7 shows relative values when swapping is enabled compared to the cases without swapping, which is represented as 1.0 in the figure. Fig. 8 shows relative values when the sensing and communication ranges are bounded compared to the results when the ranges are not bounded (swapping is disabled in Fig. 8). Capital-I-shaped bars show confidence intervals. Every confidence interval shows confidence of 95%.

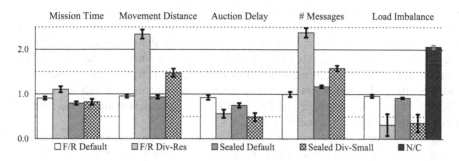

Fig. 6. Performance comparison to forward auction and default utility function

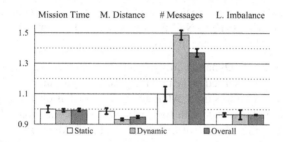

Fig. 7. Performance of swapping

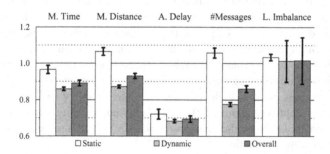

Fig. 8. Bounded vs. unbounded

N/C and forward auction with dynamic utility functions suffer from deadlock; thus, they are not represented in the figures–except for load imbalance of N/C. Reverse auction, when it is used solely, has no merit over forward auction in theory [11] and shows no better performance in the experiments. Some of the dynamic utility functions with forward/reverse auction do not complete missions before the simulation time limit; thus, forward/reverse auction with such utility functions (Division, Division-Small, and Division-Restricted and Small) are dropped from the statistics.

With data set Dense, N/C finishes missions and performs well. Sealed-bid auction with default utility function and swapping, which performed best in Dense, has 6.6±3.6% less mission time and 10.5±4.3% less movement distance than N/C. Forward auction, F/R auction, and sealed-bid auction with some of dynamic utility functions (division-restricted and linear) perform worse than N/C in mission time and movement distance. However, N/C does not perform well in other low density data sets. In Corner, N/C serves 53% of targets before the time limit; other coordination methods complete missions in about half of the time limit in Corner. N/C suffers from deadlocks in Scatter and G.Scatter and is much less efficient than other coordination methods in G.Corner (80.0±9.3% more mission time and 74.9±3.5% more movement distance than forward auction with default utility function).

Fig. 6 shows performance comparisons, which are shown by mean values compared to those of the forward auction and the default utility function. The results suggest that adding reverse auction to forward auction improves performance; F/R auction improves performance in every metric: mission time, movement distance, auction delay, number of messages, and load imbalance. Sealed-bid auction improves performance further except for the number of messages. N/C is shown with a load imbalance metric only because it cannot complete missions in most cases.

Dynamic Utility Functions. Dynamic utility functions with forward auction suffer from deadlock, which was not observed in the previous research with small-scale experiments [4]–division utility function was used. Although no deadlock is observed, dynamic utility functions do not perform well with forward/reverse (F/R) auction. This is because F/R auctions with dynamic utilities suffer from ping-pong bidding, where a bidder alternatively bids and retracts (see Section 5 for a detailed explanation). On the other hand, dynamic utility functions successfully reduce auction delay with S/B auctions except in the case when the division utility function is used. For example, when the division-restricted and small utility function is used with S/B auction, auction delay is reduced 46.3% from the default utility function with S/B auction. However, the reduction in auction delay is often not enough to reduce the mission time because the dynamic utility functions damage auction quality, which is represented by the movement distance metric–the dynamic utility functions increase the movement distance. Thus, the dynamic utility functions provide trade-offs between auction delay and auction quality. Load imbalance is improved significantly with the dynamic utility functions; the load imbalance is decreased 67% by the division-restricted with F/R auctions used and 61% by division-small with S/B auctions.

Swapping. Fig. 7 shows the performance of the swapping method. The swapping performance is shown by the mean values of the performance with swapping divided by those without swapping. Auction delay is not shown because swapping does not affect the auction process; robots do not swap while the robots are bidding. The number of messages is increased (performance deteriorated) by swapping significantly. The number of messages increases more with the dynamic utility functions (48.7%) than with the static (9.9%) and the number of swapping increases more with the dynamic (477.6) than with the static (17.4). In Dense, the number of messages increases up to 77.0%, which implies that the communication overhead of swapping can be almost as much as that of an auction. The communication overhead of swapping makes it less efficient as it can increase not only the number of messages sent, but also the mission time if the communication delays are significant. The negative effect of swapping on the mission time can be inferred by the result in Fig. 7; even though the movement distance is reduced, mission time is not as reduced. Performance improvement is more significant with dynamic utility functions, which have poor auction quality compared to the static utility function. Although the movement distance of the dynamic utility function improves with swapping, swapping does not make movement distances as short as those obtained by using the static utility function. Load imbalance is improved with swapping, which implies that swapping helps load balancing.

Bounded Sensing and Communication Ranges. When the sensing and communication ranges are bounded, the system is supposed to be more scalable because robot agents do not need to broadcast to every agent. Besides, practically, observing every target and communicating with every other robot in real-time is almost impossible in large-scale systems. Thus, we examined the mechanisms with bounded sensing and communication ranges. Fig. 8 shows how the system performs if the sensing and communication ranges are bounded by comparing the results of bounded ranges with those of unbounded ranges.

Using the static utility function, bounding ranges reduces auction delay by $27.9\pm2.8\%$ and mission time by $3.5\pm2.2\%$. However, the movement distance and the number of messages increase with bounded ranges. Because each auction has more information with global knowledge, having longer distances with bounded ranges seems to be natural. However, having too much information may lead to more delays and damages of the overall performance as Fig. 8 suggests.

Using the dynamic utility functions, bounding ranges enhances the performance in the four metrics (except load imbalance) significantly. Bounding ranges can be interpreted as filtering objects because greedy algorithms such as auction methods, usually try to choose targets closer the robots; thus, the probability to coordinate with the robots far away is relatively low. Load imbalance is increased a little with static utility and does not have significant differences in overall.

The improvement achieved by various methods in bounded ranges is compared with the improvement by them in unbounded ranges. The results suggest that bounding ranges help reduce movement distance and number of messages further except for F/R auction with static utility when the methods are compared to forward auction with static utility. This suggests that it is easier to improve performance with bounded ranges. Using dynamic utility functions, the performance improvement difference from the cases of unbounded ranges is more significant.

Swapping and Bounded Ranges. Both the number of swaps and the sum of estimated swapping benefit (ΣEB of Eq.(8)) are larger with bounded ranges using static utility function. However, using dynamic utility functions, bounding the ranges makes the two values smaller. Greater number of swapping implies worse quality of auction results. Thus, we can infer that bounding ranges gives less efficient plans with static utility function and gives more efficient plans with dynamic utility functions compared to unbounded ranges; movement distance in Fig. 8 shows the same tendency.

5   Discussion

In this section, we discuss unexpected symptoms observed during the experiments: deadlocks, unexpected delays in auctions, and other side effects of the mechanisms.

Most of them were not observed in the previous small-scale experiments. However, with large-scale experiments, more issues can be observed with the mechanisms and the variety of the mechanisms is also extended in this paper. Analyzing how such issues occur, we try to mitigate the issues and show how other versions of the mechanisms work.

N/C often suffers from deadlock unless the density of robot agents is very high (as in Dense) or the req_t values are small enough. Fig. 9 shows an example, where $req_{t1} = req_{t2} = 3$. Because each robot agent may find its own best target differently, this deadlock is not unlocked unless additional robots come in or the targets move so that the robots may change their targets. However, unless the density of robot agents is sufficiently high, unlocking does not happen frequently enough to accomplish missions.

Fig. 9. N/C suffering from deadlock

Forward auction with dynamic utility also suffers from deadlock, which is not observed in the previous small-scale experiments [4, 5]. If a target's price is higher than its value (utility), the target may not be bidden, which in turn can stop the mission progress. This happens frequently with dynamic utility functions, as such functions can cause greater increases in target prices. Table 2 shows an example. This may happen without dynamic utility function; it is observed in preliminary simulations when targets moved away too fast and robots could not finish an auction in time. Adding a reverse auction to a forward auction (F/R) helps in adapting to the dynamic environment, which prevents such deadlocks, as well as in reducing convergence time.

Table 2. Forward auction and dynamic utility

f_{util}	Target price	Actions
100	10	$r1$ bids "10".
150	10	$r2$ bids "120".
200	120	$r2$ retracts.
150	120	$r1$ retracts.
100	120	Price is too high.

Adding a reverse auction to a forward auction can alter the assignments when targets are dynamic or robots have a series of asynchronous auctions–each auction is done asynchronously with a different duration. The auctions are supposed to have the same results with a different delay [11]: forward, reverse, and F/R auction. However, if targets move, their positions, which determines the costs, become different according to each auction method because the delay varies, which in turn makes the assignments different.

Even if targets are static, assignments from a second round can be different because each robot has a series of asynchronous auctions. Fig. 10 shows an example with targets $\{a,b,c\}$, $req_a=4$, $req_b=3$, $req_c=5$, and robots 1 to 8 using different auction methods (i.e. F/R versus forward); the two auction results are different. Because the system is asynchronous and distributed, each robot incurs additional costs to wait for other auctions to converge and other robots to complete their services. In a fully distributed system with a dynamic environment, such costs can be too high. The properties of a target changes while robots are sending "confirmation of convergence", subsequently, the robots may need to cancel their confirmations and restart auctions because of the changes in the environment. As a result, given the dynamicity and asynchrony, distributed auctions may need to wait indefinitely in order to find an equilibrium. Nonetheless, adding a reverse auction to a forward auction has the advantage of converging with less delay and fewer messages. Besides, the results show that the auction quality is slightly improved. This may be a result of the fact that a faster auction can respond faster in a dynamic environment.

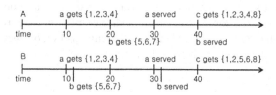

Fig. 10. Inequivalent of auctions

F/R auction can suffer from ping-pong bidding; a bidder alternatively bids to multiple targets and auctions are delayed. If a target price fluctuates, bidders may alternatively bid to different targets without completing an auction. Table 3 shows an example. Ping-pong bidding usually stops either by another bidder or by a completion of an auction; however, auctions still suffer from additional delay due to ping-pong bidding. Applying a cost for retracting a bid mitigates the problem a little. However, as shown on Table 3, ping-pong bidding still happens with the cost of retracting a bid. If the cost of retracting a bid is too high or retraction is forbidden, the algorithm cannot adapt to the change

Table 3. Ping-pong bidding

EP_{t1}	$price_{t1}$	EP_{t2}	$price_{t2}$	Actions
101	10	100	10	r bids $t1$
10	101	70*	10	r retracts bid
21	80	100	10	r bids $t2$
9*	80	10	100	$t1$ discounts
31*	40	10	100	r retracts bid
61	40	30	80	r bids $t1$
10	101	0*	80	$t2$ discounts

*: retracting cost applied. *EP*: expected profit.

in the environment; besides, an auction may spend too much time. Ping-pong bidding happens more frequently with dynamic utility because they cause greater fluctuations in the target price. With sealed-bid auctions, ping-pong bidding does not occur because bidders do not see the target price.

Sealed-bid auctions perform best in terms of mission time, movement distance, auction delay, and load imbalance. Sealed-bid auctions may have disadvantages because they do not consider the target price as a cost factor, which reflects how others bid; the more popular a target is, usually the more expensive it is. For better task distribution, overly popular targets may need to be avoided. However, because robot agents do not actually pay the price, but incurs a cost such as movement distance and pivoting, the price may be neglected by the robots.

Dynamic utility functions can distort a target's utility, which can make assignments inefficient by exaggerating the value of a target excessively. This makes movement distance longer than static utility. Fig. 11 shows an example, where $req_{t1} = 4$, $req_{t2} = 1$, and $\forall i : util_{ti}/req_{ti} = 10$. If $util_{t1}$ is boosted enough to ignore the distances by $r1$, $r2$, and $r3$, both $r4$ and $r5$ bid for $t1$ although $t2$ is better. However, although dynamic utility results in longer movement distance, shorter auction delay may compensate for the increased movement; e.g., some cases result in shorter mission time. Besides, dynamic utility functions can reduce load imbalance significantly as Fig. 6 suggests although the reason is unclear and we need further studies on this issue.

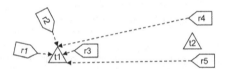

Fig. 11. Distorted utility value with dynamic utility function

A pair of robot agents sometimes repeatedly swap with each other: *ping-pong swapping*. Swap threshold TH_{swap} reduces the frequency of ping-pong swapping. However, TH_{swap} cannot completely eliminate ping-pong swapping and TH_{swap} also reduces the frequency of beneficial swaps. Ping-pong swapping is caused either by collision avoidance or by the asynchrony and delay of agents. When ping-pong swapping happens, both mission time and movement distance increase. Even when ping-pong swapping does not happen because of TH_{swap}, the initial swap may have already made the routing plans less efficient. Because some swaps are useless or harmful, the performance improvement is not as significant as the sum of EB (refer Eq. (8)) suggests.

6   Conclusion and Future Research

Various auction mechanisms and swapping for distributed multi-robot coordination, and different bidding strategies in large-scale multi-agent systems are experimented with. The results suggest that the mechanisms work with dynamic environment in large-scale systems and the mechanisms can work with larger-scale systems because the mechanisms perform well with bounded sensing and communication ranges without multi-hop communications. Table 4 summarizes the results. However, bidding strategies, which are expressed by utility functions, may include more factors such as the number of potential bidders and the number of available targets nearby (potential utility). Besides, there is a possibility that it may perform better if robot agents are heterogenous and have mixed strategies.

Table 4. Summary of strategies

Strategy		Results
Coordination method	N/C	Deadlock with non-trivial problems
	Forward	Deadlock with dynamic utility functions
	Reverse	No merit over Forward
	F/R	Better than Forward. Ping-pong bidding.
	Sealed-bid	Best except for the number of messages.
Utility function	Static	Shorter movement distance
	Dynamic	Shorter auction delay. Even workload distribution. Tradeoff between convergence speed and solution quality
Swapping		Performance improved. Ping-pong swapping occurs.

Various simulation parameters are also experimented with: sensing and communication ranges, robot agent density, and initial positions of robot agents. Table 5 summarizes the results. However, we may need to experiment further by varying more parameters such as different field sizes, static targets, and varying target speeds. This may help verify the characteristics and adaptability of the mechanisms.

Additional metrics such as the number and benefit of effective swaps, number of ping-pong bids, robot idle dime, and statistics of price-cut may help measure the performance more concretely; thus, we can find how to improve the mechanisms and verify the conjectures to explain symptoms such as ping-pong bidding and ping-pong swapping. Besides, the reason why dynamic utility improves workload imbalance significantly is not clear and further experiments are needed.

Table 5. Summary of simulation parameters

Parameters		Results
Sensing and communication ranges	Bounded	Auction methods perform better.
	Global	N/C suffers from deadlock less severely.
Robot agent density	Dense	Both N/C and auction methods work.
	Sparse	N/C fails. Auction methods perform well.
Initial positions of robots	Corner	Less performance gap between strategies.
	Scattered	N/C suffers from deadlock more severely.

Forward, reverse, and F/R auctions are known to be equivalent under certain restrictive assumptions [11]. The assumptions are that the auctions are simultaneous, the tasks are static, and each agent bids in only one auction (and for a predetermined task). In this case, the auction is used as an offline tool. In general, the auction methods do not yield the same results (equilibria) under the looser conditions of this paper: the environment is dynamic and a sequence of asynchronous auctions is used. However, it is possible that the auction methods may result in the same sets of possible assignments even though they result in different assignments. Proving that the set of possible assignments under different auction methods is the same with asynchronous auctions remains an open problem. However, even if the set of possible solutions is equal, the problem of determining the speed of convergence and the likelihood of better solutions is a more difficult problem. Given the differences that are apparent in the simulations, we conjecture that different auction mechanisms are not equivalent. This question would be much harder to resolve analytically.

Acknowledgement

This research has been supported in part by NSF under grant CMS 05-09321 and by ONR under DoD MURI award N0014-02-1-0715. We thank Liping Chen and Rajesh Karmani at UIUC and Tom Brown now at Google for useful discussions and feedback, and Andrea Whitesell for help with copy editing the paper. We would also like to thank the anonymous reviewers for their invaluable comments and advice.

References

[1] Ham, M., Agha, G.: Market-based coordination strategies for large-scale multi-agent systems. System and Information Sciences Notes 2(1), 126–131 (2007)

[2] Dantzig, G.B., Ramser, J.H.: The truck dispatching problem. Management Science 6(1), 80–91 (1959)

[3] Bertsekas, D.P., Castanon, D.A., Tsaknakis, H.: Reverse auction and the solution of inequality constrained assignment problems. SIAM Journal on Optimization (2), 268–297 (1993)

[4] Ahmed, A., Patel, A., Brown, T., Ham, M., Jang, M.W., Agha, G.: Task assignment for a physical agent team via a dynamic forward/reverse auction mechanism. In: Proc. of KI-MAS, pp. 311–317 (2005)

[5] Brown, T.D.: Decentralized coordination with crash failures. Master's thesis, Univ. of Illinois at Urbana-Champaign (2005)

[6] Palmer, D., Kirschenbaum, M., Murton, J., Zajac, K., Kovacina, M., Vaidyanathan, R.: Decentralized cooperative auction for multiple agent task allocation using synchronized random number generators. In: Proc. of IROS, vol. 2, pp. 1963–1968 (2003)

[7] Zlot, R.M., Stentz, A.T., Dias, M.B., Thayer, S.: Multi-robot exploration controlled by a market economy. In: Proc. of ICRA, vol. 3, pp. 3016–3023 (2002)

[8] Gerkey, B.P., Matarić, M.J.: Sold!: Auction methods for multirobot coordination. IEEE Trans. on Robotics and Automation 18(5), 758–768 (2002)

[9] Guerrero, J., Oliver, G.: Multi-robot task allocation strategies using auction-like mechanisms. Art. Int. Res. and Dev. 100, 111–122 (2003)

[10] Krieger, M.J.B., Billeter, J.B., Keller, L.: Ant-like task allocation and recruitment in cooperative robots. Nature 406, 992–995 (2000)

[11] Bertsekas, D.P., Castanon, D.A.: A forward/reverse auction algorithm for asymmetric assignment problems. Comp. Opt. and App. (3), 277–297 (1992)

Dynamic Pricing Algorithms for Task Allocation in Multi-agent Swarms

Prithviraj Dasgupta and Matthew Hoeing

Computer Science Department
University of Nebraska, Omaha, NE 68182
{pdasgupta,mhoeing}@mail.unomaha.edu

Abstract. Over the past few years, emergent computing based techniques such as swarming have evolved as an attractive technique to design coordination protocols in large-scale distributed systems and massively multi-agent systems. In this paper, we consider a search-and-execute problem domain where agents have to discover tasks online and perform them in a distributed, collaborative manner. We specifically focus on the problem of distributed coordination between agents to dynamically allocate the tasks among themselves. To address this problem, we describe a novel technique that combines a market-based dynamic pricing algorithm to control the task priorities with a swarming-based coordination technique to disseminate task information across the agents. Experimental results within a simulated environment for a distributed aided target recognition application show that the dynamic pricing based task selection strategies compare favorably with other heuristic-based task selection strategies in terms of task completion times while achieving a significant reduction in communication overhead.

1 Introduction

Over the past decade, multi-agent systems have emerged as an attractive paradigm for designing large scale, autonomous distributed systems [34]. Recently, several researchers have also used techniques from emergent computing such as swarming in a variety of problems including data mining [1], vehicle routing[5], telecommunications [14] and robotics [7]. In many of these swarm-based systems, mobile, coordinating swarm units, usually implemented using mobile mini-robots, perform search and execute operations on spatially and temporally distributed tasks in a dynamic environment [4,33,10,11]. The technique of swarming provides a suitable mechanism to achieve desired global objectives in a large-scale multi-agent system by embedding nature inspired behavior patterns at the level of the individual swarm units without using a centralized mechanism to coordinate the activities of the swarm units. However, in the absence of a centralized mechanism, controlling the operation of a swarm-based system to achieve the desired behavior while ensuring efficient performance becomes a challenging problem. One of the principal problems in designing swarm-based systems for environments characterized by search-and-execute tasks is to ensure efficient selection of tasks by the

N. Jamali et al. (Eds.): CCMMS 2007, MMAS 2006, LSMAS 2006, LNAI 5043, pp. 64–79, 2008.

swarm units to improve the overall performance of the system. Prior work in this direction by Gaudiano *et al* [16] have proposed a centralized shared memory to share information about tasks and coordinate the actions of the swarm units. In contrast, in a purely distributed environment with no centralized shared memory, ensuring efficient task selection by the swarm units becomes a challenging problem because of the dynamic arrival of tasks, communication delays encountered in disseminating task information across the swarm units and possible inconsistencies in task information between the different swarm units. Miller *et al* [25], have shown that a purely distributed mechanism for the task selection problem for swarmed systems characterized by search-and-execute type tasks is a NP-complete problem, and, proposed polynomial-time heuristic-based strategies to solve it. Mainland *et al* [24] have adopted a market-based pricing mechanism to address the distributed resource allocation problem in mobile sensor networks. In [12], Dasgupta and Hoeing have described a rudimentary agent-based dynamic pricing mechanism to address the distributed task selection problem in multi-agent swarms. Our work extends the model described in [12] by using computationally simple, yet efficient multi-agent based dynamic pricing strategies to solve the distributed task selection problem for swarming. Empirical results of our algorithms within a simulated environment for a distributed aided target recognition application show that dynamic pricing strategies for task selection in swarms compare favorably with other heuristic-based task selection strategies while reducing the communication overhead.

2   Multi-agent Swarming

The technique of swarming involves movement of entities (e.g., insects, or humans) individually or in small-sized units to search and act upon objects of interest such as food, prey, or enemies within a search space. We consider a search-and-execute problem domain where swarm units have to discover objects of interest individually but require to collaborate with each other to perform the actions on the objects of interest. The environment for our problem domain consists of objects of interest that are distributed randomly in a 2-dimensional environment. When an individual or unit discovers an object of interest, it communicates the information to other units. The other units then converge on the object to perform the required actions on the object(e.g., consuming food, subsuming prey, etc.) using the combined power of the congregated units. After completing the task on an object, each unit reverts to individual searching.

A computational system using swarming consists of multiple mobile units that are capable of moving within an unknown environment. Because of the dynamic nature of the environment, each unit must also be capable of continuously searching, communicating and executing tasks corresponding to objects of interest as long as it is active in the environment. Software agents provide a suitable paradigm to implement the computation units for swarming. Following are the features of the swarmed system we consider in this paper:

1. We consider a convex polygon shaped environment. The perimeter of the environment is known *a priori* by the agents. Because the focus of our work is on the task selection algorithms in swarming, we assume that agents do not need to explore and determine the perimeter of the environment. Techniques described in [6] can be easily incorporated into our agents for perimeter detection of the environment.

2. A task corresponds to a set of actions that need to be taken by agents on objects of interest. The spatial and temporal distribution of tasks is not known *a priori* and must be discovered by the agents in real-time.

3. A single agent is only capable of discovering and partially executing tasks, but lacks the computational resources required to completely execute a task.

4. A task can be completed only if multiple agents share their computational resources towards executing the task.

5. To enlist the cooperation of other agents required to complete a task, an agent that discovers a task communicates the task's information to other agents.

6. An agent is required to move to the vicinity of a task discovered by another agent to execute it. Each agent executes the tasks independently and on completing its portion of execution on the task, communicates the progress of its execution (fraction of task still incomplete) to other agents within its communication range.

Following [25] we have realized the swarming behavior in our system, using the *stigmergetic* activity of social insects such as ants [4]. Stigmergy is a communication mechanism used by insects to exchange information with each other either directly, or, indirectly through the environment. For example, ants searching for food employ an indirect form of stigmergy by using a chemical substance called pheromone to mark the path followed by them towards the food. Pheromone provides positive reinforcement to future ants, and, ants searching for the food later on get attracted to the pheromone to locate and possibly consume the food. In our system, when an agent encounters a task, it deposits a certain amount of synthetic pheromone to mark the location and priority of the task. Pheromone decays over time. The set of tasks and the corresponding pheromones that each agent is aware of is stored in a local data structure called the *pheromone landscape* within the agent and corresponds to the agent's task list. An agent communicates its task list to other agents within its communication range to disseminate task information across the swarm. The operations performed by an agent to manifest swarming can be divided into the following phases:

- **Deployment:** Agents are deployed by a central manager into the environment. Once the agents are deployed the manager does not supervise the agents. The agents revert to the manager only when their lifetime expires. For better overall coverage, the manager might choose to divide the environment into smaller sub-areas and deploy a subset of agent into each sub-area [18].

- **Search and Discovery.** In this phase, individual agents perform a blind or uninformed search within the search space to discover objects of interest. When an agent discovers an object of interest, it associates a certain amount of pheromone with the object to indicate the urgency with which other agents should arrive at the object to complete the task associated with that object.
- **Communication.** After an agent discovers a task, it has to inform other agents about the parameters of the task including the task's location and pheromone. To achieve this in a distributed manner, an agent uses a point-to-point communication model to disseminate information about tasks it is aware of to other agents within its communication range.
- **Task Selection.** An agent stores information about incomplete tasks in the search space that it receives from other agents in a task list. An agent must select a subset of tasks from its task list it wants to execute partially and the order in which to visit the selected tasks to plan its path.
- **Task Execution.** On arriving at the location corresponding to a task/object, an agent performs the actions required on the object to complete its share of the task. After completing its portion of execution for all the tasks on its task list, an agent reverts to searching.

In the rest of the paper, we focus on the task selection problem in swarming. Algorithms for deployment, search and discovery, communication and task execution for swarming are implemented in our system using the algorithms described in [10]. Functionally, each computational unit in our swarmed system is a mobile robot that contains a processor executing the algorithms implemented by an agent. Therefore, in the rest of the paper we use the terms robot and agent interchangeably.

3 Dynamic Pricing Strategies for Task Selection in Swarming

Task selection is one of the most crucial phases of the swarming mechanism as it determines the efficiency with which tasks are completed in the system. A suitable task selection mechanism ensures controlled swarming towards tasks to ensure appropriate commitment of resources to tasks, ability of the swarm to separate adaptively into sub-swarms and reduction in communication overhead.

A principal challenge in ensuring efficient performance of the task selection mechanism is to correctly update the pheromone at different tasks so that an appropriate number of robots that are close to the task start acting upon it. Most existing pheromone-based emergent systems [4] employ simple reinforcement based techniques that rely on experimental fine-tuning of the model's parameters to suitably update pheromone at the different solution points of the problem. However, such a mechanism is not guaranteed to work precisely in a swarm where tasks are time-constrained and the order of allocating resources(robots) across tasks determines the overall system performance. To address this problem, we propose to update the pheromone at different tasks in a manner that enables the tasks to attract robots rapidly to get completed while avoiding allocating excessive robots to tasks or starving some tasks by allocating too few robots for it. To develop a suitable task selection mechanism, we model pheromone update at tasks as a market-based dynamic pricing problem between the different tasks in the environment.

Our market-based task selection mechanism is based on the dynamic posted pricing model of Kephart *et al* [20] for exchange of goods in an information economy. Information goods (e.g. news items) are consumed rapidly over a short period and are characterized by prices that change dynamically with the age of the good and the number of sellers offering similar goods. In a similar manner, tasks in our swarmed system need to be completed rapidly and the urgency with which robots should visit tasks to complete them should vary dynamically depending on the task's progress and the distribution of robots and tasks in the environment. For our market-based task selection model, we assume that each task is provided with an agent. A task's agent behaves like a seller in an information economy while robots behave like buyers. The objective of a seller is to rapidly complete the task associated with it. A task is considered complete when the pheromone accumulated at it reaches a threshold value. To achieve this, each seller sells a synthetic commodity called "chips" while charging a certain price per chip. Buyers purchase chips from sellers in exchange for pheromone. The amount of pheromone that a buyer purchases from a seller depends on the price/chip offered by the seller. Each seller tries to get as much pheromone as possible from buyers to rapidly complete its task by offering an attractive price/chip to buyers. Because there are multiple sellers(tasks) in the environment trying to purchase pheromone from a finite set of buyers, each seller has to differentiate itself from its competitors and make itself attractive for buyers to purchase from. To achieve this, each seller calculates the profit or utility it obtains from selling chips at certain intervals and dynamically adjusts its unit price/chip to a value that is likely to ensure maximum possible profits during the next interval. A seller continues to sell chips in the market as long as its associated task's pheromone level does not reach the completion threshold.

The parameters used by our market-based algorithm are the following:

SU_i Utility to seller i

$\pi_{i,j,t}$ No. of chips sold by seller j to buyer i during interval t

p_{co} Base cost to a seller for procuring chips.

$BU_{i,j,t}$Utility to buyer i from seller j during interval t

$p_{j,t}$ Unit price/chip charged by seller j during interval t

$d_{i,j,t}$ Distance from buyer(robot) i to seller(task) j during interval t

$g_{i,j,t}$ Communication reqd. by buyer(robot) i to disseminate information about seller(task) j during interval t

$x_{i,j,t}$ Execution reqd. by buyer(robot) i for seller(task) j during interval t

c_d, c_g, c_x Costs for distance, communication, and execution respectively for a task to buyers

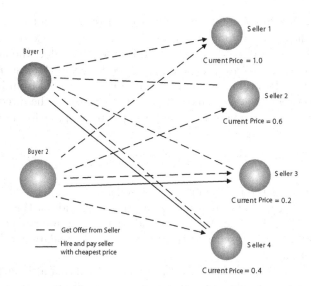

Fig. 1. A market scenario with 2 bargain-hunting buyers and 4 sellers

The utility to a seller is proportional to the amount of pheromone it accumulates during an interval t. We assume that one chip costs one unit of pheromone. Then, the utility that seller j gets by selling chips during interval t is given by:

$$SU_j = \sum_i \pi_{i,j,t} - p_{co}, \tag{1}$$

The utility to the i-th buyer from seller j during interval t is determined by the difference between the number of chips the buyer obtains from seller j and the total cost the buyer has to expend for the task corresponding to seller j, as given by the following equation:

$$BU_{i,j,t} = \pi_{i,j,t} \times p_j - (d_{i,j,t} \times c_d + g_{i,j,t} \times c_g + x_{i,j,t} \times c_x), \tag{2}$$

Figure 1 shows an example of a scenario between 2 buyers and 4 sellers in our market model. The current price/chip for each seller is shown alongside each seller. During each interval, each buyer observes the offers (price/chip) made by the sellers and selects the seller that provides the highest utility calculated using Equation 2. The buyer and seller then exchange pheromone for chips. At the end of every interval, each seller calculates the utility it obtained from the transactions with buyers during that interval using Equation 1. It then adjusts the price/chip to a value that is likely to maximize its utility during the next interval.

3.1   Dynamic Pricing Algorithms

We have used two dynamic pricing strategies to update the pheromone corresponding to the tasks(sellers) in the environment.

Derivative Following. In derivative following, a seller uses its profit information since the last price update to adjust its price in the next interval. If the profit in the last interval has increased from its previous value, the price for the next interval continues to move in the same direction as in the last interval. On the other hand, if the profit in the last interval has decreased from its previous value, the direction of the price movement is the reverse of the direction in the last interval. The equation used by seller j to update the price for interval $(t+1)$ using derivative following is:

$$p_{j,t+1} = p_{j,t} + \delta_t \times sign(\phi_{j,t} - \phi_{j,t-1}) \times sign(p_{j,t} - p_{j,t-1}) \qquad (3)$$

where $\phi_{j,t}$ represents the utility obtained by seller j during interval t calculated using Equation 1, $\delta_t \in U[0.1, 0.5]$ represents the amplitude of the price change and $sign : \mathcal{Z} \to \{-1, 1\}$. Since the prices and profits from intervals t and $(t-1)$ are already available with seller j, therefore, the price update can be done by seller j in constant time.

Previous research by Dasgupta and Das [8] has shown that although derivative following is relatively simple, it performs comparably with more computationally complex game-theory and learning based strategies where each seller requires knowledge of buyer distributions and the price and payoffs for every seller in the market to make its pricing decision at the end of every interval. However, a potential drawback of the derivative following strategy reported in [8] is that it fails to converge rapidly to an equilibrium price, if one exists.

Adaptive Derivative Following Strategy. To address the problem of derivative following, we have used the adaptive derivative following strategy from [8] to adjust sellers' prices in response to rapid fluctuations of price in the market. In adaptive derivative following, each seller uses a similar strategy to Equation 3, but the range of the distribution for the amplitude of price changes, δ_t, is dynamically adapted in proportion to the direction of the profit movement. This ensures that the price charged by a seller rapidly converges to an equilibrium(if one exists), or, diverges away from temporarily stable states.

$$\delta_t = \epsilon^{sign(\pi_t - \pi_{t-1})} \times \delta_{t-1} \qquad (4)$$

where, $\delta_{min} \leq \delta_t \leq p_{t-1}$ and $\epsilon > 1$. δ_{min} is the lower bound on the step-size for the adaptive derivative follower. The initial value of the amplitude for price changes is given by δ_0 which is chosen uniformly between $[0.1, 0.5]$. Dynamic step adjustment enables a seller to reduce the step size when the price is in the vicinity of the equilibrium and increase it otherwise.

4   Simulation Results

We have implemented our swarming algorithms for a distributed task processing application using robots [10]. The scenario consists of tasks distributed randomly in an environment. The objective of the robots is to identify all the targets.

However, each robot has limited computational resources, and, although a robot can independently discover a task, it requires the cooperation of other robots to complete the task.

4.1 Experimental Setup

All our experiments were run with 18 robots and varying number of tasks placed randomly inside a 50×50 meter^2 environment on the Webots robotic simulation platform. Robots and tasks measure 1 meter $\times 1$ meter. Each robot is simulated as a generic *DifferentialWheels* model whose speed and direction are controlled by changing the relative rotation speed between the two wheels. The maximum speed of each wheel was set to 1 meter/time unit. Each robot has the following sensors: (1) GPS: x, z location and heading, (2)Downward looking IR sensor for task detection with a measurement range between 0 and 2048, (3) Short-range radio transmitter and receiver for sending and receiving ping messages over channel 1 with a range of 1.5 units, and, (4) Long-range radio transmitter and receiver for sending and receiving gossip messages over channel 0 with a range of 7.5 units. All results were averaged over 20 runs.

Task Detection: The floor of the environment is black and corresponds to a zero intensity value on a robot's downward-looking IR sensor. Tasks are given 4 different colors (red, grey, green, purple) to simulate different task types that require different amounts of computation. When the IR sensor on a robot encounters a task, it returns a non-zero intensity value determined by the color of the task. The robot then associates a particular amount of pheromone with the task using the following values: Red= 0.8, Grey=0.6, Green= 0.4, Purple=0.2. Pheromone decays at a rate of 0.01 per simulator tick.

Task completion(Task Confirmation): When a robot encounters a task, it deposits 20 units of pheromone at its location. A task is considered confirmed when the pheromone deposited at it by different robots reaches a cumulative value > 60.0. This translates to an average of $4 - 5$ visits by different robots to a task to confirm it.

Robot Communication: When a task is found by a robot, it sends a gossip message to other robots within communication range of its long-range transmitter. Gossip messages are forwarded by robots using the probabilistic flooding algorithm described in [10] to disseminate information about a recently discovered task across the swarm. The format of the gossip message for task j sent at time t is given by: $< id, p_{j,t}, \phi_{j,t}, t_x, t_z, t_{pher}, ttl >$ where,

id	id of robot sending the message
$p_{j,t}$	price/chip offered by seller(task) j at time t
$\phi_{j,t}$	utility obtained by seller(task) j at time t
t_x, t_z	2-d coordinates of the task contained in the message
t_{pher}	Pheromone value associated with task in the message
ttl	Number of hops (time-to-live) from its source made by a gossip message before robots stop forwarding it

The heuristic strategies send three more fields per message than the market based strategy, viz., 2-d coordinates for each robot's location, a $found_i d$ corresponding to a unique identifier for the task identified and the no. of visits/task. Each field is 4 bytes.

On receiving a gossip message, a robot decrements its ttl and if $ttl > 0$, it forwards the message over its long-range transmitter after updating the values of the first three parameters of the message with its own id and location.

Obstacle and Collision Avoidance: To prevent collision between robots, each robot uses a potential field based object avoidance technique described in [10]. Collision avoidance takes precedence over all other actions.

Heuristic-based Strategies: We have used two heuristic-based task selection strategies described in [25] to compare the performance of our dynamic pricing strategies for task selection in swarms. In the *preference based* heuristic, each robot selects a task that has the minimum number of other robots in its vicinity and is also closest to completion. In the *proximity based* heuristic, each robot selects a task that satisfies the criteria for the preference based heuristic, and, additionally, is closest to the robot doing the selection.

4.2   Experimental Results

Our objective in the first set of experiments is to compare the dynamic pricing based task selection strategies with heuristic- based task selection along different performance metrics. For this set of experiments, the number of tasks in the environment is kept fixed at 20. Figure 2 shows the time required to identify all tasks within an environment using the different strategies. We observe that the dynamic pricing strategies are outperformed by the heuristic strategies. However, the market-based strategy achieves this performance while using 37.5% less communication per message than the heuristic strategies. The performance of the two dynamic pricing strategies are relatively comparable. For a small number of tasks ($5 - 10$), the derivative follower performs about $8 - 14\%$ better than the adaptive derivative follower. However, for larger number of tasks (> 15), the adaptive derivative follower dynamically adjusts the amplitude for the price changes and outperforms the derivative follower by about $11 - 30\%$.

Figure 3 compares the number of times each task is visited by different robots for the different strategies. We observe that although each task was visited by approximately 4 robots (number of robots required to complete a task for our setting) in most cases, there were variations in the exact number of visits/task both above and below the value of 4. Figure 4 shows the performance of each robot across different tasks. For our setting of 20 tasks(tasks), 18 robots and 4 robots required to complete a task, the average number of tasks that each robot should visit is given by $\lceil \frac{20 \times 4}{18} \rceil = 5$. However, we observe that some robots visited more than the average number of tasks while other robots visited far less than average. The variations observed in these two graphs around the optimum value can be attributed to two things:

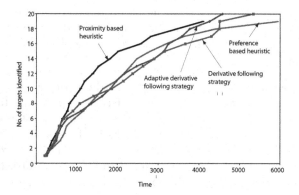

Fig. 2. Time required to identify all targets using different task selection strategies by robots

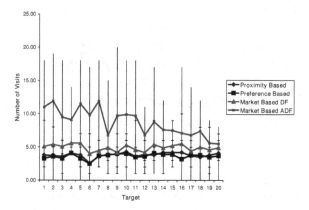

Fig. 3. Number of times each task is visited by a robot for different task selection strategies.(DF=derivative follower, ADF=adaptive derivative follower)

1. *Inadequate dispersion of robots across the environment:* With a centralized mechanism that shares robot locations and task progress across the environment, it is possible to direct the exact number of robots required to complete task towards the task. However, in a swarm, each robot decides to visit a task independently without exchanging the decision with other robots. Consequently, in some cases, more than the desired number of robots end up moving towards the same task. This triggers the collision avoidance mechanism as soon as robots reach within close range of each other before reaching the task. In such a scenario, most robots start exhibiting an oscillatory behavior moving back and forth around the task unable to reach it or to move towards another task.

2. *Communication Inefficiency:* Depending on the dispersion of robots in the environment, some robots encounter a significant delay while receiving information about a task until the task's gossip message gets flooded across all the robots.

For the next set of experiments, we compare the performance of the system using the derivative following and adaptive derivative following task selection strategy when the environment changes while keeping the number of robots fixed at 18. First, we vary the number of tasks in the system between 10 and 50 as shown in Figure 5. We observe that the system scales up favorably in the number of tasks(tasks) and the time required to identify all tasks(complete all tasks) grows linearly with the number of tasks. Figure 6 compares the effect of

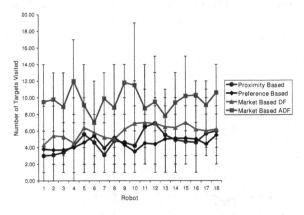

Fig. 4. Number of tasks visited by each robot for different task selection strategies.(DF=derivative follower, ADF=adaptive derivative follower)

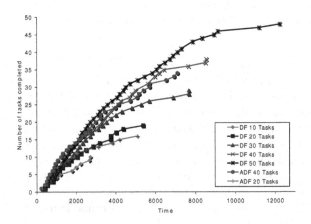

Fig. 5. Time taken to identify all tasks using the derivate and adaptive derivative follower strategy for different number of tasks in the environment

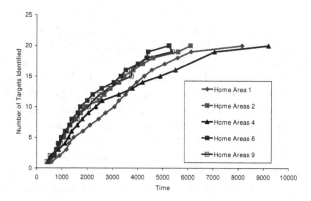

Fig. 6. Time to taken to identify all tasks for different number of home-areas into which the environment is divided using the adaptive derivative follower strategy

different coverage strategies for robots on the task completion time using the adaptive derivative following task selection strategy. We observe that the time required for task completion is comparable when we use a single deployment area, or when the environment is sub-divided into 4 *home-areas*. However, the task completion times improves significantly by about 100% when the environment is divided into 2, 6, or, 9 sub-areas. This improvement can be attributed to better distribution of robots over the environment resulting in closer initial proximity to tasks, and, consequently, better dissemination of task information across the swarm.

5 Related Work

The technique of swarming has been used extensively in nature and by humans over many years [15]. Recently, swarming-based computational systems have been used for different applications including vehicle routing [4], self-repairing formation control for mobile agents [35] and adaptive control in overlay networks [3] For most of these applications task selection among the swarm units is not of paramount importance in determining a problem solution. However, task selection is a significant issue in swarm environments comprising search and execute type tasks. For example, recent swarm-based systems for military applications such as task recognition within a reconnaissance area using unmanned aerial vehicles [10,30,33] rely on efficient task selection strategies to ensure load balancing and improve the performance of the system. Complementary to our approach of using dynamic pricing mechanisms for task allocation in swarms, Sauter *et al* [29] employ evolutionary algorithms to dynamically adapt the parameters for pheromone update equations for stigmergy based swarming systems.

Recently, the use of market-based techniques for addressing the multirobot task allocation(MRTA) problem has received considerable attention. One of the first algorithms for market based solutions for the MRTA problem was described in the MURDOCH system developed by Gerkey [17]. MURDOCH uses an auction mechanism inspired by the contract-net protocol [32] to allocate dynamically arriving tasks among multiple heterogenous robots. Gerkey also provides different classifications of the MRTA problem based on single and multiple combinations of robots and tasks. Task allocation in a multi-robot distributed system using a contract-net based protocol for the COMETS-UAV system has also been described by Lemaire et al [21]. The mechanism relies on one robot being elected as a leader(auctioneer) using a token-ring technique. In addition, the task allocation mechanism requires the leader to have knowledge about all the tasks it allocates to other robots(contractors). In contrast to contract-net protocol based approaches, the dynamic pricing based task selection strategies used in this paper do not require leader election and the information about tasks is maintained locally on each robot in a distributed manner. Kalra and Martinoli [19] compare the market based and threshold based task allocation strategies in a multi-robot setting within an environment with noisy communication. Their results show that market based approaches are particularly suitable in scenarios where task information is communicated accurately across the robots. A comprehensive review of market based approaches for multi-robot task allocation and coordination is provided by Dias et al in [13].

Independent of market-based approaches, the problem of multi-robot task allocation(MRTA) has been investigated using various techniques including physical modeling [28] and distributed planning[27]. Other approaches to multi-agent cooperation algorithms include the Martha system [2] that focuses on planning and distributed cooperation schemes, the ADOPT algorithm [26] and mediation protocol [23] that address coordination between agent teams using distributed constraint optimization techniques, and [22,31] that achieves distributed task allocation using negotiation techniques. Most of these approaches are complementary to our work and consider scenarios where an agent has to allocate shared resources across multiple tasks. Also, complementary to our work, Mainland et al [24] describe a dynamic pricing strategy called SORA(Self-Organizing Resource Allocation) to address the resource allocation problem in sensor networks. A reinforcement learning based technique is used to dynamically update a node's utility parameter and enables the node to adapt its actions in response to the payment received by the node.

6   Conclusion and Future Work

In this paper we have described multi-agent dynamic pricing strategies for task-selection in a swarmed system. Empirical results within a simulated environment show that the dynamic pricing strategies compare favorably with other heuristic-based strategies while reducing the communication overhead by as much as 37.5%. The simulation results, especially for the distribution of tasks and robots in the system, show that there remains scope for improving the performance of the system using techniques that reduce communication overhead between robots without significant loss of information. Currently, we are investigating social network based communication models and probabilistic inference based techniques to address these issues. Another potential direction to improve the performance of the system is to use more sophisiticated dynamic pricing algorithms that employ collaborative filtering based techniques for the pricing decision at each seller [9]. We envisage that with accurately engineered systems and appropriate mechanisms underlying the operations, swarm-based systems can be used to solve many challenging problems in the near future.

References

1. Abraham, A., Grosan, C., Ramos, V. (eds.): Swarm Intelligence in Data Mining, Studies in Computational Intelligence, vol. 34. Springer, Heidelberg (2006)
2. Alami, R., Fleury, S., Herrb, M., Ingrand, F., Robert, F.: Multi-robot cooperation in the MARTHA project. IEEE Robotics and Automation 5(1), 36–47 (1998)
3. Babaoglu, O., Meling, H., Montresor, A.: Anthill: A Framework for the Development of Agent-Based Peer-to-Peer Systems. In: Proc. Intl. Conf. on Distributed Computing Systems, pp. 15–22 (2002)
4. Bonabeau, E., Dorigo, M., Theraulaz, G.: Swarm Intelligence: From Natural to Artificial Systems. Oxford University Press, Oxford (1999)
5. Bullnheimer, B., Hartl, R., Strauss, C.: An improved Ant system algorithm for the vehicle routing problem. In: POM working paper no. 10/97, Vienna (1997)
6. Clark, J., Fierro, R.: Cooperative hybrid control of robotic sensors for perimeter detection and tracking. In: Proc. American Control Conference, vol. 5, pp. 3500–3505 (2005)
7. Correll, N., Martinoli, A.: Distributed Coverage: From Deterministic to Probabilistic Model. In: Proc. of the 2007 IEEE Int. Conf. on Robotics and Automation, Rome, Italy, April 2007, pp. 379–384 (2007)
8. Dasgupta, P., Das, R.: Dynamic Pricing with Limited Competitor Information in a Multi-Agent Economy. In: Proc. 7th Intl. Conf. on Cooperative Information Systems, Eilat, Israel, pp. 299–310 (2000)
9. Dasgupta, P., Hashimoto, Y.: Multi-Attribute Dynamic Pricing for Online Markets Using Intelligent Agents. In: Proc. AAMAS 2004, pp. 277–284 (2004)
10. Dasgupta, P., O'Hara, S., Petrov, P.: A Multi-agent UAV Swarm for Automatic Target Recognition. In: Thompson, S.G., Ghanea-Hercock, R. (eds.) DAMAS 2005. LNCS (LNAI), vol. 3890, pp. 80–91. Springer, Heidelberg (2006)
11. Dasgupta, P.: Distributed automatic target recognition using multi-agent UAV swarms. In: Proc. AAMAS 2006, pp. 479–481 (2006)
12. Dasgupta, P., Hoeing, M.: Market based Distributed Task Selection in Multi-agent Swarms. In: Proc. Intl. Conf. on Intelligent Agent Technology (IAT 2006), Hong Kong, pp. 113–116 (2006)
13. Dias, M.B., Zlot, R.M., Kalra, N., Stentz, A.: Market-Based Multirobot Coordination: A Survey and Analysis, Tech. report CMU-RI-TR-05-13, Robotics Institute, Carnegie Mellon University (2005)
14. Di Caro, G., Ducatelle, F., Gambardella, L.: AntHocNet: An Ant-Based Hybrid Routing Algorithm for Mobile Ad Hoc Networks. In: Yao, X., Burke, E.K., Lozano, J.A., Smith, J., Merelo-Guervós, J.J., Bullinaria, J.A., Rowe, J.E., Tiňo, P., Kabán, A., Schwefel, H.-P. (eds.) PPSN 2004. LNCS, vol. 3242, pp. 461–470. Springer, Heidelberg (2004)

15. Edwards, S.: Swarming on the Battlefield: Past, present and future. In: RAND National Security Research Division Report (2000)
16. Gaudiano, F., Bonabeau, E., Shargel, B.: Evolving behaviors for a swarm of unmanned air vehicles. In: Proc. of the 2005 IEEE Swarm Intelligence Symposium, Pasadena, CA, pp. 317–324 (2005)
17. Gerkey, B.: On multi-robot task allocation, Ph.D Thesis, Univ. of Southern California (2003)
18. Jager, M., Nebel, B.: Dynamic Decentralized Area Partitioning for Cooperating Cleaning Robots. In: Proceedings of the 2002 IEEE Intl. Conf. on Robotics and Automation, Washington, DC, USA, pp. 3577–3582 (2002)
19. Kalra, N., Martinoli, A.: A Comparative Study of Market-Based and Threshold-Based Task Allocation. In: Proc. 8th Intl. Symp. on Distributed Autonomous Robotic Systems (DARS 2006) (2006)
20. Kephart, J., Greenwald, A.: Shopbot Economics. Autonomous Agents and Multi-Agent Systems 5(3), 255–287 (2002)
21. Lemaire, T., Alami, R., Lacroix, S.: A distributed tasks allocation scheme in multi-uav context. In: IEEE Intl. Conf. on Robotics and Automation, New Orleans, LA (USA), April 2004, pp. 3622–3627 (2004)
22. Mailler, R., Lesser, V., Horling, B.: Cooperative negotiation for soft real-time distributed resource allocation. In: Proc. AAMAS 2003, pp. 576–583 (2003)
23. Mailler, R., Lesser, V.: A cooperative mediation based protocol for dynamic, distributed resource allocation. IEEE Trans. on System, Man, Cybernetics, Part C 36(1), 80–91 (2006)
24. Mainland, G., Parkes, D., Welsh, M.: Decentralized, Adaptive Resource Allocation for Sensor Networks. In: Proc. 2nd Symp. on Networked Systems Design and Implementation(NSDI 2005) (2005), http://www.usenix.org/events/nsdi05/tech
25. Miller, D., Dasgupta, P., Judkins, T.: Distributed Task Selection in Multi-agent based Swarms using Heuristic Strategies. In: Şahin, E., Spears, W.M., Winfield, A.F.T. (eds.) SAB 2006 Ws 2007. LNCS, vol. 4433, pp. 158–172. Springer, Heidelberg (2007)
26. Modi, P., Shen, W., Tambe, M., Yokoo, M.: Adopt: asynchronous distributed constraint optimization with quality guarantees. Artificial Intelligence 161(1-2), 149–180 (2005)
27. Oritz, C., Vincent, R., Morriset, B.: Task Inference and Distributed Task Management in the Centibots Robotic System. In: AAMAS 2004, pp. 870–877 (2005)
28. Parker, L.: Distributed Algorithms for Multi-Robot Observation of Multiple Moving Targets. Autonomous Robots 12(3), 231–255 (2002)
29. Sauter, J., Matthews, R., Parunak, H.V.D., Brueckner, S.: Evolving Adaptive Pheromone Path Planning Mechanisms. In: AAMAS 2000 and AAMAS 2002, pp. 434–440 (2002)
30. Sauter, J., Matthews, R., Parunak, H., Brueckner, S.: Performance of Digital Pheromones for Swarming Vehicle Control. In: Proc. AAMAS 2005, Utrecht, The Netherlands, pp. 903–910 (2005)
31. Shehory, O., Kraus, S.: Methods for task allocation via agent coalition formation. Artificial Intelligence 101(1-2), 165–200 (1998)
32. Smith, R.: The contract net protocol: High-level communication and control in a distributed problem solver. IEEE Transactions on Computers 29, 1104–1113 (1980)

33. Parunak, H., Brueckner, S., Odell, J.: Swarming coordination of multiple UAVs for collaborative sensing. In: Proc. 2nd AIAA Unmanned Unlimited Systems, Technologies, and Operations Aerospace Land and Sea Conference Workshop and Exhibits, San Diego, CA (2003),
    http://www.newvectors.net/staff/parunakv/AIAA03.pdf
34. Weiss, G. (ed.): Multi Agent Systems. MIT Press, Cambridge (1998)
35. Werfel, J., Bar-Yam, Y., Nagpal, R.: Building Patterned Structures with Robot Swarms. In: IJCAI 2005, pp. 1495–1504 (2005)

Evolve Individual Agent Strategies to Global Social Law by Hierarchical Immediate Diffusion

Yichuan Jiang[1] and Toru Ishida[2]

[1] Key Laboratory of Child Development and Learning Science of Ministry of Education,
Southeast University, Nanjing 210096, China
jiangyichuan@yahoo.com.cn
[2] Department of Social Informatics, Kyoto University, Kyoto 606-8501, Japan
ishida@i.kyoto-u.ac.jp

Abstract. A social law is a restriction on the set of strategies available to agents [1]. Each agent can select some social strategies in the operation of the systems, however, the social strategies of different agents may collide with each other. Therefore, we need to endow the global social laws for the whole system. In this paper, the social strategy is defined as the living habits of agent, and the social law is the set of living habits which can be accepted by all agents. This paper initiates a study of evolving social strategies of individual agents to global social law of the whole system, which is based on the hierarchical immediate diffusion interaction from superior agents to junior ones. In the diffusion interactions, the agents with superior social position can influence the social strategies of junior agents, so as to reduce the social potential energy of the system. The set of social strategies with the minimum social potential energy can be regarded as the global social law.

1 Introduction

The concept of *artificial social system* provides a new way to make coordination among agents, whose basic idea is to add a mechanism, called a *social law*, into the system [1][2][3]. According to [1], social law is the set of restrictions for agents' strategies which allow them enough freedom on the one hand, but at the same time constrain them so that they will not interfere with each other [5].

Each agent has its own social strategy, however, and the strategies among different agents may produce conflict. Therefore, to receive the harmony of the agent system, we will need to endow a set of social laws that can be accepted by all agents. If each agent obeys the laws, then the system can avoid collisions without any need for a central arbiter [1].

Then, how can we get the global social law? In this paper, we regard that global social law can be produced from the interactions of individual agent strategies. At the initial stage of the system, each agent has its own social strategies, but those individual social strategies may collide with each other. In the operations of the system, the social strategies will diffuse among agents. As the time goes, a global social law will be received finally.

N. Jamali et al. (Eds.): CCMMS 2007, MMAS 2006, LSMAS 2006, LNAI 5043, pp. 80–91, 2008.

There are two types of interaction, called the communication interaction and the diffusion interaction [4]. In the previous works about social law, they often focus on the communication interactions of agents, *i.e.* the negotiation mechanism of the social strategies. In this paper, we want to present a new method for the research of social law, and explore the evolution form individual social strategies to global social law by the agent diffusion interactions. Agent diffusion interaction is the large-scale of penetration of a social strategy of an agent on other agents. There are many forms for agent diffusion, in this paper we mainly capture the key characteristic of hierarchical diffusion, *i.e.* the social strategies of the superior agents may influence and change the ones of the junior agents.

2 Hierarchical Diffusion in the Society

In the society, there are so many diffusions of social phenomena, such as behavior habit, social strategies, norms, etc. There are many forms for diffusion of social phenomena, among them is the hierarchical diffusion [6]. Hierarchical immediate diffusion refers to the spread from more socially dominant actors to junior ones. The hierarchical diffusion is popular in the diffusion of knowledge, culture, and so on in the society. Another known example of this can be seen in physics, where the diffusion often takes place from the high potential energy to the low potential energy.

In the hierarchical diffusion of social phenomena, there are a small number of agents are 'experts' and are endowed with a high level of knowledge in at least one value of the vector. All individuals interact among themselves, exchanging information via a simple process of barter exchange. Barter can only take place if the first individual has superior knowledge of one type and the other individual has junior knowledge of another type [9]. A global social phenomenon will be received after continuous hierarchical diffusion from superior individuals to junior ones. Fig.1 illustrates the hierarchical diffusion structure [7][10].

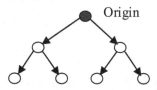

Fig. 1. The hierarchical diffusion structure

From the hierarchical diffusion structure, we can see that the direct diffusion mainly take place from the superior actor to the junior one. Certainly, there are still many other complex diffusion forms in the society, but such immediate diffusion from superior actor to junior one is one of basic forms. Therefore, in this paper, we only capture the characteristic of this basic diffusion form and initiate a study on the social law evolution by the hierarchical immediate diffusion from superior agent to junior agent.

3 Related Definitions

3.1 Social Strategy

About the social law, there are some related works about it [1][2][3]. According to [1], a social law is a restriction on the set of actions available to agents. From such definition, we can see that the social law is mainly about the restriction for the actions of agents in the previous works.

However, it is not sufficient to only restrict the actions of agents. In social agent systems, we also need to consider the living habits of the agents. The agents become more intelligent and more ubiquitous in agent systems that simulate the human life. Therefore, we may naturally endow them with some life and personality characters [8]. Among the life characters of social agent, living habits is a key factor. Each social agent has its living habits and plays its own special role. In this paper, we will define the social strategy as the living habit available to agents.

Definition 1. A social strategy is a restriction on the living habits available to the agent. The set of social strategies of all agents of the system can be denoted as a matrix: $S = [s_{ik}], 1 \le i \le n, 1 \le k \le m$, where n denotes the number of agents and m denotes the number of living habits.

$$s_{ij} = \begin{cases} 1 \ \ where \ agent \ i \ like \ the \ living \ habit \ of \ k; \\ 0 \ \ where \ agent \ i \ cares \ nothing \ about \ the \ living \ habit \ of \ k \\ -1 \ where \ agent \ i \ doesn't \ like \ the \ living \ habit \ of \ k \end{cases} \qquad (1)$$

Obviously, the social strategies on an agent i can be denoted as a vector $S_i = \bigcup_k s_{ik}$.

We can also use some predications to represent the agent social strategies for their living habits.

$like(i, j)$: agent i likes the living habit of j;

$notcare(i, j)$: agent i cares nothing about the living habit of j;

$unlike(i, j)$: agent i unlikes the living habit of.

Therefore, we have:

$$s_{ij} = 1 \Rightarrow like(i, j); s_{ij} = 0 \Rightarrow notcare(i, j); s_{ij} = -1 \Rightarrow unlike(i, j).$$

Now, if $s_{ij}=1$ and $s_{i+1,j}=-1$, i.e. $like(i,j)$ and $unlike(i+1,j)$, therefore, the social strategies of i and $i+1$ will collide.

For example, Fig.2 shows an agent system with 3 agents and three living habits {drinking, smoking, noisiness}. Let a be superior to b, i.e. the social position of a is higher than the one of b. From Fig.2, we can see that b likes to smoke and make noise, but a doesn't like these habitis, therefore, their social strategies collide with each other at this time. Since a is superior to b, a will influence the living habits of b. Therefore, b's social strategy will be changed by the diffusion interactions between a and b.

\	drinking	smoking	noisiness
a	1	−1	−1
b	0	1	1
c	1	0	−1

Fig. 2. An agent system with 3 agents and 3 kinds of living habits

In the system, since the imbalance of the social strategies and positions among agents, the social strategies are not fixed but change as the time goes. In the operations of the system, the agents with higher social positions will diffuse their social strategies to the agents with lower social positions continuously.

3.2 Social Position and Potential Energy

In the system, each agent has different social position. The agents with different social positions in the system may take different effects; the superior agents may influence the living habits of the junior agents.

Definition 2. Position of agent i can be a function: $p_i \to [0, \vartheta]$, where ϑ is a natural number. The set of the positions of all agents in the system can be denoted as: $P = [p_i], where\ 1 \le i \le n$, and n denotes the number of agents in the system. $p_i > p_j \Rightarrow the\ position\ of\ i\ is\ \sup erior\ to\ j$. Obviously, the higher the position of an agent is, the more probably its social strategy will influence other agents.

However, it is not realistic that all the superior agents will diffuse their social strategies to the junior agents. The diffusion between two agents will be determined by some forces between them. The forces will be defined by their social positions, their social strategies, their geographical distance, etc. Only when the strength of the force is more than a degree, the superior agent will diffuse its social strategy to the junior agent.

We can use the concept of social potential energy to describe the force between two agents that influences the social strategy diffusion. *Potential energy (PE)* exists whenever an object which has a position within a force field. Potential energy functions are often used as global optimization problems in search of the stable structure [11]. Therefore, in this paper, we want to use the potential energy function to search the stable social strategy structure, *i.e.* a global social law. Our aim is the determination of the global minimum social energy configuration.

We can think that our agents are located within a social law field and each agent has its social potential energy. In this paper, we consider the social potential energy between two agents is energy which results from the following factors: *distance of the two agents' social positions, distance of the two agents' social strategies, and geographical distance between the two agents' localities.* The bigger the distance of the two agents' social positions is, the more the potential energy between them is; the bigger the distance of the two agents' social strategies is, the more the potential energy between them is; however, the bigger the geographical distance between the two agents' localities is, the less the potential energy between them is.

According to the common definitions of potential energy [12], the potential energy should be defined between the object and the zero-potential energy position. In this paper, the social potential energy is also comparative, *i.e.* the social potential energy is defined by the distance between two agents. The set of distance between all agent pairs can be denoted as a matrix $D = [D_{ij}]$. The distance between two agents can be defined by the following three factors:

$D_{SS}(i,j)$: Distance of the social strategies between two agents i and j,

$$D_{SS}(i, j) = \sum_k \left| s_{ik} - s_{jk} \right| ;$$

$D_{SP}(i,j)$: Distance of the social positions between two agents i and j,

$$D_{SP}(i, j) = \left| p_j - p_i \right| ;$$

$D_{GL}(i,j)$: Distance of the geographical localities between two agents i and j.

At last, the distance of two agents can be defined as:

$$D_{ij} = \frac{\sigma_{SS} D_{SS}(i, j) + \sigma_{SP} D_{SP}(i, j)}{\sigma_{GL} D_{GL}(i, j)} \tag{2}$$

Where $\sigma_{SS}, \sigma_{SP}, \sigma_{GL}$ are the three parameters that decide the comparative effects of the three kinds of distances to the D_{ij}.

From (2), we can see that:

$$D_{SS} \uparrow \cup D_{SP} \uparrow \cup D_{GL} \downarrow \Rightarrow D \uparrow \Rightarrow PE \uparrow .$$

Definition 3. Let the distance between agent i and j be D_{ij}, and we can also assume the social potential energy between two agents i and j is only determined by the distance D_{ij}.

$$PE_{ij} = f(D_{ij}) \tag{3}$$

Obviously, the PE_{ij} is a monotonous increasing function of D_{ij}. The bigger D_{ij} is, the more PE_{ij} is.

The social potential energy of the whole system is the sum of the social potential energy of all agent pairs. Since $PE_{ij}=PE_{ji}$, therefore, the social PE of the whole system can be defined as:

$$PE = \frac{1}{2} \sum_{i=1}^n \sum_{j=1}^n PE_{ij} \tag{4}$$

PE_{ij} decides the probability that the diffusion between i and j will take place.

3.3 Social Law

As said above, the individual social strategies of agents may collide with each other. Fox example, an agent with a higher social position doesn't like to smoke, but a nearby agent with a lower position like to smoke. Obviously, the former agent shall influence the living habit of the latter agent since the former has a higher social position. After the diffusion interactions of social strategies among agents go continuously, the global social law may be achieved. A global social law should collectively apply to the system members A. For instance, if $A=\{a_1, a_2... a_n\}$, then the social law has the set of social strategies X, if and only if, $a_1, a_2, ..., a_n$, collectively obey X. Certainly, the real social law that can be fully accepted by all agents is hard to reach. We can only make the social law be accepted by majority agents. In our view, our aim for the social law is "*good enough*" but not "*fully perfect*".

Global social law (GSL) is the set of social strategies which produce the minimum collisions among agents, which emerges from the interactions of local agent strategies. There are two types of interaction, called the communication interaction and the diffusion interaction [4]. In our paper, we mainly consider the diffusion interaction, *i.e.* the superior agents influence the social strategies of the other junior agents step by step. At last, the collisions of the social strategies among agents will be minimized, and then we can say that the global social law is achieved.

According to our definition of social potential energy, the minimum collision is corresponding to the minimum PE. Therefore, the desired law is the one that minimizes overall system social potential energy.

$$SL = \{S^* \mid \forall S \ PE(S) > PE(S^*)\} \tag{5}$$

When the PE is minimized, the conflicts of the social strategies among different agents can also be minimized. In the agent diffusion interaction, the evolution of the social laws will go toward the goal of minimizing the potential energy of the whole system, and the global social law will be achieved eventually.

4 Diffusion from Superior Agent to Junior One

4.1 Agent Diffusion Interaction

When two agents make diffusion interaction, the superior agent will influence the social strategy of the junior agent. Diffusion can only take place if the source agent has superior position and the potential energy between them is more than a degree. In the diffusion process, the superior agent will penetrate its social strategy into the one of the junior agent, and change the social strategies of junior agentS through some desired rules which can reduce the potential energy between them.

Each agent is characterized by a social strategy vector that evolves over time through diffusion interactions among the agents. Therefore, now we extend the definition for the agent social strategy in Section 3.1 by including the time factor. Formally, let

$$S_i(t) = \bigcup_j s_{ij}(t), 1 \le j \le m,$$

denote agent i's social strategies endowment at time t, and m is the number of living habits. $S(t) = \bigcup S_i(t)$ denotes the set of social strategies of the system at time t. Also, we will use $PE_{ij}(t)$ to denote the social potential energy between agent i and j at time t, and $PE(t)$ to denote the social potential energy of the whole system at time t.

Therefore, the goal of the agent diffusion interaction is: $PE(t+1) < PE(t)$. The diffusion interaction is formally denoted as:

1) Diffusion interaction between two agents i (superior one) and j (junior one):

$$S_j(t) \xrightarrow{\text{\textit{penetrated by } } S_i(t)} S_j(t+1),$$

and the social strategies of i keep fixed, i.e. $S_i(t) = S_i(t+1)$. Obviously, the distance of the social strategies between the two agents will be reduced, so as to the PE between them can also be reduced.

2) Diffusion interactions of the whole system: $S(t) \rightarrow S(t+1)$, so as to $PE(t+1) < PE(t)$.

As said above, in the diffusion interaction, the social strategy of the agent with higher social position keeps constant, and the social strategy of the agent with junior social position will be penetrated by the superior agent. Then, how can the social strategy of the junior agent be changed? For example, if the superior agent likes to smoke, and the junior agent doesn't like to smoke, the junior agent only can select the new habit "cares nothing about smoking" or "likes to smoke" after their diffusion interactions; if the superior agent doesn't like to smoke, and the junior agent likes to smoke, so the junior agent only to select the new habit "cares nothing about smoking" or "doesn't like to smoke". To avoid the drastic change of the living habit of junior agent that may increase the PE between it and other agents, it will select the new living habit "cares nothing about smoking".

Formally, let i be the superior agent and j be the junior agent, and $S_{ik}(t)$ denote the kth living habit of agent i at time t. Then, we can have the following diffusion penetration rules for the social strategies:

$$S_{ik}(t+1) = S_{ik}(t);$$
$$S_{jk}(t+1) = \begin{cases} S_{jk}(t), & \text{if } S_{jk}(t) == S_{ik}(t) \text{ or } S_{ik}(t) == 0 \\ 0, & \text{otherwise} \end{cases} \qquad (6)$$

The diffusion penetration rules for the social strategies between two agents can also be shown as Table 1.

For example, let there be two agent a and b, a have a superior position and b have a junior position. Their social strategies are show as Fig.3 (a) and (b). According to the diffusion penetration rules in Table 1, the social strategy in b will be changed as Fig.3 (c).

Table 1. Diffusion penetration rules of the social strategies

Before diffusion interaction		After diffusion penetration	
Superior agent	Junior agent	Superior agent	Junior agent
1	1	1	1
1	0	1	0
1	-1	1	0
0	1	0	1
0	0	0	0
0	-1	0	-1
-1	1	-1	0
-1	0	-1	0
-1	-1	-1	-1

1	-1	-1	0	1	(a) Social strategy of a
1	1	-1	1	-1	(b) Social strategy of b before diffusion interaction
1	0	-1	1	0	(c) Social strategy of b after diffusion interaction

Fig. 3. An example for the diffusion interaction of social strategies between two agents

4.2 Algorithm for the Global Social Law Evolution

According to our definition of PE, reducing PE of the whole system can also reduce the conflicts of the social strategies among agents. Therefore, to get the global social law, we will need to reduce the PE of the whole system. To reduce the PE of the whole system, we will select the agent pair with the highest PE to make diffusion interaction, and change the social strategy of the junior agent.

Algorithm 1

Input: S, P, D_{GL}, Degree.
1. Compute the PE of the system (at first we will need to compute the D_{SS} and D_{SP});
2. Select the agent pair (i,j) with the highest PE;
3. If there is chance for diffusion between i and j, then goto 4, else select other agent pair with the second highest PE, until all agent pairs are considered. If there are no chances for diffusion for all the agent pairs, then end.
4. Change the social strategy of the junior agent according to the diffusion penetration rules;
5. Compute the PE, If the $PE<Degree$ or there aren't any changes for the S, then end; else, goto 2;
Output: the new S, which can be regarded as the global social law.

5 A Simple Case

Now we take a simple example to demonstrate our model. Fig.4 is the S, P and D_{GL} of the example.

$$S(t) = \begin{Bmatrix} / & drinking & smoking & noisiness \\ a_1 & 0 & -1 & 0 \\ a_2 & 1 & 1 & -1 \\ a_3 & -1 & 1 & 1 \end{Bmatrix}$$

(a)

$$P = \begin{Bmatrix} a_1 & a_2 & a_3 \\ 1 & 2 & 3 \end{Bmatrix}$$

(b)

$$D_{GL} = \begin{Bmatrix} / & a_1 & a_2 & a_3 \\ a_1 & 0 & 2 & 1 \\ a_2 & 2 & 0 & 1 \\ a_3 & 1 & 1 & 0 \end{Bmatrix}$$

(c)

Fig. 4. An example to demonstrate our model

We compute the distances among all agents, shown as Fig.5. To simplify the problem, in the computation of D, we let $\sigma_{SS}, \sigma_{SP}, \sigma_{GL}$ be all 1.

$$D_{SS} = \begin{Bmatrix} / & a_1 & a_2 & a_3 \\ a_1 & 0 & 4 & 4 \\ a_2 & 4 & 0 & 4 \\ a_3 & 4 & 4 & 0 \end{Bmatrix}, \quad D_{SP} = \begin{Bmatrix} / & a_1 & a_2 & a_3 \\ a_1 & 0 & 1 & 2 \\ a_2 & 1 & 0 & 1 \\ a_3 & 2 & 1 & 0 \end{Bmatrix}, \quad D = \begin{Bmatrix} / & a_1 & a_2 & a_3 \\ a_1 & 0 & 5/2 & 6/1 \\ a_2 & 5/2 & 0 & 5/1 \\ a_3 & 6/1 & 5/1 & 0 \end{Bmatrix}, \quad PE(t) = f(13.5)$$

(a)   (b)   (c)   (d)

Fig. 5. The initial potential energy at time t

From Fig.5, the potential energy between a_1 and a_3 is the highest and there is chance for diffusion between them, therefore now we will change the social strategy of a_1 according to the diffusion penetration rules. At last, the new S is shown as Fig.6 (a). Then we compute the new D_{SS}, D and PE, shown as Fig.6 (b), (c), and (d).

From Fig.6, we can see that the potential energy between a_1 and a_3 is still the highest, but there aren't any diffusion penetrations between their social strategies. Therefore,

$$S(t+1) = \begin{cases} / & drinking & smoking & noisines \\ a_1 & 0 & 0 & 0 \\ a_2 & 1 & 1 & -1 \\ a_3 & -1 & 1 & 1 \end{cases},$$

(a)

$$D_{SS} = \begin{cases} / & a_1 & a_2 & a_3 \\ a_1 & 0 & 3 & 3 \\ a_2 & 3 & 0 & 4 \\ a_3 & 3 & 4 & 0 \end{cases},$$

(b)

$$D = \begin{cases} / & a_1 & a_2 & a_3 \\ a_1 & 0 & 4/2 & 5/1 \\ a_2 & 4/2 & 0 & 5/1 \\ a_3 & 5/1 & 5/1 & 0 \end{cases},$$

(c)

$$PE(t+1) = f(12)$$

(d)

Fig. 6. The social strategies and potential energy at time $t+1$

$$S(t+2) = \begin{cases} / & drinking & smoking & noisines \\ a_1 & 0 & 0 & 0 \\ a_2 & 0 & 1 & 0 \\ a_3 & -1 & 1 & 1 \end{cases} = GSL,$$

(a)

$$D_{SS} = \begin{cases} / & a_1 & a_2 & a_3 \\ a_1 & 0 & 1 & 3 \\ a_2 & 1 & 0 & 2 \\ a_3 & 3 & 2 & 0 \end{cases}$$

(b)

$$D = \begin{cases} / & a_1 & a_2 & a_3 \\ a_1 & 0 & 2/2 & 5/1 \\ a_2 & 2/2 & 0 & 3/1 \\ a_3 & 5/1 & 3/1 & 0 \end{cases},$$

(c)

$$PE(t+2) = f(9)$$

(d)

Fig. 7. The social strategies and potential energy at time $t+2$

we select the agent pair with the second highest potential energy, $i.e$, a_2 and a_3, to make diffusion penetration. The result is shown as Fig.7 (a).

Now, there are no chances for diffusion penetration of the social strategies among different agents. Therefore, we can said that $S(t+2)$ is the global social law (GSL). From the GSL of Fig.7 (a), we can see that there are no conflicts among the social strategies of the agents.

6 Conclusion and Future Work

Social strategies among agents may collide with each other; therefore, a global social law is needed. This article regards the global social law as the set of social strategies that will produce the minimum conflicts among agents, and presents a method for evolving individual social strategies to global social law based on the agent diffusion. In the model, we mainly consider how the superior agents diffuse their social strategies to the junior agents, and which is demonstrated by a case study.

Certainly, there are several issues that need future work:

- In this article, only the superior agents can diffuse their social strategies to the junior agents. However, in the real situation, the social strategies shared by many junior agents can also diffuse to the superior agents. Therefore, it is necessary to discover how this diffusion from junior agents to the superior agents may take place and the diffusion principles.
- In this article, we only consider the diffusion between two agents, *i.e.* agent pair. However, in real system, the forms of agent diffusion interactions are very complex. There are many forms for the agent diffusion interaction, such as, team diffusion and concurrent diffusion, cooperative and competitive diffusion, homogeneous and heterogeneous agent diffusion, etc. Therefore, in the future, we will make systemic research on the different forms of those complex agent diffusions and the dynamics of diffusion.

Acknowledgements

This work is supported by JSPS Research Grant No.17-05282, JSPS Grant-in-Aid for Scientific Research (18200009) and the Strategic Information and Communications R&D Promotion Program.

References

1. Shoham, Y., Tennenholtz, M.: On the emergence of social conventions: Modeling, analysis and simulations. Artificial Intelligence 94, 139–166 (1997)
2. Shoham, Y., Tennenholtz, M.: On social laws for artificial agent societies: off-line design. Artificial Intelligence 73, 231–252 (1995)
3. Onn, S., Tennenholtz, M.: Determination of social laws for multi-agent mobilization. Artificial Intelligence 95, 155–167 (1997)
4. Morone, P., Taylor, R.: Knowledge diffusion dynamics and network properties of face-to-face interactions. Journal of Evolutionary Economics 14(3), 327–351 (2004)
5. Boella, G., van der Torre, L.: The evolution of artificial social systems. In: Proceeding of the Nineteenth International Joint Conference on Artificial Intelligence, Edinburgh, Scotland, 30 July-5 August (2005)

6. Wallace, R., Huang, Y.-S., Gould, P., Wallace, D.: The hierarchical diffusion of AIDS and violent crime among U.S. metropolitan regions: inner-city decay, stochastic resonance and reversal of the mortality transition. Soc. Sci. Med. 7(44), 935–947 (1997)

7. Hornsby, K.: Spatial diffusion: conceptualizations and formalizations, http://www.spatial.maine.edu/~khornsby/KHI21.pdf

8. Hayes-Roth, B., Doyle, P.: Animate Characters. Autonomous Agents and Multi-Agent Systems 1(2), 195–230 (1998)

9. Morone, P., Taylor, R.: Knowledge Diffusion Dynamics and Network Properties of Face-to-Face Interactions. In: Nelson and Winter Conference, Aalborg, June 12-15 (2001)

10. Cliff, A.D., Haggett, P., Ord, J.K., Versey, G.: Spatial Diffusion: An Historical Geography of Epidemics in an Island Community. Cambridge University Press, Cambridge (1981)

11. Moloi, N.P., Ali, M.M.: An iterative global optimization algorithm for potential energy minimization. Computational Optimization and Applications 30, 119–132 (2005)

12. Viegas, J.: Kinetic and Potential Energy: Understanding Changes within Physical Systems, Jan 1, 2005. The Rosen Publishing Group (2005)

Team Formation Strategies in a Dynamic Large-Scale Environment

Chris L.D. Jones and K. Suzanne Barber

The University of Texas at Austin
Laboratory for Intelligent Processes and Systems
1 University Station C5000, Austin, TX, 78712-0240
{coldjones,barber}@lips.utexas.edu

Abstract. In open markets and within business and government organizations, fully autonomous agents may form teams to work on large, multifaceted problems. Factors such as uncertain information, bounded rationality and environmental dynamicism can lead to sudden, unforeseen changes in both solution requirements and team participation. Accordingly, this paper proposes and examines strategies for team formation strategies in a large-scale, dynamic environment. Strategies control how agents select problems to work on and partners to work with. The paper includes an experimental evaluation of the relative utility of each strategy in an increasingly dynamic environment, and concludes that a strategy which combines greedy job selection with adaptive team selection performs best in highly dynamic environments. Alternatively, greedy job selection combined with selecting smaller teams performs best in environments with little to no dynamicism.

Keywords: Coalition formation, Task selection, Partner selection, Fault-tolerance, Dynamic environments, Large-scale environments, Request for Proposal.

1 Introduction

Individual agents and multi-agent systems increasingly represent mature technologies, capable of competently solving problems in their specific domains and operating with a high degree of autonomy. Therefore, as computing becomes more ubiquitous and agents consequently become more pervasive, there is an increasingly high probability that an agent exists to help solve any given problem.

These trends, combined with the basic Request For Proposal domain described in [1] suggests the potential for a huge electronic marketplace, where a constant stream of questions or problems is handled by thousands or millions of humans and self-interested agents, each taking on different roles such as general contractor or service provider, each buying or selling skills, expertise, and other services as needed. The potential for such markets arises within government institutions, the military, and business corporations as well.

While many job requests submitted to such a market might be trivial, many are likely to be complex, requiring multiple skills from multiple providers. Furthermore,

N. Jamali et al. (Eds.): CCMMS 2007, MMAS 2006, LSMAS 2006, LNAI 5043, pp. 92–106, 2008.

many of these problems are likely to be novel, undertaken with incomplete information about the problem and a limited understanding of the solution requirements, both of which will almost certainly change as the problem is worked on. Real world problems also occur in dynamic environments, where unexpected changes occur to both the problem and the personnel involved in solving it.

In this type of market environment, many issues arise. Even given a way to accurately determine which agents possess what skill set, how can an agent seeking to maximize its own utility select the best jobs to work on, and the best agents to partner with? How do the partners available to work on different possible jobs influence which job an agent should pursue? How should a team of agents be structured to handle difficulties such as sudden changes to a problem, or defections from the team? And how can these varying requirements be balanced against each other?

One initial attempt at addressing this combination of factors may be found in [2], which draws on previous work in the field in areas such as task selection [3, 4, 5], coalition formation in dynamic environments [6, 7], bottom-up team formation between autonomous agents [8], and team formation in environments with imperfect information [9, 1, 10]. This paper therefore continues the work started in [2] and creates an experimental framework that simulates a decentralized problem-solving marketplace within a very large organization. More particularly, the paper introduces a set of strategies for team formation between autonomous agents in a large-scale, dynamic, decentralized environment, and seeks to determine the relative performance of different classes of agents utilizing these strategies as the rate of change ("dynamicism") of jobs in the environment increases.

This paper is organized as follows. In section two, it discusses related work in the multi-agent systems community. In section three, it describes several job and team selection heuristics, and how these heuristics combine to form team formation strategies in a dynamic environment. In section four, it describes the setup and parameters of a simulation to test the relative utility of the proposed strategies. In section five it discloses the results of the simulation, and analyzes those results. Finally, section six suggests several ideas to expand upon these strategies, and investigate their utility in different settings.

2 Related Work

Coalition formation has been studied both inside and outside of the multi-agent systems community for some time. Some research has focused on the formation of optimal coalitions by a centralized authority, [11] while other research has focused on the formation of coalitions to solve jobs by a hierarchical structure of agents [3]. Still further research has been focused coalition formation between selfless agents in a dynamic [7] or open environment, [5] or between agents willing to delegate their autonomy to a centralized controller or consensus decisions among groups of agents [12].

However, such research has limited applicability to decentralized selfish agents, which may be unwilling or unable to take direction from a centralized authority. Other work has therefore examined selfish agents operating in various environments. Research has focused on building coalitions of agents who lack a common view of a coalition's value, [19] as well as coalitions developed between rationally-bounded agents, [10] or agents who lack full knowledge about the abilities of potential partner agents [11]. Others have examined the interaction between agents in market environments [13]. Such research frequently focuses on relatively small groups of agents, although still other research has focused on the use of congregations, [14] adaptive social networks, [15] and even physics-motivated mechanisms to allow large groups of agents to form large, mutually beneficial coalitions [16]. It should be noted, however, that such work is frequently focused on only one possible task at a time, or does not occur in dynamic, unpredictable environments.

In contrast, Klusch and Gerber focus on the formation of coalitions of agents to work on multiple possible tasks in dynamic environments, by utilizing a simulation-based scheme to determine the utility of various potential coalitions in a given state of a dynamic environment [6]. This work allows for complex negotiations between the different potential partners of a coalition, and takes risk vs. reward considerations into account when considering different potential coalitions. However, it differs substantially from the work below in that the coalitions formed are not adaptive once formed, nor are jobs selected based on the potential teams available to solve a given job.

Tambe's work is likewise relevant, wherein selfish agents are collected into a team by an initial authority, often a human programmer. The agents may then be delegated by software algorithms into roles which pursue various sub-goals critical to the overall mission [17]. As will be shown in further detail below, the strategies described below build on this research by allowing agents to form adaptive teams without the need for an initial organizing authority.

In addition, Soh and Tsatsoulis have focused on the possibility of hastily-formed coalitions in response to new problems or events [18]. This research forms the basis for one of our heuristics for job selection, as will be described in further detail below.

3   Team Formation Strategies

This paper introduces a set of strategies for team formation between fully autonomous agents in a large-scale, dynamic, unpredictable environment, which is described with a simple, but widely applicable model similar to that used in [15]. Consider a set of general tasks $T = \{T_i\}$, where $1 \leq i \leq \alpha$. Each general task T_i represents a type of job that an agent might carry out: if T is limited to tasks involved in building construction, for example, T_1 might be building a driveway, while T_2 might be constructing a roof, and so on. Each general task T_i is therefore a set of task instances $\{T_{ij}\}$, where each T_{ij} is a specific instance of general task T_i associated with a job J_j, and where each job J_j is part of a set of jobs $J = \{J_j\}$, where $1 \leq j \leq \beta$. For example, if T represents the set of all tasks associated with building a building, and if J is the set of all buildings under construction, then T_{11} might be building a driveway at a first building under construction, T_{12} might be building a driveway at a second building under construction, T_{21} is constructing a roof at the first building, and so on.

Each job J_j in set J contains a potential task instance T_{ij} of every possible task T_i in T, but only a subset of these tasks need to be completed to finish the job. Again, returning to the building example, every building in existence could conceivably have a swimming pool, or a loading dock, or a conference room, but in practice factories and offices rarely have swimming pools, and houses rarely have loading docks. Accordingly, within each job J_j, task instances T_{ij} are separated into a set of active task instances *ActiveTasks$_j$*, all of which must be completed for the job to be finished, and a set of inactive task instances *InactiveTasks$_j$*, which are irrelevant to the job's completion status. For any job J_j, *ActiveTasks$_j$* $\cup$ *InactiveTasks$_j$* $= \{T_{ij}\}$ for all i, and *ActiveTasks$_i$* $\cap$ *InactiveTasks$_i$* $= \varnothing$.

Continuing on, a set of skills $S = \{S_i\}$ and a set self-interested of agents $A = \{A_k\}$ are introduced, where once again $1 \leq i \leq \alpha$ and $1 \leq k \leq \chi$. Each skill S_i is associated with a general task T_i, and may be used to work on and eventually complete any task instance T_{ij} in T_i. Furthermore, each agent A_k has an associated set of skills *AgentSkills$_k$* that A_k is capable of doing, where *AgentSkills$_k$* is a subset of S. Each agent A_k has the same number of skills, and each skill in S equally common among agents in A.

Each task instance T_{ij} has an associated TaskLength$_{ij}$, where $1 \leq$ TaskLength$_{ij} \leq \gamma$. To complete task instance T_{ij}, an agent A_k must use an appropriate skill S_i on the task instance for TaskLength$_{ij}$ timesteps. Accordingly, function $C(T_{ij})$ is defined as a value ranging from 0 to TaskLength$_{ij}$, and represents the amount of time that one or more agents have worked on T_{ij}. Different tasks are worth the same amount of credit, but agents earn rewards proportional to the TaskLength$_{ij}$ of any task instance T_{ij} they have finished. For example, an agent that completes a task over five timesteps earns five credit points, while an agent that completes a task over eight timesteps earns eight credit points.

To simulate the end results of uncertain information, bounded agent rationality and dynamic, unpredictable environments, jobs in J are dynamic and unpredictable. More particularly, task instances T_{ij} in J_j are randomly moved between *ActiveTasks$_i$* and *InactiveTasks$_i$* on a periodic basis. This may be best understood as a sudden change to a job's solution requirements. For example, despite the best efforts of project management and requirements engineering, software development projects frequently change their required functionality in the middle of development, making some already-completed portions of the project obsolete and requiring new modules to be built from scratch. Similarly, task instances T_{ij} which are moved from *InactiveTasks$_j$* to *ActiveTasks$_j$* must be done from scratch, while only active task instances which have been fully completed are immune from being moved to *InactiveTasks$_j$*. (Admittedly, it is not unheard-of for fully-completed portions of many different types of projects to be discarded, but it is also reasonable to argue that work which has been fully completed is often used in some way, somehow, whereas partially completed work is often abandoned entirely.) Note that the number and types of tasks that must be completed for an individual job to be completed is therefore continually changing.

3.1 Agent Strategies

Accordingly, a set of strategies for bottom up team formation between agents in dynamic environments is defined as follows. A strategy is a combination of a job selection heuristic that orders potential jobs in J, and a team selection heuristic that ranks a set of potential teams capable of completing a specific job. More particularly, self-selected foreman agents from A each utilize a job selection heuristic to select one or more top-ranked jobs from J, depending on if one or more jobs are tied for the top ranking. This creates a set of jobs $P = \{J_w\}$.

For each J_w in P, each foreman agent then generates ε agent teams capable of solving J_w. More specifically, these agent teams each include the foreman agent which generated the team, and one or more other agents A_k, such that the combined skills of all the agents in the team are capable of completing the task instances in *ActiveTasks*$_w$ of associated job J_w. These teams thus form a set of teams $Q = \{Team_x\}$. Furthermore, each agent A_k in a $Team_x$ is associated with a set *AssignedInstances*$_{kw}$, which, after a team has been formed, represents the set of task instances T_{iw} that each agent A_k in the team is assigned to complete in job J_w. Teams are currently assembled via a semi-random approach that seeks to satisfy the various solution requirements one at a time, but nearly any constraint satisfaction solver could also be used. Once Q is generated, each foreman agent uses a team selection heuristic to select the top-ranked team from Q, which it then attempts to form through protocols described in further detail below.

The first job selection heuristic is a Greedy heuristic (Eqn. 1) that maximizes the expected reward from a job J_j. While a naive heuristic would simply choose jobs that require the greatest amount of work (and thus the greatest amount of associated reward), the Greedy heuristic takes the dynamicism of the environment into account by giving double weight to portions of a task that have already been completed, thereby giving preferential treatment to large jobs that are less likely to undergo changes before the job is complete.

$$\text{Greedy heuristic: } \max_{J_j \in J} \sum_{T_{ij} \in AssignedInstances_{kj}} (TaskLength_{ij} + C(T_{ij})) \qquad (1)$$

The second job selection heuristic is a Lean heuristic (Eqn. 2) that minimizes the amount of work needed to complete a job, thereby letting agents opportunistically form teams to quickly solve simpler problems, similar to [22].

$$\text{Lean heuristic: } \min_{J_j \in J} \sum_{T_{ij} \in AssignedInstances_{kj}} (TaskLength_{ij} - C(T_{ij})) \qquad (2)$$

Note that these mechanisms stand in contrast to previous work in task selection under uncertain conditions, such as Hannah and Mouaddib [4], where a problem's uncertain elements are explicitly modeled probabilities. Instead, the heuristics described here operate under any level of uncertainty, from any source. However, future work is possible where the above heuristics are adaptive based on a known or suspected level of uncertainty in the environment, or in a specific problem.

The first team selection heuristic is a Null heuristic that does not rank the teams, but rather keeps teams ordered according to how the strategy's job selection heuristic ranked the jobs associated with each team. This effectively randomly selects one of the teams generated to handle the top-ranked job from P.

The second team selection heuristic is a Fast heuristic (Eqn. 3) that minimizes the maximum amount of work that any member of a $Team_x$ needs to complete. Alternatively, the Fast heuristic could be said to minimize the amount of time needed before the entire team has completed work on associated job J_w.

$$\textbf{Fast heuristic: } \min_{x} \left| \max_{\substack{A_k \in Team_x \\ T_{iw} \in AssignedInstances_{kw}}} \sum (TaskLength_{iw} - C(T_{iw})) \right| \qquad (3)$$

The third team selection heuristic is a Redundant heuristic (Eqn. 4) that seeks to maximize the number of redundant skills in $Team_x$. In other words, the Redundant heuristic prefers teams with multiple agents capable of working on active task instances, thereby increasing the ability of a team to deal with the defection of an agent.

$$\textbf{Redundant: } \max_{x} \left| \bigcup_{A_k \in Team_x} AgentSkills_k \cap ActiveTasks_w \right| \qquad (4)$$

The fourth team selection heuristic is an Auxiliary heuristic that seeks to maximize the number of auxiliary skills in $Team_x$. In other words, the Auxiliary heuristic (Eqn. 5) tries to maximize the combined skills of a team that are not immediately applicable to task instances in $ActiveTasks_w$, thereby increasing the ability of the team to deal with newly added task instances.

$$\textbf{Auxiliary: } \max_{x} \left| \bigcup_{A_k \in Team_x} AgentSkills_k \cap InactiveTasks_w \right| \qquad (5)$$

Note that, intuitively, the Fast, Redundant, and Auxiliary heuristics each prefer a greater number of partners in a team, since this increases the amount of work that can be done in parallel and the number of unused skills for each partner. Alternatively, the MinPartner heuristic (Eqn. 6) prefers teams with the smallest number of partners, thereby implicitly using a greater number of skills per partner and thus a greater amount of potential profit per partner.

$$\textbf{MinPartner heuristic: } \min_{x} \left[|Team_x - 1| \right] \qquad (6)$$

Each of these five team selection heuristics is combined with each of the job selection heuristics for experimental comparisons, as described in further detail below.

4 Experimental Setup

To evaluate the relative utility of each of the team formation strategies described above, these strategies are tested in a simulation environment wherein agents compete to form teams and solve jobs according to the described strategies. More particularly, a set of agents is divided into ten different classes, each of which contains an identical number of agents, and each of which implements a different team formation strategy. By assigning agents credit for completing task instances, the relative utility of each strategy may be determined by comparing the average amount of credit earned by each class of agents. Furthermore, by varying the rate of change of the solution requirements for different jobs ("dynamicism"), the relative performance of these strategies in a dynamic environment can be determined.

Agents in set A operate in a simulation environment that is divided into discrete timesteps, or rounds. During each round, each agent may coordinate with other agents in A to form teams, or, if it is part of a team, may work on a task instance associated with a specific job in J. Each agent in A can belong to, at most, one team at a time, and each team works on only one job at a time. This is arguably a simplistic assumption, since real world providers of valuable skills or expertise frequently multitask between different projects at the same time. However, many problem solutions require complete focus from the workers involved, or security or other constraints may require exclusivity. Furthermore, requiring each agent to be part of only one team at a time allows us to clearly delineate where an agent is making a contribution. Determining to what degree an agent's partial efforts require task reassignments touches on complex multidimensional trust issues [19], and as such is too complex to be addressed here.

During each round, an agent A_k may work on a job J_j by utilizing a skill S_i found in *AgentSkills*$_k$ to work on a task instance T_{ij} found in set *ActiveTasks*$_j$. Each agent utilizes only one skill in any given round. After A_k has worked on T_{ij} for a given number of rounds, T_{ij} is completed.

Credit is distributed to agents when a job J_j is completed, which, in turn, occurs when all task instances in *ActiveTasks*$_j$ are completed. Upon job completion, credit points for each active, completed task are given to the agent which completed the task. As described above, these credit points are proportional to the length of the completed task (e.g. a completed task of length five would give five credit points). No credit is given for work on task instances that were moved to *InactiveTasks*$_j$ before completion, or to agents who worked on, but did not finish, a completed task instance. Accordingly, agents in the simulation may be said to work in a "pay-for-play" environment, where credit is distributed directly to those who have fully completed a given job.

Once a job J_i has been completed and paid out its credit, it is removed from J and a new J_j is created and inserted in J. Each new J_j starts with the same number of task instances randomly placed in *ActiveTasks*$_j$, and task instance in the new job must be completed from scratch.

As described above, the simulation incorporates unpredictability by shuffling task instances between *ActiveTasks*$_j$ and *InactiveTasks*$_j$. More particularly, each round a given percentage of jobs in J are randomly selected to be shuffled. This percentage is referred to as the dynamicism of the simulation. Each task instance in each selected job J_j has a random chance of being selected for shuffling between *ActiveTasks*$_j$ and *InactiveTasks*$_i$, such that, on average, one task instance per selected job is shuffled. However, as described above, task instances that have been fully completed cannot be moved from *ActiveTasks*$_j$.

4.1 Team Formation

As described above, teams are formed by a foreman agent. The opportunity to act as a foreman agent is randomly distributed among agents, such that any given round of the simulation a given percentage of agents will have the opportunity to form teams. Once the foreman agent has used its associated team formation strategy to select a potential team *Team*$_x$, the foreman sends proposal messages to potential partners in

$Team_x$ indicating the $AssignedInstances_{kw}$ that a potential partner would work on. Note that, to encourage agents to form teams, $|AgentSkills_k|$ is constant for all k, and the initial value of $|ActiveTasks_i| > |AgentSkills_k|$.

When these proposal messages are received, each agent ranks the $AssignedInstances_{kw}$ it is currently working on (if any) against one or more proposed $AssignedInstances_{kw}$ using the job selection heuristic associated with that class of agent. If the agent finds that its current assigned tasks are preferable to any of the proposals, it continues working on its current job, and the lack of a response is taken as a decline message by the foreman which sent the proposal. If the agent receives a proposal it finds more attractive than its current job assignment, the agent returns an accept message to the foreman which sent the proposal.

Accordingly, it is noted that agents may stop work on their current assignments at any time upon receiving a more attractive proposal (or, if they become a foreman agents, upon finding a more attractive job to work on). This obviously runs counter to a significant amount of work which his been done in contract negotiation and breaking contracts [20]. However, such work usually involves complete information, and/or occurs between a relatively small number of agents. In contrast, the scheme described here allows for agents which are better able to take advantage of new opportunities, and better simulates many environments where contracts are largely nonexistent or unenforceable (i.e. informal task forces and many Internet transactions). This lack of commitment between agents, combined with the dynamicism and unpredictability of jobs within the simulation, also makes it desirable for agents to assemble teams that can survive agent defections and changes in the task instances required to finish the job.

If the foreman does not receive accept messages back from all potential partners, the team formation process has failed and the foreman, as well as the agents which accepted the team proposal, must wait for new team proposals or for their next chance to be a foreman. If the foreman receives accept messages from all of its potential partners, the team is successfully formed and the foreman claims J_w, thereby making it off limits to other teams. Jobs may be claimed only by foremen who have successfully formed full teams. Note that during this process, other agents may be attempting to assemble a team to handle the same job, thereby simulating a realistic "churn" in which a degree of effort is unavoidably lost to competition. Jobs are claimed by means of a lock mechanism which prohibits "ties" between agents trying to claim a job.

Once agents have formed $Team_x$, they begin to work on the task instances associated with J_w. Non-foreman agents may work on J_w until they have completed all task instances in $AssignedInstances_{kw}$. In contrast, the foreman agent may stay with J_w until the job is complete, even if the foreman has completed its assigned tasks. While J_w is incomplete, if a non-foreman agent defects from the job, or a new task instance is moved into $ActiveTasks_w$ set, the foreman is responsible for finding an agent to work on the new or abandoned task instance. The foreman may therefore assign the new task instance to the $AssignedInstances_{kw}$ set of itself or a partner agent, in a manner similar to the team reformation strategies in [17]. If no team member has the skill required to handle the new task, the team has failed and dissolves with the job uncompleted. A new team which later tries to claim the job must begin the job from scratch. It therefore follows that teams must handle defections and new task instances to be successful.

Furthermore, it should be noted that a balance must be achieved when forming a new team with regard to the number of agents recruited. Because only one decline message will prohibit the formation of a new team, or will break an existing team seeking to recruit an outside member, larger teams are more difficult to form. Furthermore, team members running the Greedy job selection heuristic are more likely to defect from a larger team, since, on average, they will be assigned less work and thus have less opportunity for profit. However, larger teams are better able to handle agent defections and new task instances within the team, making them more stable once formed.

Table 1. Experimental parameters

Parameter	Value
Number of classes	10
Agents per class	250
Per round chance of agent acting as foreman	1%
Jobs	1000
$|T|$	20
$|AgentSkills|$	5
Initial size of $|ActiveTasks|$	10
Range of TaskLength	1 to 10 rounds
Credit received per round of completed task instance	1
Number of potential teams examined per top-rank job	15
Dynamicism range	0% to 100%, 25% increment
Number of rounds per simulation	2500
Number of simulations per dynamicism step	20

Experiments were conducted using the basic parameters in Table 1, which were selected to broadly model a problem-solving market internal to an organization such as a large corporation or a moderately large number of freelance agents. The experiments tested all strategies against each other simultaneously to see which strategies were most successful in a field of heterogeneous agents. More particularly, a two-factor ANOVA analysis was carried out, and the Fisher LSD method was used to determine significant differences between different strategies at the same dynamicism level.

5   Results and Discussion

Figure 1 displays the average credit earned by each agent class at different levels of dynamicism, along with standard deviation bars for each value. A cursory examination of the data indicates that the credit earned by each class decreased as the level of dynamicism in the environment increased, and that while GreedyMinPartners was the most successful strategy for 0% and 25% dynamicism, GreedyAuxiliary was

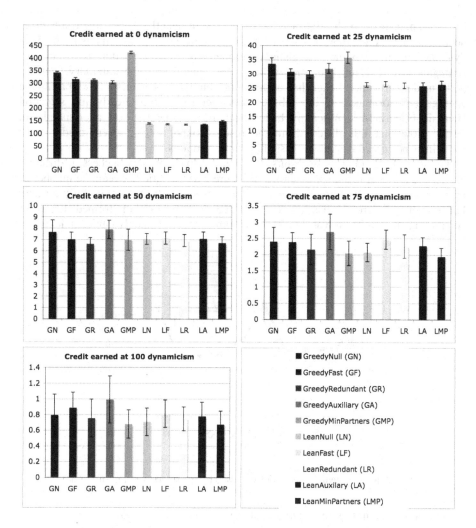

Fig. 1. Strategy performance as a function of dynamicism

the most successful strategy for all other dynamicism levels. ANOVA analysis (alpha = .05) indicates that the strategy selection causes statistically significant differences in the results.

Furthermore, Fisher LSD tests (alpha = .05 for all comparisons below) indicate that the top-performing strategy for each dynamicism level was statistically significant from all other strategies, with the exception of 50% dynamicism, where GreedyAuxiliary and GreedyFast were statistically significant from all other strategies but not from each other, and 100% dynamicism, where GreedyAuxiliary was significantly better than all other strategies, save GreedyFast.

Similar results can be seen when examining the aggregate performance of each team selection heuristic, regardless of the job selection heuristic it was paired with: at

0% dynamicism, the MinPartner performed significantly better than all other heuristics, and better than all but the Null heuristic at 25% dynamicism. At 50% dynamicism, the Auxiliary heuristic performed significantly better than all other strategies save the Null heuristic, while at 75%, and 100%, the Auxiliary heuristic performed significantly better than all heuristics but the Fast heuristic. Comparing the aggregate performance of the job selection heuristics, the Greedy job selection heuristic performed significantly better than the Fast heuristic at all dynamicism levels. Note that this differs from the results found in [2], where credit could sometimes be earned from unsuccessfully completed jobs.

To better understand these results, it is helpful to know how successful different classes are at forming teams, as shown in Figure 2 as the ratio between the number of team formation requests by a foreman and the number of teams successfully formed. Furthermore, Figure 3 displays the average success rate of formed teams at completing an assigned job as a function of both agent class and dynamicism level.

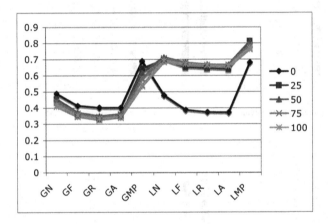

Fig. 2. Ratio of teams successfully formed by class and dynamicism level

As can be seen in Figure 2, certain patterns are immediately obvious. Agents using Lean job selection strategies are significantly more successful at forming teams than Greedy job selection strategies, except at 0% dynamicism, when job requirements do not change. This may be due to the fact that, in dynamic environments, a subset of jobs will have a lower than average number of tasks, which are more attractive to agents using the Lean job selection heuristic, thereby improving the probability that these agents will join a team.

Furthermore, agents using the MinPartner team selection heuristic are far more likely to successfully form a team. As discussed below, this is likely due in part to the fact that a smaller number of partners means a smaller number of potential rejections, any one of which can break team formation. In addition, a smaller number of agents means a higher number of tasks assigned to each agent, and accordingly, a greater amount of profit for each agent.

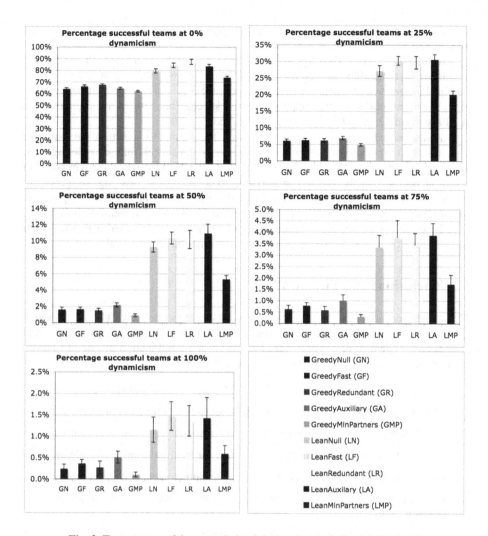

Fig. 3. Teams successful at completing jobs by class and dynamicism level

Conversely, Figure 3 shows that, although agents which utilize the MinPartners team selection heuristic are the most successful at forming teams, they are consistently the least successful agents at forming teams which successfully complete their assigned jobs. Alternatively, agents which utilize the Fast, Redundant, and Auxiliary heuristics are consistently the most successful at forming successful teams. In fact, ANOVA and LSD analysis (alpha = .05) indicates that, although agents utilizing these three heuristics do not have success rates that are always significantly different from each other, they are almost always significantly different from agents using the Null and MinPartner heuristics. Again, as discussed above, this is likely due to the fact that teams formed according to the Fast, Redundant and Auxiliary heuristics are more likely to have team members with unused skills that can be used in the event that another team member leaves the team, or a new task is added to the list of *ActiveTasks*.

This result suggests that agents which can recognize a team with significant redundant or adaptable characteristics may be more successful than agents which cannot. In other words, agents which can recognize a proposed team that has a lower offered reward but a greater opportunity for success because of its redundant or auxiliary resources may be able to earn more credit.

It is also noted that, although agents using the Lean job selection heuristic are significantly more successful at both forming teams and successfully completing jobs, these agents are generally less successful than agents which use the Greedy job selection heuristic. This may be in part due to the fact that Lean agents generally select jobs with far less work involved, and thus earn far less credit per job. Accordingly, it may be possible to determine under what circumstances a Lean vs. Greedy job selection heuristic is preferred, or even to find an optimal heuristic which combines the two considerations, based on environmental characteristics.

6   Conclusions and Future Work

This paper presented a set of strategies for team formation between fully autonomous agents in a large-scale dynamic environment. Strategies prioritized which jobs and partners each agent selected, and were composed of a combination of one of two job selection heuristics and one of five team selection heuristics:

- Greedy job selection, which selects jobs according to profit potential
- Lean job selection, which selects jobs for minimal time to completion
- Null team selection, which defers to the associated job selection heuristic
- Fast team selection, which selects teams for minimal time to completion
- Redundant team selection, which selects teams to best handle partner failures
- Auxiliary team selection, which selects teams most capable of adapting to new tasks
- Minimum Partner team selection, which selects teams with the fewest number of partners

The paper then analyzed the relative performance of the strategies, as executed by different classes of agents, in an experimental test bed. Results indicated that a strategy combining the Greedy and Auxiliary heuristics performed the best in highly dynamic environments, while a strategy combining the Greedy and MinPartner heuristics performed better in environments with low or no dynamicism.

Furthermore, the paper showed that, although agents using the MinPartner heuristic were more successful at forming teams, these teams were significantly less successful at completing jobs than teams formed by agents using the Fast, Redundant, and Auxiliary team selection heuristics.

This paper therefore examined an unpredictable, dynamic domain of independent heterogeneous agents, and proved which of a given set of strategies for team formation best maximized agent utility in such a domain. These strategies work with very large groups of agents (>2500) and may potentially be applied to request for proposal (RFP) environments where teams of autonomous agents continually seek to solve dynamic problems by forming multi-skilled teams. These market environments potentially include Internet-wide open markets, and markets internal to large organizations such as corporations and government agencies.

A number of possible avenues of further investigation suggest themselves. One possibility is to modify the mechanism by which agents decide between joining potential teams; agents may be more successful if they can balance the reward a team offers for membership against that team's ability to adapt to change. Other potential work involves determining in what circumstances a Lean job selection heuristic is preferable to a Greedy job selection heuristic, and potentially finding an optimal balance between the two.

Acknowledgments. This research is sponsored in part by the Defense Advanced Research Project Agency (DARPA) Taskable Agent Software Kit (TASK) program, F30602-00-2-0588. The U.S. Government is authorized to reproduce and distribute reprints for Governmental purposes notwithstanding any copyright annotation thereon.

References

1. Kraus, S., Shehory, O., Taase, G.: Coalition Formation with Uncertain Heterogeneous Information. In: Proceedings of the Second International Joint Conference on Autonomous Agents and Multiagent Systems, pp. 1–8. ACM Press, New York (2003)
2. Jones, C., Barber, K.: Bottom-up Team Formation Strategies in a Dynamic Environment. In: AAMAS 2007 Workshop on Coordination and Control in Massively Multiagent Systems, pp. 60–72. ACM Press, New York (2007)
3. Abdallah, S., Lesser, V.: Organization-Based Cooperative Coalition Formation. In: Proceedings of the IEEE/WIC/ACM International Conference on Intelligent Agent Technology, pp. 162–168. ACM Press, New York (2004)
4. Hanna, H., Mouaddib, A.: Task Selection Problem Under Uncertainty as Decision-making. In: Proceedings of the First International Joint Conference on Autonomous Agents and Multiagent Systems, pp. 1303–1308. ACM Press, New York (2002)
5. Shehory, O., Kraus, S.: Methods for Task Allocation via Agent Coalition Formation. Artificial Intelligence 101, 165–200 (1998)
6. Klusch, M., Gerber, A.: Dynamic Coalition Formation among Rational Agents. IEEE Intelligent Systems 17, 42–47 (2002)
7. Nair, R., Tambe, M., Marsella, S.: Team Formation for Reformation. In: Proceedings of the AAAI Spring Symposium on Intelligent Distributed and Embedded Systems (2002)
8. Rathod, P., desJardins, M.: Stable Team Formation Among Self-Interested Agents. In: Working Notes of the AAAI 2004 Workshop on Forming and Maintaining Coalitions in Adaptive Multiagent Systems. AAAI, Menlo Park (2004)
9. Ketchpel, S.: Forming Coalitions in the Face of Uncertain Rewards. In: Proceedings of the Twelfth National Conference on Artifical Intelligence, pp. 414–419. AAAI, Menlo Park (1994)

10. Sandholm, T., Lesser, V.: Coalitions among Computationally Bounded Agents. Artificial Intelligence 94, 99–137 (1997)
11. Sen, S., Dutta, P.: Searching for Optimal Coalition Structures. In: Proceedings of the Fourth International Conference on Multi Agent Systems, pp. 287–292. ACM, New York (2000)
12. Martin, C.: Adaptive Decision Making Frameworks for Multi-Agent Systems. Ph.D. Thesis, University of Texas, Austin, TX (2001)
13. Wellman, M., Wurman, P.: Market-Aware Agents for a Multiagent World. Robotics and Autonomous Systems 24, 115–125 (1998)
14. Brooks, C., Durfee, E., Armstrong, A.: An Introduction to Congregating in Multiagent Systems. In: Proceedings of the Fourth International Conference on Multi Agent Systems, pp. 79–86. MIT Press, Cambridge (2000)
15. Gaston, M., desJardins, M.: Agent-Organized Networks for Dynamic Team Formation. In: Proceedings of the fourth international joint conference on Autonomous Agents and Multiagent Systems, pp. 230–237. ACM Press, New York (2005)
16. Lerman, K., Shehory, O.: Coalition Formation for Large-Scale Electronic Markets. In: Proceedings of the Fourth International Conference on Multi Agent, pp. 167–174. MIT Press, Cambridge (2000)
17. Tambe, M., Pynadath, D., Chauvat, N.: Building Dynamic Agent Organizations in Cyberspace. IEEE Internet Computing 4, 65–73 (2000)
18. Soh, L., Tsatsoulis, C.: Satisficing Coalition Formation among Agents. In: Proceedings of the first international joint conference on Autonomous Agents and Multiagent Systems, pp. 1062–1063. ACM Press, New York (2002)
19. Griffiths, N.: Task Delegation using Experience-Based Multi-Dimensional Trust. In: Proceedings of the fourth international joint conference on Autonomous Agents and Multiagent Systems, pp. 489–496. ACM Press, New York (2005)
20. Faratin, P., Klein, M.: Automated Contract Negotiation and Execution as a System of Constraints. MIT, Cambridge (2001)

Using Swarm-GAP for Distributed Task Allocation in Complex Scenarios

Paulo R. Ferreira Jr.[1,2], Felipe S. Boffo[1], and Ana L.C. Bazzan[1]

[1] Instituto de Informática, Universidade Federal do Rio Grande do Sul
Caixa Postal 15064, CEP 91501-970, Porto Alegre, RS, Brasil
{prferreiraj,fboffo,bazzan}@inf.ufrgs.br
[2] Instituto de Ciências Exatas e Tecnológicas, Centro Universitário Feevale
RS239, 2755, CEP 93352-000, Novo Hamburgo, RS, Brasil

Abstract. This paper addresses distributed task allocation in complex scenarios modeled using the distributed constraint optimization problem (DCOP) formalism. It is well known that DCOP, when used to model complex scenarios, generates problems with exponentially growing number of parameters. However, those scenarios are becoming ubiquitous in real-world applications. Therefore, approximate solutions are necessary. We propose and evaluate an algorithm for distributed task allocation. This algorithm, called Swarm-GAP, is based on theoretical models of division of labor in social insect colonies. It uses a probabilistic decision model. Swarm-GAP is experimented both in a scenario from RoboCup Rescue and an abstract simulation environment. We show that Swarm-GAP achieves similar results as other recent proposed algorithm with a reduction in communication and computation. Thus, our approach is highly scalable regarding both the number of agents and tasks.

1   Introduction

It is shown in [1] that optimal distributed coordination is associated with a high computational complexity, especially when agents lack full observability of the environment they operate. Even the less restrictive situations are proved to be NEXP-complete. However lack of full observability is a characteristic of many problems in the real world, where agents must reason with incomplete and uncertain information, in a timely fashion in order to cope with dynamic environments. Given these issues, Lesser [3] points out the fundamental principles for the construction of a multiagent system: agent flexibility. Flexibility would enable agents to react dynamically to the emerging state of the coordination effort.

When one exchanges centralized for distributed control, or trade total observability by local information, *self-organization* becomes key. To show good performance in realistic applications, multiagent systems must have a certain level of self-organization. Since the most natural way to organize work among agents is the decomposition of the objective in tasks, task allocation is an important part of the coordination problem. Research regarding multiagent systems

N. Jamali et al. (Eds.): CCMMS 2007, MMAS 2006, LSMAS 2006, LNAI 5043, pp. 107–121, 2008.
© Springer-Verlag Berlin Heidelberg 2008

coordination through distributed task allocation has shown significant advances in the last few years. One successful direction, under the multiagent community perspective, has been the distributed constraint optimization problem (DCOP) framework.

Models of task allocation in complex environments, when modeled as a DCOP, yield hard problems, which cannot be treated with the traditional optimal/complete approaches to DCOP [5]. Thus complex DCOP scenarios introduce new challenges for the DCOP research. We see a complex scenario in distributed task allocation as the one in which, even small instances formalized as a DCOP generate large problems with exponentially growing number of parameters. Given that in the real-world we usually have large instances and these are dynamic, it is easy to conclude that new techniques are necessary.

We propose Swarm-GAP, an approximated algorithm for distributed task allocation based on theoretical models of division of labor in social insects colonies. This method is highly scalable regarding both the number of agents and tasks, and can solve the E-GAP (see next section) for dynamic task allocation in complex DCOP scenarios. Cooperative agents running our algorithm can coordinate their actions with low communication and computation.

We empirically evaluated the Swarm-GAP method on an abstract, domain-independent simulator, as well as in a scenario of the RoboCup Rescue simulator. Swarm-GAP is compared mainly to LA-DCOP [8], another approximated method for DCOP.

This paper is organized as follows: Section 2 discusses the use of the E-GAP model for task allocation in dynamic environments, and how it leads to a complex DCOP scenario. Section 3 presents our motivation to use swarm based heuristics and introduces the Swarm-GAP. The empirical evaluation of Swarm-GAP is shown in Section 4, together with a discussion on the results, while Section 5 presents our conclusions and future directions of this work.

2   Task Allocation Models and Complex DCOP Scenarios

In many real-world scenarios, a large number of agents must perform a large number of tasks. Besides, these tasks and their characteristics change over time and little information about the whole scenario, if any, is available to all agents. Each agent has different capabilities and limited resources to perform each task. The problem is how to find, in a distributed fashion, an appropriate tasks allocation that represents the best match among agents and tasks. This kind of scenario is becoming ubiquitous in manufacturing, robotics, computing, etc.

The Generalized Assignment Problem (GAP) deals with the assignment of tasks to agents, respecting agents resources, in order to maximize the total reward. GAP is known to be NP-complete [9]. It can be formalized as follows. Let us define $\mathcal{J}$ as the set of tasks to be allocated and $\mathcal{I}$ the set of agents. Each agent $i \in \mathcal{I}$ has a limited amount of resource r_i (a single type of resource is used). When a task $j \in \mathcal{J}$ is executed by agent i, task j consumes c_{ij} units of

i's resource. Each agent i also has a capability k_{ij} $(0 \leq k_{ij} \leq 1)$ to perform each task j.

The allocation matrix A, where a_{ij} is the value of the i-th row and j-th column, is given by Equation 1.

$$a_{ij} = \begin{cases} 1 \text{ if } j \text{ is allocated by } i \\ 0 \text{ otherwise} \end{cases} \tag{1}$$

An optimum solution to the problem is given by matrix A^*, which maximizes the system reward as stated by Equation 2, subject to the agents resource limitations and the constraint of having only one agent allocated to each task.

$$A^* = \operatorname{argmax}_{A'} \sum_{i \in \mathcal{I}} \sum_{j \in \mathcal{J}} k_{ij} * a'_{ij} \tag{2}$$

such that

$$\forall i \in \mathcal{I}, \ \sum_{j \in \mathcal{J}} c_{ij} * a_{ij} \leq r_i \text{ and } \forall j \in \mathcal{J}, \ \sum_{i \in \mathcal{I}} a_{ij} \leq 1$$

The GAP was extended by [8] to capture dynamic domains and interdependence among tasks. This extension, called Extended-GAP (E-GAP), improves the model in two ways:

Allocation constraints among tasks. Tasks in E-GAP can be interrelated by an AND constraint. All interrelated tasks by this constraint must be allocated at the same time to be considered by the reward computation. Following [8], let us define $\bowtie \ = \{\alpha_1, ..., \alpha_p\}$, where $\alpha_k = \{j_{k_1}, ..., j_{k_q}\}$ denotes the k-th set of an AND constrained tasks. Thus, the partial reward w_{ij} for allocating task j to agent i is given by Equation 3.

$$w_{ij} = \begin{cases} k_{ij} * a_{ij} & \text{if } \forall \alpha_k \in \ \bowtie, j \notin \alpha_k \\ k_{ij} * a_{ij} & \text{if } \exists \alpha_k \in \ \bowtie \text{ with } j \in \alpha_k \wedge \\ & \forall j_{k_u} \in \alpha_k, a_{x j_{k_u}} \neq 0 \\ 0 & \text{otherwise} \end{cases} \tag{3}$$

Reward dynamically computed over time. The total reward W is computed in E-GAP as the sum of the agents partial rewards (Eq. 3) in the last t time steps. In this case, the sequence of allocations over time is considered against the single allocation used in the GAP. Additionally, a delay cost d_j is used in order to punish the agents when task j was not allocated by time t. The objective of the E-GAP is to maximize the total reward W given by Equation 4.

$$W = \sum_t \sum_{i^t \in \mathcal{I}^t} \sum_{j^t \in \mathcal{J}^t} w_{ij}^t * a_{ij}^t - \sum_t \sum_{j^t \in \mathcal{J}^t} (1 - a_{ij}^t) * d_j^t \tag{4}$$

such that

$$\forall t \forall i^t \in \mathcal{I}^t, \quad \sum_{j^t \in \mathcal{J}^t} c_{ij}^t * a_{ij}^t \leq r_i^t \tag{5}$$

and

$$\forall t \forall j^t \in \mathcal{J}^t, \quad \sum_{i^t \in \mathcal{I}^t} a_{ij}^t \leq 1 \tag{6}$$

Several task allocation situations in large scale and dynamic scenarios can be modeled as an E-GAP [8]. Thus, the question now is how to find the best solution to E-GAP. The choice to model the E-GAP as a DCOP is mainly motivated by the recent advances in DCOP algorithms.

DCOP consists of n variables $V = \{x_1, x_2, ..., x_n\}$ that can assume values from a discrete domain $D_1, D_2, ..., D_n$ respectively. Each variable is assigned to one agent which has the control over its value. The goal of the agents is to choose values for the variables to optimize a global objective function. This function is described as the sum over a set of valued constraints related to pairs of variables. Thus, for a pair of variables x_k, x_l, there is a cost function defined as $f_{kl} : D_k \times D_l \to N$.

In DCOP, an E-GAP can be formalized as follows:

- Each variable $x_i \in V$ represents each agent i;
- Let us define a global domain D, whose elements are the set of all possible subsets of $\mathcal{J}$. The domain D_i of x_i is the set of elements from D, such that $\forall d \in D_i, \sum_{j \in d} c_{ij} \leq r_i$. This means that, to include d in D_i, the agent i must have enough resources to perform the entire task subset (each agent can allocate more than one task in E-GAP).
- The constraint cost function f_{kl}, related to the variables x_k and x_l, is given by the inverse of the sum of the reward obtained by each agent (Eq. 3). Besides, f_{kl} must prevent that more than one agent allocate the same task. Equation 7 defines f_{kl}.

$$f_{kl} = \begin{cases} -(\sum_{j \in D_k} w_{kj} + \sum_{j \in D_l} w_{lj}) & \text{if } a_{kj} \neq a_{lj} \\ \infty & \text{otherwise} \end{cases} \tag{7}$$

- There is one constraint to each pair of variables in V. We compute the cost as the inverse of reward because DCOP searches for minimizing the cost and E-GAP for maximizing the reward.

As we can see, an E-GAP formalized as a DCOP yields a large number of constraints, since there must be one for each pair of variables (a complete graph). The total number of required constraints can be computed as $\frac{n(n-1)}{2}$, where n is the number of agents (represented as variables). The size of variables' domain in the worst case, where agents have enough resources to allocate all tasks simultaneously, is $|\mathcal{P}(\mathcal{J})| = 2^{|\mathcal{J}|}$. The number of constraints grows exponentially according to the number of agents, while the size of variables' domains grows exponentially according to the number of tasks.

An important question about all DCOP algorithms is whether they are fast enough to be applied in complex scenarios. This translates to whether the number and size of exchanged messages turns the approach feasible and efficient. In distributed approaches, communication among agents usually imposes demands that can cause network overload. Complex problems usually mean that the planning (for allocation) and action should be treated as quickly as possible. Most of the proposed approaches yields good results in simple scenarios, but there is a lack of analysis regarding complex ones.

Most complete algorithms for DCOP were tested in small scenarios like the MaxSAT 3-coloring problem. It is an interesting one as this problem can be considered a benchmark, but it is not enough to deal with more complicated problems. The largest and hardest scenario reported in the literature where the DCOP algorithms were applied are related to distributed meeting schedule (DMS) [4,7].

In [4], the authors analyze the performance of the Adopt algorithm with an instance of DMS problem with 47 variables, an 8-element domain and 123 constraints. It was shown that using Adopt, agents exchange about 750.000 messages to compute the solution. In [7] the DPOP was experimented with a DMS instance of 136 variables, an 8-element domain and 161 constraints. In this case, 132 messages were exchanged by the agents. According to the authors, the number of messages grows linearly according to the number of constraints. However, the size of messages grows exponentially and the time necessary to compute and send this messages are critic to the performance.

Complex scenarios, as we define, result in problems dramatically more hard then the ones cited above. Let us suppose an E-GAP scenario with 100 agents and 100 tasks. This is a small scenario if thinking in large scale (thousands of tasks and agents). The number of variables is equal to the number of agents. The total number of constraints can be computed, as we mentioned before, as $\frac{n(n-1)}{2}$ where n is the number of agents: 4950 for 100 agents. Assuming that each agent has, on average, enough resources to perform only 3 tasks simultaneously, the size of the variables domain is equal to the number of possible tasks' subsets (each with 1, 2 or 3 tasks), namely 166,750 elements. These figures are much higher than the ones related to the DMS problem. The amount of messages or their size as well as the computational effort in DCOP algorithms grow exponentially with those numbers. Thus, to deal with complex scenarios, it is necessary to minimize the communication (including the messages size) among the agents as much as possible. Besides, in this kind of problem, it is better to get an approximated solution as fast as possible than to find the optimal one in an unfeasible time.

Most DCOP algorithms have approximated it is possible to define an upper bound for the number or size of messages. However, normally the mechanisms used by those algorithms become very inefficient as the scale of a complex scenario grows. Since it is not possible to use the optimal algorithms, nor their variants, we must look for other heuristic approaches, based on different mechanisms.

In [8], authors present an approximated algorithm called Low-communication Approximation DCOP (LA-DCOP) to solve instances of E-GAP. LA-DCOP outperforms DSA, another approximated algorithm able to deal with E-GAP, both regarding solutions' quality and number/size of messages. LA-DCOP uses a token based protocol to improve communication performance. Agents perceive a task in the environment, and either create a token to represent it or they receive a token from another agent. An agent decides whether to allocate a task based on a threshold and tries to maximize the use of its resources. After an agent decides whether or not to allocate a task, it sends the token to another randomly chosen agent.

3   Swarm-GAP

3.1   Motivation: Division of Labor in Swarms

Nature often rely on self-organization. There are several examples of self-organized biological systems. We focus here on the social insect colonies – also called swarms. A social insect colony with hundreds of thousand of members operates without any explicit coordination. An individual worker cannot assess the needs of the colony; it just has a fairly simple local information, and no one is in charge of coordination. From individual workers aggregation, the colony behavior emerges without any type of explicit coordination or planning. The key feature of this emergent behavior is the plasticity in division of labor inside the colony. Colonies respond to changing conditions by adjusting the ratios of individual workers engaged in the various tasks. Observations regarding this behavior are the basis of the theoretical model described in [11]. In this model, interactions among members of the colony and the individual perception of local needs result in a dynamic distribution of tasks. This model describes task distribution among individuals using the stimulus produced by tasks that need to be performed and an individual response threshold related to each task. The intensity of this stimulus can be associated with a pheromone concentration, a number of encounters among individuals performing the task, or any other quantitative cue sensed by individuals. An individual that perceives a task stimulus higher than its associated threshold, has a higher probability to perform this task.

Assuming the existence of $\mathcal{J}$ tasks to be performed, each task j has a s_j stimulus associated. $\mathcal{I}$ different individuals can perform them, each individual i having a response threshold θ_{ij} associated to a task j, according the task's type. Individual i engages in the task j with probability:

$$T_{\theta_{ij}}(s_j) = \frac{s_j^2}{s_j^2 + \theta_{ij}^2} \qquad (8)$$

Each insect in the colony can potentially perform all types of tasks. However, it is possible for individuals to specialize in some type of tasks based on morphological aspects (polymorphism). Polymorphism plays a key rule to determine the division of labor in ant colonies. It is possible to capture the physical variety in the theoretical model by differentiating individual thresholds. The threshold θ_{ij} of the individual (i) for the task i decreases proportionally to the individual capability to perform these tasks $capability_i(j)$. Thus, individuals with large capability for a set of tasks have higher tendency to perform tasks of this set.

$$\theta_{ij} = 1 - capability_i(j) \tag{9}$$

where $capability_i(j)$ is the capability of individual i regarding to task j.

Social insects behavior seems to fit the requirements of complex problems since they are the result of millions of years of survival-of-the-fittest evolution.

3.2   Swarm-GAP Algorithm

The aim of Swarm-GAP is to allow agents to decide individually which task to execute in a simple and efficient way, minimizing computational and communication efforts. As in [8], we assume that the communication does not fail. In the future we intend to relax this assumption and perform tests with unreliable communication channels. Agents in Swarm-GAP decide which task to execute based on the same mechanism used by social insects as shown in Equation 8. Each task has the same associated stimulus, there is no priority on task allocation. The stimulus s is the same for every task j and its value was empirically determined to maximize the system reward, through direct experimentation. Swarm-GAP uses polymorphism to setup the agents thresholds according to agents capabilities. Equation 9 sets the agents threshold θ_{ij} as 1 minus the capability $capacity_i(j)$ of agent i to perform task j. This is so because threshold and capability are inversely proportional values.

Algorithm 1 details Swarm-GAP. Agents running Swarm-GAP communicate using a token based protocol, and react to two events: task perception and message arriving. When an agent perceives some tasks, it creates a token composed by these tasks (line 5), or it receives the token from another agent (line 10). Once this is done, the agent has the right to determine which tasks to allocate (lines 14 to 21) according to their tendency given by Equation 8. This decision also depends on whether the agent has the resource which is required to perform the task. The quantity of resource one agent has is decreased by the amount required by the task (line 19). Afterwards, the agent is marked as visited (line 23). This prevent deadlocks, since it avoids passing the token to agents that already received the token. At the end of this process, if the token still has available tasks, a token message is sent to an agent randomly selected among those agents which have not received the token in the current allocation (lines 24 to 29). The size of the token message is proportional to the number of tasks.

Algorithm 1. Swarm-GAP($agentId$)

```
1: loop
2:     ev ← waitEvent()
3:     if ev = task perception then
4:         J ← set of new tasks
5:         token ← newToken()
6:         for all j ∈ J do
7:             token.addTask(j, -1)
8:     else
9:         token ← receiveToken()
10:
11:     r ← avaiableResources()
12:     τ ← token.avaiableTasks()
13:     for all t ∈ τ do
14:         θ_t ← 1− capability(t)
15:         if roulette() < T_{θ_t(s)} and r ≥ c_t then
16:             token.aloc(j, agentId)
17:             r ← r − c_t
18:
19:     token.visited(agentId)
20:     τ ← token.avaiableTasks()
21:     if |τ| > 0 then
22:         ı ← token.avaiableAgents()
23:         i ← rand(ı)
24:         sendToken(i)
```

---

4   Experiments and Results

Empirical evaluations of Swarm-GAP were conducted in an abstract, domain-independent simulator, and in the RoboCup Rescue Simulator [2,10].

The abstract simulator allows experimentation with a large number of agents and tasks. In general, we have 2000 tasks in each experiment, with 5 different classes randomly assigned to the tasks, and a variation in the number of agents from 500 to 4000 (that means, the latter is twice the number of tasks). Tasks cost are assigned uniformly from $\{0.25, 0.50, 0.75\}$. Each agent has 60% probability of having a non-zero capability for each class. Capabilities are uniformly assigned, with values ranging from 0 to 1. 60% of the tasks are AND inter-related in groups of 5. When new tasks arise at each simulation cycle they are randomly perceived by agents. The total number of tasks is kept constant, which means we modify the tasks characteristics (10% of the tasks has a probability of 10% to have their classes and demanded resources changed). At each simulation cycle, agents are constrained in the number of messages they can send to a maximum of 20.

Rewards are computed over 1000 simulation cycles, where in each cycle one allocation is performed. All data is averaged over 20 runs. Swarm-GAP is compared with three methods: LA-DCOP, a distributed greedy algorithm, and a centralized greedy algorithm. In the distributed greedy strategy, agents allocate the local perceived tasks for which they have highest capability. The central greedy strategy, used to benchmark other methods, allocates the appearing tasks to the most capable available agent, i.e. it does this in a centralized way. This simulation has exactly the same setup used by [8] to experiment LA-DCOP and, according the authors, different values for these parameters do not affect the results.

The other scenario used is the RoboCup Rescue [2]. The goal of the RoboCup Rescue Simulation League is to provide a testbed for agent rescue teams acting in large urban disasters. RoboCup Rescue is a complex multiagent domain characterized by: agents' heterogeneity, restricted access to information, long-term planning, and real-time. In the RoboCup Rescue, each agent has perception limited to its surroundings. Agents are in contact by radio, but they are limited on the number of messages they can exchange. As a cooperative multiagent system, efficiency can be achieved with the correct coordination. Approaches based on communication are not appropriate, because of the high communication constraints. According to [6], the challenge imposed by the environment can be decomposed into a task allocation problem. The allocation sub problem that we use in this paper concerns to the efficient assignment of fire brigade agents to the task of extinguishing fire spots. Swarm-GAP is also compared with LA-DCOP in this case and both methods are benchmarked by a greedy algorithm. This algorithm considers a heuristic where brigade agents decide always to tackle their shortest distant fire spots.

4.1 Abstract Simulator

In the first experiment, the aim is to find the best stimulus value (Equation 8) that maximizes the reward when the number of agents changes regarding the number of tasks. In this case there are no tasks with AND constraints.

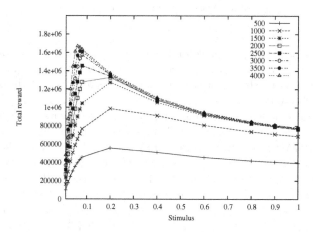

Fig. 1. Total reward *versus* task stimulus, for different number of agents

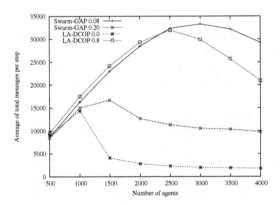

Fig. 2. Average number of messages per simulation cicle *versus* the number of agents

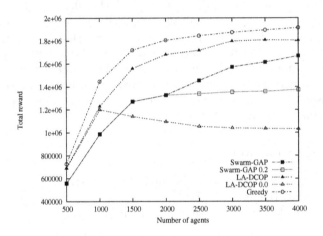

Fig. 3. Total reward for different number of agents

Figure 1 shows the rewards achieved for different values of stimulus and different number of agents. We use different quantities of agents to experiment different proportions related to the number of tasks (500 means 25% of the 2000 tasks, 1000 means 50%, and so on.)

In the second experiment, we measure the average number of messages per simulation cycle, according to the number of agents, for different setup parameters of Swarm-GAP (stimulus 0.2 and 0.08) and LA-DCOP (threshold 0.0 and 0.8). As we can see in Figure 2, when LA-DCOP works with threshold equal to zero, the number of messages exchanged is the smallest. Only on this case the average number of messages exchanged by Swarm-GAP is significantly greater than that of LA-DCOP. However, as we can see further on Figure 3, in this specific case, the total reward is significantly lower for LA-DCOP in comparison with Swarm-GAP. The total reward in E-GAP is computed as the sum of the agents capabilities to each task they allocated.

In the third experiment, we evaluate Swarm-GAP comparing its results with those achieved by the greedy centralized algorithm and LA-DCOP. Figure 3 shows the total reward, for different number of agents, achieved by Swarm-GAP, with the best stimulus for each number of agents and LA-DCOP, also with the best threshold for each number of agents. As expected, the greedy approach outperforms both Swarm-GAP and LA-DCOP. Swarm-GAP performs well achieving rewards that are only 20% lower (on average) than those achieved by the greedy, and 15% lower than those of LA-DCOP.

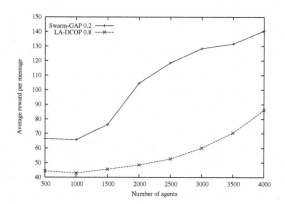

Fig. 4. Average reward divided by total number of exchanged messages, for different number of agents

To illustrate the advantages of Swarm-GAP related to LA-DCOP regarding the number of exchanged messages, Figure 4 shows the average reward divided by the total number of exchanged messages for different number of agents achieved by Swarm-GAP with stimulus 0.2 and LA-DCOP with threshold 0.8. We use this setup because in this case, both algorithms achieve to similar rewards. As we can see, Swarm-GAP exchanges a significant lower number of messages.

Furthermore, as Swarm-GAP uses a probabilistic decision process, the computation necessary for agents to make their decision is significantly lower than in LA-DCOP. As mentioned in Section 2, an agent running LA-DCOP chooses to allocate tasks which maximize the sum of its capabilities, while respecting its resource constraints. This is a maximization problem that can be reduced to a Binary Knapsack Problem (BKP), which is proved to be NP-complete. The computational complexity of LA-DCOP depends of the complexity of its function to deal with BKP. Each agent solves several instances of BKPs during a complete allocation. Agents running Swarm-GAP chooses to allocate tasks according to a probability computed by Equation 8, constrained by its available resources. This is a simple one-shot decision process.

Regarding the average number of allocated tasks per simulation step, both algorithms allocate almost the same number of tasks.

The last experiment with the abstract scenario measures the impact that AND-constrained tasks have over the reward. In this experiment, 60% of the

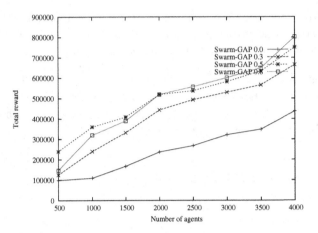

Fig. 5. Total reward for different number of agents in the presence of AND constrained tasks

tasks are AND constrained in groups of 5. Figure 5 shows the expected decrease in the performance of Swarm-GAP when we consider the AND constraints and several values for ω (Equation 8). Rewards improve when $\omega \neq 0$, improving the average performance in 25%.

4.2   Experiments on the RoboCup Rescue Simulator

In the following experiments, we evaluate Swarm-GAP comparing its results with those achieved by LA-DCOP. Both methods are benchmarked by a greedy approach based on a shortest distance heuristic.

We run our experiments in two partial maps of the Japanese city of Kobe (commonly used in RoboCup Rescue simulations), using 30 fire brigade agents in the first ($Kobe$) and twice this number in the second and largest map ($Kobe\_4$). For each map, we have tested two different scenarios for fire ignition points: 30 fires ($Kobe_1$), 42 fires ($Kobe_2$), 43 fires ($Kobe\_4_1$) and 59 fires ($Kobe\_4_2$). These points were uniformelly distributed. To measure performance, we use a metric which is the building area left (e.g. after an earthquake followed by a fire and the intervention of the fire brigades). Table 1 and 2 list results obtained in the above described scenarios. On the algorithm name column we also show the differents threshold values for LA-DCOP and stimulus value for Swarm-GAP that were experimented. All data is averaged over 20 runs of the simulator. Figure 6 depicts only the best performance for each method, for different scenarios.

To compute agents capabilities in the RoboCup Rescue we use the Euclidian distance from the fire brigade to the fire spot. Equation 10 show how this measure is normalized by agents.

$$capability(t) = \frac{\max\{distance(t_i), \forall t_i \in tasks\} - distance(t)}{\max\{distance(t_i), \forall t_i \in tasks\}} \quad (10)$$

Table 1. Results from the *Kobe* map, showing the average building area left

	$Kobe_1$ (30 fires)	$Kobe_2$ (42 fires)
Swarm-GAP 0.1	$1.35 \times 10^7 \pm 0.08 \times 10^7$	$0.66 \times 10^7 \pm 0.89 \times 10^7$
Swarm-GAP 0.2	$1.25 \times 10^7 \pm 0.14 \times 10^7$	$0.65 \times 10^7 \pm 0.12 \times 10^7$
Swarm-GAP 0.3	$1.26 \times 10^7 \pm 0.14 \times 10^7$	$0.58 \times 10^7 \pm 0.12 \times 10^7$
Swarm-GAP 0.4	$1.13 \times 10^7 \pm 0.29 \times 10^7$	$0.57 \times 10^7 \pm 0.90 \times 10^7$
Swarm-GAP 0.5	$1.25 \times 10^7 \pm 0.18 \times 10^7$	$0.60 \times 10^7 \pm 0.11 \times 10^7$
Swarm-GAP 0.6	$1.12 \times 10^7 \pm 0.42 \times 10^7$	$0.59 \times 10^7 \pm 0.12 \times 10^7$
LA-DCOP 0.1	$1.04 \times 10^7 \pm 0.22 \times 10^7$	$0.45 \times 10^7 \pm 0.11 \times 10^7$
LA-DCOP 0.2	$1.09 \times 10^7 \pm 0.19 \times 10^7$	$0.50 \times 10^7 \pm 0.72 \times 10^7$
LA-DCOP 0.3	$1.08 \times 10^7 \pm 0.23 \times 10^7$	$0.51 \times 10^7 \pm 0.10 \times 10^7$
LA-DCOP 0.4	$0.97 \times 10^7 \pm 0.21 \times 10^7$	$0.51 \times 10^7 \pm 0.83 \times 10^7$
LA-DCOP 0.5	$0.77 \times 10^7 \pm 0.14 \times 10^7$	$0.48 \times 10^7 \pm 0.11 \times 10^7$
LA-DCOP 0.6	$0.70 \times 10^7 \pm 0.15 \times 10^7$	$0.46 \times 10^7 \pm 0.12 \times 10^7$
Shortest distance	$1.31 \times 10^7 \pm 0.10 \times 10^7$	$0.97 \times 10^7 \pm 14 \times 10^7$

Table 2. Results from the *Kobe_4* map, showing the average building area left

	$Kobe\_4_1$ (43 fires)	$Kobe\_4_2$ (59 fires)
Swarm-GAP 0.1	$4.80 \times 10^7 \pm 0.09 \times 10^7$	$2.04 \times 10^7 \pm 0.09 \times 10^7$
Swarm-GAP 0.2	$4.78 \times 10^7 \pm 0.04 \times 10^7$	$1.96 \times 10^7 \pm 0.11 \times 10^7$
Swarm-GAP 0.3	$4.77 \times 10^7 \pm 0.14 \times 10^7$	$1.89 \times 10^7 \pm 0.18 \times 10^7$
Swarm-GAP 0.4	$4.76 \times 10^7 \pm 0.10 \times 10^7$	$1.78 \times 10^7 \pm 0.12 \times 10^7$
Swarm-GAP 0.5	$4.75 \times 10^7 \pm 0.10 \times 10^7$	$1.80 \times 10^7 \pm 0.08 \times 10^7$
Swarm-GAP 0.6	$4.76 \times 10^7 \pm 0.08 \times 10^7$	$1.78 \times 10^7 \pm 0.11 \times 10^7$
LA-DCOP 0.1	$4.64 \times 10^7 \pm 0.14 \times 10^7$	$1.65 \times 10^7 \pm 0.09 \times 10^7$
LA-DCOP 0.2	$4.57 \times 10^7 \pm 0.18 \times 10^7$	$1.62 \times 10^7 \pm 0.08 \times 10^7$
LA-DCOP 0.3	$4.48 \times 10^7 \pm 0.24 \times 10^7$	$1.61 \times 10^7 \pm 0.09 \times 10^7$
LA-DCOP 0.4	$4.52 \times 10^7 \pm 0.17 \times 10^7$	$1.64 \times 10^7 \pm 0.10 \times 10^7$
LA-DCOP 0.5	$4.40 \times 10^7 \pm 0.23 \times 10^7$	$1.61 \times 10^7 \pm 0.10 \times 10^7$
LA-DCOP 0.6	$4.51 \times 10^7 \pm 0.03 \times 10^7$	$1.61 \times 10^7 \pm 0.13 \times 10^7$
Shortest distance	$4.78 \times 10^7 \pm 0.05 \times 10^7$	$2.39 \times 10^7 \pm 0.15 \times 10^7$

Swarm-GAP, in the first scenario of each map ($Kobe_1$ and $Kobe\_4_1$), outperforms other methods by a slight difference. These are a very simple situations with few fire spots and all methods perform almost equally well.

In the scenarios $Kobe_2$ and $Kobe\_4_2$, Swarm-GAP outperforms LA-DCOP, but not the shortest distance heuristic. When there are more fires and they get bigger, there is a demand for more agents concentrated in clusters. Here, the stochastic decision of Swarm-GAP agents keep them from performing a more concentrated effort, and make them waste more simulations cycles to go from one spot to another. When we increase task stimulus, Swarm-GAP performance get worse. In LA-DCOP, the agents simply reject tasks for which their capabilities are lower than the associated threshold. In LA-DCOP there is always the possibility that agents do not allocate any task during a time step, or keep from accepting distant tasks for a long time. Swarm-GAP agents can also allocate

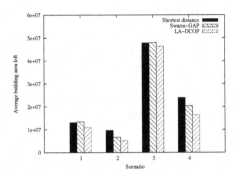

Fig. 6. Best performance of each method, for the scenarios $Kobe_1(1)$, $Kobe_2(2)$, $Kobe\_4_1(3)$, and $Kobe\_4_2(4)$

zero tasks during a time step or neglect far tasks, but when the number of tasks is high (like in scenario of $Kobe\_4_2$ map), this occurs with lower probability. In fact, in an overall average, LA-DCOP number of non-allocated tasks was almost 80% higher than Swarm-GAP.

Our results points that Swarm-GAP, by doing more flexible allocation choices, enable agents to better divide the tasks, sometimes outperforming LA-DCOP or performing equally well in comparison to the shortest distance in some situations.

5   Conclusions and Further Work

The approach introduced here – Swarm-GAP – deals with task allocation in complex scenarios modeled as DCOPs based on the theoretical models of division of labor in swarms. This algorithm solves complex DCOPs in an approximated and distributed fashion.

The experimental results show that the probabilistic decision, based on the tendency and polymorphism models, allows the agents to make reasonable coordinated actions. In the abstract simulation, Swarm-GAP performs well in comparison with LA-DCOP. However, by the nature of its mechanisms, Swarm-GAP uses less communication and computation than LA-DCOP.

Next, we intend to introduce failures in the simulation regarding the communication channel and agents task perception. This failures contribute to a realistic analysis of all algorithms. The idea is to evaluate our intuition that swarm like algorithms are able to deal with communication failures.

Acknowledgments

This research is partially supported by the Air Force Office of Scientific Research (AFOSR) (grant number FA9550-06-1-0517).

References

1. Goldman, C., Zilberstein, S.: Decentralized control of cooperative systems: Categorization and complexity analysis. Journal of Artificial Intelligence Research 22, 143–174 (2004)
2. Kitano, H.: Robocup rescue: A grand challenge for multi-agent systems. In: Proc. of the 4th International Conference on MultiAgent Systems, Boston, USA, pp. 5–12. IEEE Computer Society, Los Alamitos (2000)
3. Lesser, V.: Cooperative multiagent systems: A personal view of the state of the art. IEEE Transactions on Knowledge and Data Engineering 11(1), 133–142 (1999)
4. Maheswaran, R.T., Tambe, M., Bowring, E., Pearce, J.P., Varakantham, P.: Taking DCOP to the real world: Efficient complete solutions for distributed multi-event scheduling. In: Third International Joint Conference on Autonomous Agents and Multiagent Systems, Washington, DC, USA, July 2004, vol. 1, pp. 310–317. IEEE Computer Society, Los Alamitos (2004)
5. Modi, P.J., Shen, W.-M., Tambe, M., Yokoo, M.: An asynchronous complete method for distributed constraint optimization. In: Proc. of the Second International Joint Conference on Autonomous Agents and Multiagent Systems, pp. 161–168. ACM Press, New York (2003)
6. Nair, R., Ito, T., Tambe, M., Marsella, S.: Task allocation in the rescue simulation domain: A short note. In: Birk, A., Coradeschi, S., Tadokoro, S. (eds.) RoboCup 2001. LNCS (LNAI), vol. 2377, pp. 751–754. Springer, Heidelberg (2002)
7. Petcu, A., Faltings, B.: A scalable method for multiagent constraint optimization. In: Kaelbling, L.P., Saffiotti, A. (eds.) Proceedings of the Nineteenth International Joint Conference on Artificial Intelligence, Edinburgh, Scotland, August 2005, pp. 266–271. Professional Book Center (2005)
8. Scerri, P., Farinelli, A., Okamoto, S., Tambe, M.: Allocating tasks in extreme teams. In: Proc. of the Fourth International Joint Conference on Autonomous Agents and Multiagent Systems, pp. 727–734. ACM Press, New York (2005)
9. Shmoys, D.B., Tardos, V.: An approximation algorithm for the generalized assignment problem. Mathematical Programming 62(3), 461–474 (1993)
10. Skinner, C., Barley, M.: Robocup rescue simulation competition: Status report. In: Bredenfeld, A., Jacoff, A., Noda, I., Takahashi, Y. (eds.) RoboCup 2005. LNCS (LNAI), vol. 4020, pp. 632–639. Springer, Heidelberg (2006)
11. Theraulaz, G., Bonabeau, E., Deneubourg, J.: Response threshold reinforcement and division of labour in insect societies. In: Royal Society of London Series B - Biological Sciences, vol. 265, pp. 327–332 (1998)

Mousetrap 2.0

Venkatesh G. Rao[1] and Brian Petty[2]

[1] www.ribbonfarm.com
vgururao@gmail.com
[2] www.artstopllc.com
colonelpaws@aol.com

The chapters in this book describe a variety of algorithms, infrastructure ideas, and applications involving large numbers of coordinated agents: Massive Multi Agent Systems (MMAS) in short. History tells us though, that powerful technological revolutions, like MMAS promises to be, often shape up in ways we cannot imagine. What Einstein said about nature holds for future technology as well – it is not only weirder than we imagine, but weirder than we *can* imagine. Vannevar Bush, for instance, first imagined something like the Internet in his idea for a 'Memex' in a popular article, *As We May Think*, published in the Atlantic Monthly back in 1948. While his vision inspired the original architects of the Internet, what we see today, 60 years later, would certainly dazzle even an exceptional visionary like Bush.

As scientists exploring the possibilities of MMAS, narrative explorations and storytelling are one way we can imagine the future of this technology beyond what our technical explorations can reveal, and perhaps get closer to imagining the unimaginable. What might research labs look like in an age of mature MMAS? What sort of issues might become important? How might political and cultural implications play out? These are all fascinating questions for the scientist interested in the socially-situated implications of his/her work.

We hope you enjoy one such narrative exploration in the mini-comic-book that follows in this chapter. Inspired by the nugget of common wisdom that says "build a better mousetrap and the world will beat a path to your door," we imagine the tumultuous career of a hypothetical invention, Mousetrap 2.0, in a future world dominated by mature MMAS technologies.

N. Jamali et al. (Eds.): CCMMS 2007, MMAS 2006, LSMAS 2006, LNAI 5043, pp. 122–130, 2008.

Mousetrap 2.0

VENKATESH G. RAO* AND BRIAN L. PETTY**

ABSTRACT

IN THIS PAPER WE SURVEY THE HISTORY OF ONE OF THE MOST FAMOUS INVENTIONS OF THE 21ST CENTURY:

INTRODUCTION:
IT ALL BEGAN IN THE LAST SEASON OF THE POPULAR SHOW AMERICAN INVENTOR...

* WRITER, www.ribbonfarm.com, vgururao@gmail.com

**ARTIST, colonelpaws@aol.com, www.artstopllc.com

Application of a Massively Multi-Agent System to Internet Routing Management

Osamu Akashi[1], Kensuke Fukuda[2], Satoshi Kurihara[3], Toshio Hirotsu[4], and Toshiharu Sugawara[5]

[1] NTT Network Innovation Labs., 3-9-11 Midori-cho, Musashino-shi, Tokyo 180-8585, Japan
`akashi@core.ecl.net`
[2] National Institute of Informatics, 2-1-2, Hitotsubashi, Chiyoda, Tokyo 101-8430, Japan
`kensuke@nii.ac.jp`
[3] ISIR, Osaka University, 8-1, Mihogaoka, Ibaragi, Osaka 567-0047, Japan
`kurihara@ist.osaka-u.ac.jp`
[4] Toyohashi University of Technology/JST CREST, Tempaku, Toyohashi, Aichi 441-8580, Japan
`hirotsu@ics.tut.ac.jp`
[5] Waseda University, (Previously NTT CS Labs.,) 3-4-1 Ohkubo, Shinjuku, Tokyo 169-8555, Japan
`sugawara@waseda.jp`

Abstract. Diagnosing the anomalies of inter-AS (autonomous system) routing and flexibly controlling its behavior to adapt to environmental changes are difficult, because this information changes spatially and temporally over different administrative domains. Multi-agent-based systems that coincide with this control architecture have been applied to these domains, but the number of deployed agents is small and more accurate analysis taking into consideration the actual Internet structure is desirable. To enable better analysis, cooperation among tens of thousands of agents is needed. This paper proposes a cooperative routing management system, called NetManager-M, which enables detailed analysis by using massively deployed agents on the Internet. NetManager-M can diagnose the routing flows around suspicious areas through cooperation among dynamically organized agents. This cooperation, which is conducted based on the current and previous routing topology, enables monitoring of routing update messages at neighboring observation points and the identification of the causes of problems in more detail. This system is thus an effective means of detailed analysis for typical scenarios of inter-AS routing failures.

1 Introduction

The Internet consists of more than 20000 autonomous systems (ASs) that correspond to independent network management units such as ISPs. IP messages reach their destinations by transiting among some ASs based on inter-AS routing information. The inter-AS routing information is locally exchanged among

N. Jamali et al. (Eds.): CCMMS 2007, MMAS 2006, LSMAS 2006, LNAI 5043, pp. 131–145, 2008.

neighboring ASs and distributed through the Internet in a hop-by-hop manner. There is no centralized control system and no global view. Currently, this routing information is generated and propagated by the Border Gateway Protocol (BGP) [1]. This is designed to take into account not only path vectors for transition to all destinations but also routing policies that, for example, reflect the contracts and capital relationships between ISPs. However, the actual routing information changes spatially and temporally because it is affected by network traffic (congestion), link failures, and instability caused by normal operation or misconfiguration. Moreover, inconsistent routing among ASs and unintended traffic flows can easily occur. Given this policy-based and dynamically changing routing, topology- and path-based static verification is not sufficient for observing and diagnosing routing inconsistency. More importantly, a coordination framework among ASs for monitoring, analyzing, and controlling inter-AS routing is strongly required.

Cooperative distributed problem solving (CDPS) provided by multi-agent system (MAS) can adequately deal with such problems because 1) CDPS coincides with the control architecture and monitoring methods should be managed on a request-and-accept basis rather than centralized control approaches, 2) observed results that include statistical analysis should be shared after local calculation to improve efficiency and scalability, and 3) operation availability such as message relaying among agents, whose effectiveness was verified through deployment, should be established. The integration of observed results from several ASs can provide more accurate network views for effectively inferring the behaviors of BGP information flow. For this reason, we developed the ENCORE and ENCORE-2 systems [2,3], which are MAS-based routing anomaly detection systems. More recently, we have also applied CDPS to a cooperative inter-AS routing management system called AISLE[4]. Ideally, ENCORE-2 and AISLE agents should be deployed in all ASs, each playing a representative role for its AS, because deploying more agents to cover the nodes on the BGP topology map will enable more precise diagnosis and control of inter-AS routing. Thus, these agent systems can be regarded as a massively multi-agent system (MMAS). Hence we have integrated the diagnostic functions of ENCORE-2 with the policy control functions of AISLE and have designed a massively deployed network-service agent system called NetManager-M.

An important concern regarding a MMAS like NetManager-M is how to ensure the collaboration can be achieved through many agents appropriately selected based on their network locations, abilities, and workloads. In practice, all NetManager-M agents have to communicate with other agents in their neighboring ASs for constant daily health checks and to find any abnormal variations. When an anomaly is detected, they must connect to the agents in the ASs suspected of being the origin (or the vicinage) of the anomaly. Since many agents will observe the same anomaly and have the same task of figuring out the observed problem, teamwork among neighboring agents can enable more efficient and effective problem solving. Recent Internet research indicates that cooperation among simple neighborhood-based agents is not scalable. The Internet has a scale-free property [5], so it has a small number of hub ASs, each having many direct connections with a huge number of other ASs. The agents in hub ASs become overloaded, especially when routing is instable, under the simple local iteration strategy of a MMAS, but almost all other agents have extremely low workloads. Moreover, because a MAS like ENCORE-2 or AISLE is deployed gradually, performance bottlenecks are exposed only after many agents are installed and in operation.

In this paper, we describe the difficulties that arise in inter-AS routing management and analyze this domain. We then explain current multi-agent-based approaches to cope with these problems and the requirements for solutions obtained through massively deployed agents used to more accurately diagnose and control inter-AS routing. After that, we introduce the cooperative model and architecture of NetManager-M, our massively multi-agent system, and discuss their effectiveness in allowing a more detailed level of analysis by focusing on two typical action scenarios.

2   Difficulties in Inter-AS Routing Management

The difficulties in understanding inter-AS routing can be summarized as follows.

1. [**Spatial changes**] Routing information is physically and geographically distributed and varies depending on the observation points.
2. [**Temporal changes**] Routing information changes over time.
3. [**Administrative domain**] Routing is controlled independently by each AS. Operators in other ASs cannot directly access these routing data.
4. [**Local trends**] Each observation point has its own local trends regarding the dynamics of routing information. Information about these trends can be acquired only through actual observation at each point and statistical analysis of the observed data.
5. [**Limitations of human operators**] Detection and diagnosis require human operators to repeatedly observe and analyze large amounts of routing information, including raw data such as BGP update messages. They also require operators to have sophisticated expertise concerning where and how to collect and analyze data.

The spatial changes easily lead to inconsistent routing states among several ASs, even though each AS is working consistently with respect to its neighboring ASs. Moreover, the ASs experiencing anomalies might not be those causing the anomalies. Therefore, we need to infer part of a global view of the routing information to verify whether advertised routing information is spreading as the originating AS intends. The temporal changes make advance analysis invalid. Overcoming this problem requires verification at multiple observation points on an on-demand basis. Operators can use tools such as `ping`, `traceroute`, and `looking glass` [6], but they have to use these tools repeatedly over a long period to confirm their own AS's advertisement and find an anomaly as quickly as possible.

There are also the following problems regarding the control of intra- and inter-AS routing based on the network status. Solutions to these problems are required concurrently or after gaining an understanding of the routing behavior.

6. [**Feedback based on network status changes**] Router primitives only configure the routing protocol at a low level. There are no control frameworks to describe adaptive actions on the observed results.
7. [**Policy description over router primitives**] More abstract policies, such as contractual restrictions, cannot be described.
8. [**Coordination framework among ASs**] Cooperative actions among ASs are required to control inbound traffic. Furthermore, control fluctuation should be avoided.

Our earlier analysis of BGP-related troubleshooting records [3] revealed 72% of the records could not be analyzed without BGP information obtained from outside the AS. These records therefore suggest that inter-AS coordination was established in this domain. To implement these collaborative actions in our system, the agent has to integrate locally observed data with information from other agents that reside outside the AS. These cooperative partners should be determined based on the current and previous BGP topology by considering how an anomaly affects their status. In general, as the number of agents deployed in the Internet becomes large enough to cover almost all ASs, the system can infer the causes of anomalies more precisely. Therefore, massively deployed agents that exist in almost all ASs, which exceed 12000 in number according to our full-route BGP routing information, can know the behavior of inter-AS routing flows more precisely. In the first step of analyzing inter-AS anomalies, each agent tries to find indications of anomalies through continuous observation within its environment and the integration of information exchanged with other agents. If it finds any such indications, it issues a warning to the appropriate agent. It then starts executing various types of cooperative analysis with the agents of other ASs. In many cases, it is necessary to change the cooperating partner agents during the diagnosis process. Planning activities should gradually generate these diagnostic actions based on required information, because there are a huge number of possible hypotheses and candidates for cooperative actions and the system must narrow down the list of hypotheses and candidates during the analysis process.

3   Multi-agent-based Diagnosis and Control

3.1   Current Multi-agent-based Diagnosis

As explained in Section 2, a global view of the current routing information that is spread among different administrative domains is essential for diagnosing inter-AS routing anomalies. Since a complete understanding of the global view is impossible, we use routing information observed almost simultaneously at multiple ASs. By integrating these observed results, we can infer a part of the global view for the purpose of diagnosis. To achieve these coordinated actions,

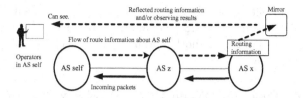

Fig. 1. Reflector model: basic idea for observing the spread of information

we have proposed a diagnostic system called ENCORE which uses a multi-agent architecture and utilizes cooperative actions to resolve the problems described in Section 2. Here, we briefly introduce the model and architecture of the currently deployed ENCORE system and its extension ENCORE-2. These systems were experimentally tested on the actual Internet and then have been commercially deployed [7], but the number of cooperative agents is currently less than 10 due to contractual reasons. A detailed analysis is therefore sometimes impossible, though the feasibility and effectiveness of the basic diagnostic functions on the actual Internet have been verified through them.

The system is based on the reflector model as shown in Fig 1. The essence of this model is to provide a function which allows an agent to request that a remote agent observe routing information about a specific AS, usually the AS of the requesting agent. The routing information observed and analyzed by remote agents is sent to the requesting agent. Although the reflector model can provide a cooperative function, this function is performed on an on-demand basis. Thus, a function that enables an agent to request that a remote agent continuously observe the routing information of a specified AS and notify the requesting agent when specified events occur is required for efficient verification and rapid detection. For example, if the remote agent finds a change in the origin AS number of the BGP attribute value of a specified IP address, it notifies the requesting agent of this observed change. This function is effective because a remote AS receiving routing information usually becomes aware of a failure sooner than the originating AS.

Another useful function enables the relay of messages to appropriate agents. The relay function is needed to cooperatively deliver important messages to destination agents even when direct IP routes for message delivery are unavailable. This function, enabled by having agents act as application gateways, is useful because 1) the system can use paths that are not used in the usual IP routing, and these paths can include non-transit ASs; and 2) messages whose source IP addresses have changed can pass misconfigured filters with a high probability. Message loops and a significant increase in the number of copied messages are prevented by using information about the path that a message has traversed and restricting the maximum number of hops over which a message can be delivered. When failures are caused by filter setting errors, which are typical configuration mistakes, exchanging messages at the end-to-end level is sometimes impossible. In the case of Fig 1, if an intermediate AS filters routing information advertised from AS_{self}, AS_{self} cannot exchange messages with AS_x to verify the reachability. In this situation, AS_{self} can exchange messages with AS_x by having an agent in an intermediate AS relay messages because the source IP address of relayed messages changes to another address and this enables the relayed messages to pass the filter.

3.2   Required Functions When Using Massively Multi-Agent Systems

Although the basic functions for verifying routing reachability and diagnosing some class of causes of an anomalous routing state are achieved through the cooperation described above, a more detailed diagnosis of anomalous states is required. In MMAS, each agent needs a strategy that defines how to cooperate with other agents because agents cannot act with a large number of agents in all diagnosis and/or control phases. Therefore, a NetManager-M agent first accesses a small number of agents for diagnosis or control. When an agent starts performing detailed analysis, the agent searches for other topologically suitable agents. Such agent location information on the BGP topology map is maintained by an agent organization management system called ARTISTE [8], which is an independent system of another MAS such as NetManager-M. ARTISTE can search for agents that match a given requirement, such as "Find agents that can relay messages and are located within two AS-hops from ASx."

NetManager-M is typically required to diagnosis the detailed causes of unusual traffic flow changes. Although the systems in our previous architecture can determine whether advertised routing information reaches remote ASs by applying the reflector model or its extended actions among several agents, it can only point out the unintended state of routing tables in several ASs. The important point is that the absence of some BGP entry can be caused due to several reasons and more detailed causes cannot be identified in this framework. Such an absence may simply reflect the policy of the AS where the AS intentionally declines to receive the BGP entry based on the AS's contract with other BGP peers. The entry may be filtered due to router setting errors in an intermediate AS, or it may be temporarily suppressed by the route dampening algorithm [9] applied in intermediate routers when such an entry is flapped and penalty values individually calculated in these routers exceed pre-defined values.

These situations require the system to monitor the BGP update sequence and analyze them from a temporal viewpoint. In addition, a dense population of observing points around an anomalous area is needed as shown in Fig 2. In this example, the agent in AS_{self} recognizes that $ASself$ advertised its BGP entry concerning prefix-1 (that is, the network portion of the IP address) to AS_i. The most recent sequence of the BGP update messages is "advertise, withdraw, advertise". When all agents in other ASs peering with AS_i (i.e., AS_x, AS_y, and AS_z) find there is no BGP entry concerning prefix-1 in their routing tables, there are various possible causes. If none of the agents in AS_x, AS_y, or AS_z have observed prefix-1 in their routing tables in the past, there should be some management policy in AS_i where AS_i should refuse to receive prefix-1 from AS_{self}. If the agents have observed prefix-1 in their routing table but have

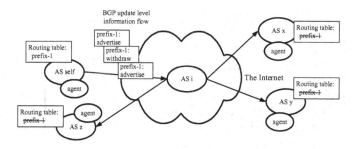

Fig. 2. NetAgent-M deployment for detecting route damping

not received any reasonably recent update messages, there should be a filter setting error in AS_i. If some agents have seen only the preceding part of the update message sequence, an update concerning prefix-1 should be temporarily damped in AS_i. Note that the agent in AS_i cannot easily identify the damped router and directly extract that damping state, because an AS usually consists of several BGP routers and there are many possible BGP information flows. Therefore, route damping can be performed at any BGP router, which might be configured with different damping control parameters. The important point is that those agents can be located in all peer ASs of AS_i, where they can observe the BGP flows from AS_i. If AS_i is replaced with a set of ASs, all BGP paths surrounding this cluster of ASs similarly need to be monitored. If any paths are not monitored, the certainty of the diagnosis gradually deteriorates. Therefore, a massively multi-agent system enables more detailed analysis and dynamical organization based on the place where an anomalous state is found is important.

4   Diagnosis and Control by Massively Deployed Agents

4.1   Agent System Structure

The NetManager-M agent system uses the same platform used to construct the ENCORE-2 system [3]. The agent consists of several modules classified according to their functions as shown in Fig 3. This architecture has been realized as a hybrid system for diagnosis functions and policy control functions. The knowledge-processing component for diagnosis consists of an inference engine, an observation strategy controller, a cooperation controller, an execution module, and knowledge description. This knowledge description should be independent of the system operation so as to allow knowledge to be added or modified for the purpose of flexibly adapting to the local environment. This is represented by using variables, whose values represent the agent's local environment state. These values are acquired at run time and are determined when accessed. The body consists of environment-dependent components, including the observed data, data acquired through statistical analysis, some monitor modules, and sensing and analysis tools. For controlling the BGP information, the agent modifies several BGP attribute information to reflect policy and to adjust to environmental

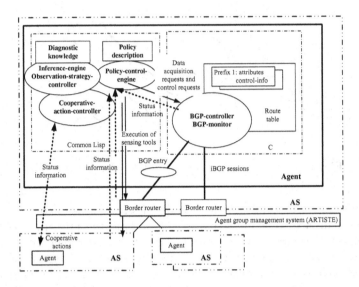

Fig. 3. NetManager-M agent architecture for diagnosis and routing control

changes. The selection rules of the best path from multiple BGP entries, which have different attribute values, are strictly defined in RFC [1] and NetAgent-M can communicate with border routers within these rules.

The knowledge-processing component of the agent is based on the BDI (belief, desire, and intention) architecture [10]. It makes plans for verifying hypotheses or satisfying policy descriptions, schedules the execution of verification rules or policy-control rules, and controls monitoring and statistical analysis based on the given descriptions. The actions of an agent are invoked by events from other agents or the `monitoring-planner`. The `monitoring-planner` selects the rules for observation, while the `diagnosis-planner` selects the rules for analyzing causes. The `policy-control-engine` interprets the policy description and determines rules for adjusting routing under the given policy. The `scheduler` then assigns a set of rules to execution threads. The `executor` executes threads if locally executable, or else the `coordinator` performs cooperative actions by requesting other agents using basic action primitives. The execution system is optimized using the tabulation technique and adaptive control. These internal modules also work as threads.

The agent module is constructed on a network agent platform that provides basic action primitives in distributed environments. They are implemented by using Allegro Common Lisp/CLOS. The agents use RPC/SSL for authentication and secure communication with each other.

4.2   Cooperative Action Management

For practical deployment reasons, ENCORE-2 agents use diagnostic knowledge that enables an effective cooperative strategy even if cooperation is organized among only several agents. This means that for effective collaboration in MMAS, suitable partners should be carefully selected among the large number of deployed agents based on their BGP topological position and the observed phenomena caused by routing-related anomalies.

The agent's roles in the basic cooperative strategy in ENCORE, which are *investigation*, *relay*, and *friend*, are statically assigned so that the functions required for inter-AS diagnosis can be performed. ENCORE-2 dynamically searches for agents suitable for these three roles based on their functional capability and topological conditions. In NetManager-M, role assignments are also flexible because dynamical searching for suitable active agents is performed on an on-demand basis according to topological requirements from each agent's viewpoint. When cooperative diagnosis is performed, an agent sends a query to ARTISTE which responds with a list of active agents that can fill the requested role and satisfy a given topological requirement on the BGP map. The formation of groups is possible, and this is useful for political reasons because the list of potential cooperative agents can be restricted and separate management information is provided to each group.

An investigation agent is used to send back requested information observed in its environment. This role is typically assigned to agents located in major transit ASs, because they can observe the large amount of routing information exchanged there. NetManager-M agents also deploy investigation agents in transit ASs and use them at an early stage of each diagnostic action. Therefore, they are considered as the first contact points. However, a transit AS is a hub and a NetManager-M agent assigned the investigation role receives many queries and tends to become overloaded. In this case, it simply replies with a reject message, which tells the requesting agent that the requested agent is currently overloaded. The requesting agent must then try to find other investigation agents that reside near the first one. In addition, the overloaded agent in the hub can set a flag in ARTISTE denoting that it is overloaded and recommending the use of an agent having the same role which is located in the same neighborhood, especially upstream. An agent matching this description will work well because it has almost the same BGP view including the view from that hub AS. The diagnosis then starts and the next investigation agents will be designated for isolating the cause of anomalies in detail and/or identifying an area where these anomalies affect routing. A friend agent is used to continuously observe the state from outside the AS. Candidates to become friend agents can be selected using topological requirements such as agents in a neighboring AS, a transit AS, or an AS on the other side of the central ASs of the Internet. A relay agent is used to control the routing at the application level. If an agent cannot obtain results within a predefined time, the agent selects other investigation or relay agents and requests that they do the job. An initial set of relay agents can also be selected in the same way as candidates to become friend agents.

An agent may need to find 1) other investigation agents located in ASs that are downstream from the initially selected investigation agent; or 2) other investigation agents located near an AS in which hijacked routes were observed.

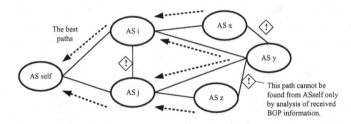

Fig. 4. Problem of finding hidden paths

These newly selected agents are considered suitable because they could have BGP data needed to determine the location of the anomaly's cause or the extent to which the anomalous state, such as a hijacked route, is spreading. More comprehensively, these agents are able to issue search queries to ARTISTE including condition terms such as `group`, `role`, `designated-AS`, `AS-hop-count`, and `topology`, where `topology` is `downstream`, `upstream`, or `neighbor`. Conditions can be combined using logical terms such as `and` and `or`.

For diagnosis in a massively deployed environment, the *neighbor* concept is important. It is directly expressed as a query to ARTISTE such as "Find agents that exist within x AS-hop from ASy." Therefore, it is important to know the entire network topology map for finding suitable agents. On the other hand, it is difficult to find all paths on the BGP topology map by only analyzing BGP information received at a single observation point, because the received BGP information consists of the best path entries, each of which only includes a single AS path per destination from an AS. Therefore, a single agent can only see a spanning tree of the BGP best paths from an AS. In the example shown in Fig 4, AS_{self} cannot see the links between AS_i and AS_j, AS_x and AS_y, and AS_y and AS_z since these links are not selected as the best paths in the BGP information received at AS_{self}. Therefore, the BGP information observed at different ASs must be integrated to consider the possible BGP paths more accurately. As well as target agent systems, ARTISTE is also a multi-agent-based system and performs this path-searching over the Internet environment. Basically there is a design assumption that an available ARTISTE agent exists within one AS-hop from a managed agent like a NetManager-M agent. ARTISTE agents cooperate with other agents to integrate the BGP best-path trees observed from other observation points. They can also cooperate to find BGP peers of an AS, whose information may not be delivered if they are not selected as the best paths. Therefore, ARTISTE agents can also find agents within a specified number of AS-hops more precisely if they are deployed more densely.

4.3   Cooperative Scenario

In the case of hijacked routes. Each NetManager-M agent autonomously acts based on monitoring strategies that are given by operators in their ASs or are requested from other agents. For example, an agent R_1 in AS_1 requests that

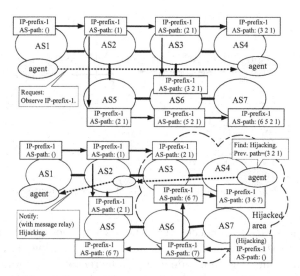

Fig. 5. Contamination by hijacked route delivery

a friend agent R_4 observe BGP entries in AS_1. R_1 notifies R_4 of the target IP prefixes in AS_1 and trap conditions for which agent R_4 is requested to invoke a warning action. The BGP topology is assumed as shown in Fig 5. A typical trap condition is "Notify R_1 if the origin AS number, which should be AS_1, in any BGP entries concerning target IP prefixes is changed or any of these BGP entries disappear."

In this example, AS_1 advertises its IP-prefix-1 to AS_2. AS_2 advertises it to AS_3 and AS_5. Then IP-prefix-1 is delivered and arrives at AS_4 with AS path (3, 2, 1). It also arrives at AS_7 with AS path (6, 5, 2, 1). If AS_7 mis-advertises the same prefix IP-prefix-1 to AS_6 and AS_6 does not filter it, this prefix from AS_7 is selected as the best path for IP-prefix-1, because the BGP entry of IP-prefix-1 from AS_7 has a shorter AS path than the one from AS_1 and so has priority as the best path according to the default selection rules [1]. Similarly, it is diffusing and contaminating routing tables in some other ASs. In these contaminated ASs, packets destined for IP-prefix-1 are forwarded to AS_7. In this example, this mis-advertised prefix also reaches AS_3 and AS_5. AS_3 and AS_5 have two BGP entries concerning destination IP-prefix-1 and one is selected as the BGP best path. If the mis-advertised route is selected in AS_3, AS_4 is also contaminated. In this situation, R_1 is notified that the origin AS number, which should be AS_1, was changed to AS_7 in AS_4. Then R_1 extracts possible hypotheses and starts verification. More specifically, the contaminated routing table prevents direct communication between AS_1 and AS_4, since packets in AS_3 destined for AS_1 are forwarded to AS_7. In this case, AS_1 and AS_4 can communicate indirectly by using a relay agent such as in AS_2. As shown in Fig 6, a suspicious AS is found by comparing the AS paths of the two BGP entries acquired from the current BGP routing table in AS_4 and the previously existing one. In this case, these are (3, 6, 7) and (3, 2, 1). The separation point of these two paths

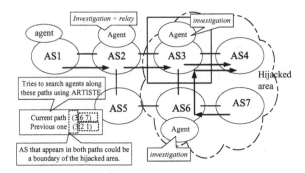

Fig. 6. Cooperative analysis of a hijacked route

is AS_3. Therefore, R_1 first checks AS_3 and its neighboring AS, namely AS_2. Then along with the current path, AS_6 and its neighboring AS_5 are checked. Therefore, R_1 can infer the contaminated area by repeatedly sending inquiries to investigation agents which are near from the ASs located along the path where unintentional advertisement is detected. In such partially hijacked cases, relay agents can effectively work to deliver messages among agents.

Although fatal accidents or attacks like the 1997 failure that disturbed the entire Internet through the unintentional advertisement of full-routes might not occur because of the careful filtering employed by several major ISPs, cases of small-scale or partial-area mis-advertising have been observed several times in the past few years. Thus, continuous observation and diagnosis by an adequate number of sufficiently distributed agents are still needed. Massively deployed NetManager-M agents suitably covering almost all ASs can detect these partial failures, and such a deployment is needed to maintain reachability in the Internet. After detection and analysis, operators of a misadvertising AS should be notified of their mistake as soon as possible. On the other hand, some countermeasures should be applied to allow rapid though temporary recovery. Although ASs neighboring around the misadvertising AS can try to filter any misadvertising, all paths connecting border routers in neighboring ASs should be filtered and this is not possible in all cases. Therefore, an originating AS that has a hijacked route advertises longer prefixes that include the hijacked address space. These longer prefixes can overwrite misadvertised routes, because longer prefixes precede the currently advertised shorter ones according to the BGP best path selection rule.

Detailed analysis of hijacked-route behavior from the viewpoint of the AS adjacency topology of an actual Internet structure are described in [11]. Its simulation results using an actual Internet topology show the effectiveness of an agent-deployment strategy based on connectivity information. These results demonstrate that our routing management system using massively multi-agents can be applied to the real Internet topology.

In the case of route information disappearing. A NetManager-M agent R_{self} in stub-AS AS_{self} observes various network status parameters to find any indication of anomalies. In this example, suppose a border router in a transit AS located upstream from AS_{self}, failed, and previous router configurations, in which a newly connected AS_{self} was not described, were restored. The advertisement from AS_{self} is then filtered. R_{self} finds that it cannot access some hosts, because the rule utilizing `ping` fails. At the same time, friend agent R_n, which observes AS_{self} from the viewpoint of AS_n, can also find these routing changes and try to send a notify message to R_{self}. If this leads to a timeout, R_n then uses relay agents.

By checking a previous BGP path stored in R_n, R_{self} can find that the previous path was $(.., AS_i, AS_j, .., AS_{self})$. R_{self} then issues queries to agents along this path and finds that AS_i is suspicious, because every AS appeared in the sequence from AS_{self} to AS_j currently has the BGP entry from AS_{self} and it has the same AS path as the previously observed one. In the next step, R_{self} tries to find neighboring agents peering with AS_i and gets a list $\{AS_x, AS_y, AS_z\}$. As described in subsection 3.2, neighboring agents check previous update messages concerning AS_{self} from AS_i. In this example, the neighboring agents have not seen recently flapped update messages and know that no BGP entry concerning AS_{self} exists in the routing tables in their ASs. These agents know, though, that a BGP entry existed in all of their routing tables before the warning message from AS_n, which notified them of the disappearance of the route, was issued. Thus, R_{self} can determine that the cause of the problem was some filter in AS_i.

5   Related Work

There are several diagnostic tools for analyzing inter-AS routing anomalies. WWW-based systems such as looking glass [6], RIS tools [12], RouteViews [13], and various visualization tools are widely used by network operators to monitor routing information and the states at specific points. These systems, however, are designed for use by humans and cannot be straightforwardly applied. Although analysis of the temporal and topological behavior of BGP path-changes [14] and centralized analysis approaches [15] have been reported, all possible cases are not covered. To provide real-time anomaly detection by analyzing BGP updates, the signature-based method and statistics-based method were proposed [16]. These methods can effectively identify anomalous BGP events, but they also cannot cover all cases. Our analysis approach concerning BGP update events, which utilizes a kind of learned parameters and human operator heuristics, is less automatic than these methods, but can be used to complement them. Such a hybrid system of human and statistically analyzed results [17] is unique and effective. Although it is a kind of visualization tool and cannot be directly applied, it could become a valuable complement if some patterns are extracted as interpretable rules. Listen and Whisper [18] can eliminate a large number of problems due to misconfiguration by considering the network topology, but Listen only treats verification in the data plane. Whisper can verify routes in the control plane, but requires another protocol over BGP.

Several advantages provided by the CDPS-based approach would be a useful supplement for them. From the viewpoints of data availability and cooperation among different administrative domains, some agent-based intra-AS diagnostic systems have been proposed, but these systems only offer restricted cooperation to obtain targeted information. These systems operate under the assumption that targeted information exists in the management domain of the agent recognizing a problem. This means that the agents in these systems cannot deal with situations in which an anomaly or its effect is observed in a different management domain from that in which the cause exists. This situation is actually quite common in inter-AS diagnosis.

Although community attribute extension for policy control has been proposed [19], it only defines the mechanism for distributing additional values on BGP and does not discuss inter-AS routing adjustment or coordination functions. A path selection mechanism for BGP paths and overlay routing has been reported in [20], but routing only at a fine-grained level such as units of sessions or packets was discussed. In addition, there was no treatment of inter-AS control. The NetManager-M system focuses on control of the inter-AS routing at the mass traffic level, considering observed results and the given policy description. Intelligent routers [21,22] are also capable of controlling outgoing packets by modifying received BGP information based on a given policy description, but they do not provide cooperative actions among multiple ASs and they assume special devices are available. On the other hands, the NetManager-M architecture works with conventional routers without any protocol extensions. RAML [23], a meta description approach cannot express control according to the observed network status. Active network approaches [24] provide similar control functions, but do not consider the control structure like ASs. A CDPS approach in NetManager-M applies the request-and-acceptance based cooperation and it coincides with the actual network management structure.

6 Conclusion

To effectively support inter-AS routing management and control, we have proposed a massively deployed multi-agent-based system called NetManager-M. By cooperating with other massively deployed agents that are located in suitable positions on the BGP topology map, NetManager-M can diagnose the specific causes of anomalies which are difficult to analyze with conventional multi-agent-based systems.

References

1. Rekhter, Y., Li, T.: A Border Gateway Protocol 4 (BGP-4) (RFC1771) (1995)
2. Akashi, O., Sugawara, T., Murakami, K., Maruyama, M., Koyanagi, K.: Agent System for Inter-AS Routing Error Diagnosis. IEEE Internet Computing 6(3), 78–82 (2002)
3. Akashi, O., Terauchi, A., Fukuda, K., Hirotsu, T., Maruyama, M., Sugawara, T.: Detection and Diagnosis of Inter-AS Routing Anomalies by Cooperative Intelligent Agents. In: Schönwälder, J., Serrat, J. (eds.) DSOM 2005. LNCS, vol. 3775, pp. 181–192. Springer, Heidelberg (2005)

4. Akashi, O., Fukuda, K., Hirotsu, T., Sugawara, T.: Policy-based BGP Control Architecture for Autonomous Routing Management. In: SIGCOMM workshops on Internet Netwrok Management, September 2006, pp. 77–82. ACM, New York (2006)
5. Watts, D.: Small Worlds: The Dynamics of Networks between Order and Randomness. Princeton Univ. Pr, Princeton (2004)
6. Kern, E.: http://nitrous.digex.net
7. http://www.ntt.com/release_e/news04/0002/0226.html
8. Terauchi, A., Akashi, O., Maruyama, M., Fukuda, K., Sugawara, T., Hirotsu, T., Kurihara, S.: ARTISTE: An Agent Organization Management System for Multi-agent Systems. LNCS (LNAI), vol. 4078. Springer, Heidelberg (accepted for publication, 2006)
9. Villamizar, C., Chandra, R., Govindan, R.: BGP Route Flap Damping, RFC2439 (1998)
10. O'Hare, G.M.P., Jennings, N.R.: Foundations of Distributed Artificial Intelligence. Wiley-Interscience, Chichester (1996)
11. Akashi, O., Fukuda, K., Hirotsu, T., Sugawara, T.: Analysis of Diagnostic Capability for Hijacked Route Problem. In: Medhi, D., Nogueira, J.M., Pfeifer, T., Wu, S.F. (eds.) IPOM 2007. LNCS, vol. 4786, pp. 37–48. Springer, Heidelberg (2007)
12. RIPE: http://www.ripe.net/
13. Meyer, D.: http://www.routeviews.org
14. Chang, D., Govindan, R., Heidemann, J.: The Temporal and Topological Characteristics of BGP Path Changes. In: Proc. of Int'l Conf. on Network Protocols, November 2003, pp. 190–199. IEEE, Los Alamitos (2003)
15. Feldmann, A., Maennel, O., Mao, Z., Berger, A., Maggs, B.: Locating Internet Routing Instability. In: Proc. of SIGCOMM, August-September 2004, pp. 205–218. ACM, New York (2004)
16. Zhang, K., Yen, A., Zhao, X., Massey, D., Wu, S., Zhnag, L.: On Detection of Anomalous Routing Dynamics in BGP. In: Proc. of Networking, IFIP, pp. 259–270 (2004)
17. Teoh, S., Ma, K., Wu, S., Massey, D., Zhao, X., Pei, D., Wang, L., Zhang, L., Bush, R.: Visual-Based Anomaly Detection for BGP Origin AS Change (OASC) Events. In: Brunner, M., Keller, A. (eds.) DSOM 2003. LNCS, vol. 2867, pp. 155–168. Springer, Heidelberg (2003)
18. Subramanian, L., Roth, V., Stoica, I., Shenker, S., Katz, R.: Listen and Whisper: Security Mechanisms for BGP. In: Proc. of Networked Systems Design and Implementation, USENIX, November 2004, pp. 127–140 (2004)
19. Sangli, S., Tappan, D., Rekhter, Y.: BGP Extended Communities Attribute (2005), draft-ietf-idr-bgp-ext-communities-08.txt
20. Akella, A., Pang, J., Maggs, B., Seshan, S., Shaikh, A.: A Comparison of Overlay Routing and Multihoming Route Control. In: Proc. of SIGCOMM, August-September 2004, pp. 93–105. ACM, New York (2004)
21. RouteScience Technologies, Inc.: RouteScience PathControlm, http://www.routescience.com/products
22. radware: Peer Director, http://www.radware.com/contents/products/pd/
23. Griffin, T.G., Sobrinho, J.L.: Metarouting. In: Proc. of SIGCOMM, August 2005, pp. 1–12. ACM, New York (2005)
24. Tennenhouse, D.L., Smith, J.M., Sincoskie, W.D., Wetherall, D.J., Minden, G.J.: A Survey of Active Network Research. IEEE Communications Magazine 35(1), 80–86 (1997)

An Agent-Based Approach for Range Image Segmentation

Smaine Mazouzi[1], Zahia Guessoum[2], Fabien Michel[1], and Mohamed Batouche[3]

[1] MODECO-CReSTIC, Université de Reims, B.P. 1035, 51687, Reims, France
{mazouzi,fmichel}@leri.univ-reims.fr
[2] LIP6, Université de Paris 6, 104, av. du Président Kennedy, 75016, Paris, France
zahia.guessoum@lip6.fr
[3] Département d'informatique, Université de Constantine, 25000, Algérie
batouche@wissal.dz

Abstract. In this paper an agent-based segmentation approach is presented and evaluated. The approach consists in using a high number of autonomous agents for the segmentation of a range image in its different planar regions. The moving agents perform cooperative and competitive actions on the image pixels allowing a robust extraction of regions and an accurate edge detection. An artificial potential field, created around pixels of interest, allows the agents to be gathered around edges and noise regions. The results obtained with real images are compared to those of some typical methods for range image segmentation. The comparison results show the potential of the proposed approach for scene understanding in range images regarding both segmentation efficiency, and detection accuracy.

Keywords: Image segmentation, Multi-agent systems, Range image, Artificial potential field.

1 Introduction

The segmentation of an image is often necessary to provide a compact and convenient description of its content, suitable for high level image analysis and understanding. It consists in assigning image pixels to homogenous and disjoint subsets, which form an image partition. The pixels which belong to the same region share a common feature called the region homogeneity criterion. In range images, segmentation methods can be divided into two distinct categories: edge-based segmentation methods and region-based segmentation methods. In the first category, pixels which correspond to discontinuities in depth or in surface normals are selected and chained in order to delimit the regions in the image [8,4,10]. Edge-based methods are well known for their low computational cost, however they are very sensitive to noise.

Region-based methods use geometrical surface descriptors to group pixels with the same proprieties in disjoint regions [22,11,13,3,1]. Compared to edge-based methods, region-based methods are more stable and less sensitive to noise. However, their efficiency depends strongly on the selection of the region seeds. Most

N. Jamali et al. (Eds.): CCMMS 2007, MMAS 2006, LSMAS 2006, LNAI 5043, pp. 146–161, 2008.

of the time, the segmentation results in an over-partition of the image. So, it is necessary to perform an iterative fusion of homogenous regions. Such an approach does not facilitate the distribution of the used algorithms, and leads to high computational costs [7].

Furthermore, most of the proposed methods model surface proprieties by computing image derivatives of different orders. Such techniques result in a highly noise-sensitive detection. It is then necessary to perform some preprocessing tasks, which consist mostly in image smoothing and noise filtering. However, in the case of highly noisy images such as range images [7], a strong noise smoothing can erase the roof edges (at discontinuities of surface normals), and the smooth edges (at discontinuities of curvature) whose detection remains a challenge. Moreover, if the noise is under-smoothed the distortions, which remain in the image, result in inaccurate or erroneous segmentation results. This difficulty, which is an open issue in image segmentation [14], results from the restriction of computation and decision to the local neighborhood of the processed pixel. In range images, several recent segmentation methods fail because they do not correctly address and resolve this problem [9].

To deal with this problem, some authors have proposed agent-based solutions for 2-D image segmentation. Agent-based solutions inherit the advantages of the agent-oriented systems for collective problem solving. In such systems a single agent has a limited perception and limited capabilities, and it is not designed to solve an entire problem. Agents cooperate thus in order to provide a collective solution. Contrary to conventional systems, solutions in agent-based systems emerge from collective action of interactive agents [12].

In this paper, a new agent-based solution for range image segmentation is presented and discussed. It consists in the use of reactive agents, which move over the image, and act on the visited pixels. While moving over the image, an agent adapts to the planar region on which it moves, and memorizes its proprieties. When an agent encounters a pixel which does not belong to its current region, an agent alters this pixel in order to align it to its current region. At the boundaries between the regions the agents will be in competition to align the pixels of the boundaries to their respective regions. The resulting alternative alignment of the boundary pixels preserves the region boundaries against erasing. Noise regions that are characterized by small sizes or by aberrant depths (outliers) prevent the agents from adapting. Thus, these regions continuously contract by aligning their pixels to the planar regions which surround them.

Our aim is to overcome the difficulty related to the local perception around the processed pixel. A pixel is therefore processed according to both its neighborhood, and the agents that visit this pixel. An agent acts on pixels with more certainty, acquired from its move on large areas on the image regions. The combination of the global information memorized within the agent, and the local information, provides more reliable decisions. To optimize the agent movements, an artificial potential field inspired from the electrostatic potential field is used. It allows to rationalize the movements of the agents by directing them to be gathered around the regions of interest (edges and noise regions) and to concentrate their actions around these regions. The utilization of a large number of reactive and weakly coupled agents provides a massively multi-agent system, allowing a parallel and distributed image segmentation. Extensive experimentations have been performed using real images from the ABW database [7]. The obtained results show the high potential of the proposed approach for an efficient and accurate segmentation of range images.

The remainder of the paper is organized as follows: In Section 2, we review the agent-based approaches for image segmentation. Section 3 introduces the surface proprieties modeling. Section 4 is devoted to the proposed approach. It describes the behavior of the agents and shows the underlying collective mechanism to deal with the edge detection and the noise removal. The experimental results are introduced in Section 5, in which we discuss the selection of the used parameters, and we analyse and comment the obtained results. Finally, a conclusion summarizes our contribution.

2   Related Work

Several agent-based systems have been proposed for image analysis and object recognition. They propose interesting solutions to deal with several problems, such as multiple domain knowledge handling, control automation over the image interpretation tasks, collective segmentation, and distributed and parallel image processing. In this review we consider only works which have addressed a solution in image segmentation.

Liu et al. [16] introduce a reactive agent-based system for brain MRI segmentation. They underline that the employed agents are more robust and more efficient than the classical region-based algorithms. Four types of agents are used to label the pixels of the image according to their membership grade to the different regions. When finding pixels of a specific homogenous region an agent creates offspring agents into its neighborhood. In this system, the agents neither interact directly between them nor act on the image. Their actions depend only on their local perception. Nevertheless, each agent is created so that it becomes more likely to meet more homogenous pixels. For the same type of images, Richard et al. [18] propose a hierarchical architecture of situated and cooperative agents for brain MRI segmentation. Three types of agents have been used: global control agent, local control agent, and tissue dedicated agent. The role of the global control agent is to partition the volume of data into adjacent territories and to assign one local control agent to each territory. The role of a local control agent is to create the tissue dedicated agents which perform a local region growing. The statistical parameters of the image data distribution, needed to perform region growing are updated according to the interaction between neighboring agents. Using several types of agents has allowed to deal with both the control over the high-level segmentation tasks and the low-level image processing tasks.

The two previous systems are well optimized to brain MRI segmentation. They can provide interesting results because region characteristics are regular in the different brain anatomic parts. In addition, most of the edges in such images are jump edges (at discontinuities of image data) which are easy to detect, compared to roof and smooth edges.

Rodin et al. [19] using the oRis langauge [6], have presented a reactive agent-based system for edge detection in biological images. According to some prior on image content, the system provides an edge detection which is better than that provided by traditional detectors. Two groups of agents, called darkening agents and lightning agents follow respectively the dark regions and the light regions. Their actions aim at reinforcing regions by stressing their contrast, allowing a reliable detection of these regions. In this system, agents are fully independent from each other, and never interact. The system can be considered as a parallel segmentation algorithm which was well optimized for the detection of roof edges in some biological images. However, agents were not designed to detect discontinuities of image data. So, the system may fail to detect jump edges. Furthermore, the number and the topology of the expected regions must be known, and hard coded within the agents.

Based on the cognitive architecture Soar [17], Bovenkamp et al. [2] have developed a multi-agent system for IntraVascular UltraSound (IVUS) image segmentation. They aim to elaborate a high knowledge-based control over the algorithms of low-level image processing. In this system, an agent is assigned to every expected object in the image. Agents cooperate and dynamically adapt the segmentation algorithms, according to contextual knowledge, local information and their personal believes. In this work, the problem of the control over segmentation algorithms seems to be well resolved. However, no agent or even behavior has been proposed to deal with the problem of uncertain and noisy data.

The proposed agent-based systems for image segmentation are specific to image contents. Following a supervised approach, these systems aim at segmenting images in known and previously expected regions. The system proposed in this paper claims to be general and unsupervised. It aims to segment an image into its several regions by using some invariant surface proprieties. The adaptive and competitive behavior of the agents allow overcoming the constraint related to the restriction of the treatments to the local neighborhood of pixels. We show in this work that despite the simplicity of the model used to represent surfaces, the obtained results are better than those provided by conventional approaches. We believe that interactions between agents provide an alternative way for image segmentation to that of methods based on complicated and costly models [15].

3   Surface Modeling

A range image is a discretized two-dimensional array where at each pixel (x, y) is recorded the distance $Z(x, y)$ between the range finder and the corresponding point of the scene. Regions in such an image represent the visible patches of object surfaces. To attenuate the white and the impulsive noise contained in the image, a Gaussian filter and a median filter are applied to the depth raw data. A new image $Z^*(x, y)$, called plane image is then derived from the range image.

Each pixel (x, y) of the new image records the tangent plane to the surface at (x, y). The best tangent plane at (x, y) is obtained by the multiple regression method using the set of neighboring pixels $\chi(x, y)$. The neighborhood $\chi(x, y)$ is made up of pixels (x', y') situated within a 3×3 window centred at (x, y), and whose depths $Z(x', y')$ are close, according to a given threshold (Tr_D).

The plane equation in a $3 - D$ coordinate system may be expressed as follows:

$$ax + by + cz = d \tag{1}$$

where $(a, b, c)^T$ is the unit normal vector to the plane $(a^2 + b^2 + c^2 = 1; c < 0)$ and d is the orthogonal distance between the plane and the coordinate origin. First, Parameters α, β and γ of the surface $z = \alpha x + \beta y + \gamma$ at (x_0, y_0) are obtained by the minimization of the function Φ, defined as follows:

$$\Phi(\alpha, \beta, \gamma) = \sum_{(x_i, y_i) \in \chi(x_0, y_0)} [\alpha x_i + \beta y_i + \gamma - Z(x_i, y_i)]^2 \tag{2}$$

with

$$\chi(x_0, y_0) = \{(x_0 + i, y_0 + j); (i, j) \in \{-1, 0, +1\} \text{ and } |Z(x_0 + i, y_0 + j) - Z(x_0, y_0)| < Tr_D\}$$

Parameters a, b, c and d are thus obtained as follows:

$$(a, b, c, d)^T = \frac{1}{\sqrt{\alpha^2 + \beta^2 + 1}}(\alpha, \beta, -1, \gamma)^T \tag{3}$$

The tasks performed on the plane image are based on the comparison of planes. Indeed, we consider that two planes $ax + by + cz = d$ and $a'x + b'y + c'z = d'$ are equal if they have, according to given thresholds, the same orientation and the same distance to the coordinate origin. Let θ be the angle between the two normal vectors, and D the distance between the two planes: $\sin(\theta) = \|(a, b, c)^T \otimes (a', b', c')^T\|$ and $D = |d - d'|$. So, the two planes are considered equal if $\sin(\theta) \leq Tr_\theta$ and $D \leq Tr_D$, where Tr_θ and Tr_D are respectively the angle and the distance thresholds. Plane comparison is first used to test if a given pixel belongs to a planar region, given its plane equation. It is also used to test if the pixel is, or is not, a pixel of interest (edge or noise pixel). In this case, the pixel in question is considered as a pixel of interest if at least one of its neighbors has a different plane equation, according the previous thresholds.

4 Multi-agent Range Image Segmentation

The plane image is considered as the environment in which agents are initialized at random positions. An agent checks if it is situated within a planar region, and adapts this region if planar, by memorizing its plane equation. Next, the agent performs actions which depend on both its state and the state of the pixel on which it is located. At each time t, an agent is characterized by its position (x_t, y_t) over the image, and by its ability A_t to act on the encountered pixels. At the beginning of the process, all the agents are unable to alter the image pixels. After having been adapted to a planar region, an agent becomes able to modify the first pixel not belonging to this region (A_t=true). When an agent alters a pixel, it loses its alteration ability (A_t=false) and starts again searching for a new planar region. An agent having modified a pixel records in an appropriate array I at the position (x_t, y_t) the last state of the visited pixel: $I(x_t, y_t) \in$ {smoothed, aligned, unchanged}. We show next, that this simple behavior of the agents allow both the detection of the image edges, and the removal of the noise regions.

4.1   Agent Behavior

An agent adapts to the region of the image on which it is moving by computing and storing the proprieties of this region, and by adopting the suited behavior to the local image data. Fig. 1 depicts the behavior of an agent according to its state and the state of the pixel on which it is located.

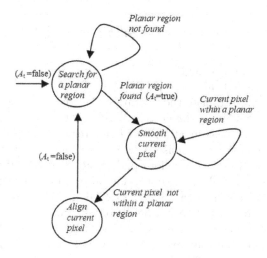

Fig. 1. Agent behavior according to its state and position

Searching for a Planar Region. After its creation, an agent randomly moves within the image and searches for a planar region around its current position. The seed of the searched region is formed of the last L pixels visited by the agent. L is called the adaptation path-length. It represents the confidence degree that the agent is situated within a planar region. The agent considers that it is within a planar region if the pixels of the seed form a planar surface. The agent memorizes the new region and considers it as its current planar region. It agent becomes then able to alter the first encountered pixel which does not belong to its planar region (A_t=true).

Moving on a Planar Region. While moving inside a planar region, an agent smoothes the pixel on which it is located by updating the equations of both the memorized plane and the plane at the pixel position. This is done by replacing the two equations by their weighted average. Let (a', b', c', d') and (a, b, c, d) be the parameters respectively of the memorized plane and the plane at the current pixel. Resulting parameters of the weighted average plane, before normalization, are obtained as follows:

$$(a'', b'', c'', d'') = \frac{1}{1+l}(a + la', b + lb', c + lc', d + ld') \tag{4}$$

where l is the length of the path crossed by the agent on the planar region.

Pixel Alignment. Pixels of interest are edge pixels or pixels within noise regions. When an agent meets a pixel of interest (i.e. not belonging to its current planar region) it alters it in order to partially align it to the planar region on which it is moving. Parameters (a'', b'', c'', d'') of the new plane equation at the pixel position are obtained by linear combination of the current parameters (a, b, c, d) and the parameters of the memorized plane equation (a', b', c', d'):

$$(a'', b'', c'', d'') = \frac{1}{1+\xi}(a + \xi a', b + \xi b', c + \xi c', d + \xi d') \tag{5}$$

where ξ is the alteration strength.

The agent loses then its alteration ability (A_t=false) and starts again to search a new planar region. Further to the alteration of a pixel, the agent can pass into another region, or remain in the current region. If the altered pixel is an edge pixel, the agent likely pass in an other planar region. However, if the altered pixel is on the boundary of a noise region, the agent crosses the noise region and most likely end up in the previous planar region, except if the noise region is situated between two planar regions. The alteration strength ξ is a critical parameter which affects the quality of the results and the time of computation. Indeed, high values of ξ lead to a fast detection of regions. However the resulting region boundaries are distorted and badly localized (Fig. 2c). Low values of ξ result in a slow detection, but region boundaries in this case are well detected and correctly localized (Fig. 2d). In order to speed up the segmentation process, and avoid edge distortion, an agent chooses the alteration strength among ξ_{min} and ξ_{max} according to the information recorded by other agents in the array I. So, an agent assumes that the current planar region is adjacent to a noise region and thus uses ξ_{max} as alteration strength, if the number of "unchanged" pixels (situated in a noisy region) around the agent is greater than a given threshold (fixed to 3 in our experimentations). Indeed, pixels labeled "unchanged" in the adjacent region mean that this latter is a noise region for which agents have not adapted and consequently have not smoothed its pixels. Otherwise the agent assumes that the current planar region is adjacent to another one, where other agents have labeled the pixels as "smoothed" or "aligned". In this case the agent uses the alteration strength ξ_{min}.

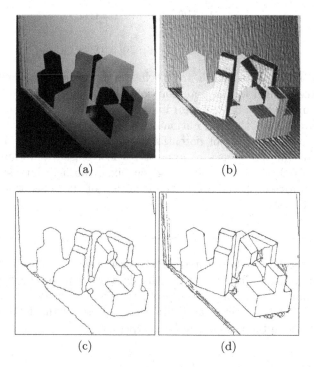

Fig. 2. The impact of the alteration strength on the segmentation results: (a) Range image (abw.test.8); (b) Rendered range image; (c) Segmentation results with $\xi_{min} = \xi_{max} = 4$ at t=2500; (d) Segmentation results with $\xi_{min} = 0.3$ and $\xi_{max} = 5$ at t=13000

4.2 Agent Coordination by Artificial Potential Field

To endow the agents with a self-organization mechanism, an artificial electrostatic like potential field is used. It is created and updated around the aligned pixels. It allows agents to be gathered around pixels of region boundaries, and concentrate their actions at these pixels. Contrary to other works, where the potential field is created at known positions of objects (goals and obstacles) [5,21,20], the potential field in our case results from the interaction of agents with the objects in the environment (pixels). The intensity $\Psi(x, y)$ of the potential field at position (x, y) created by a set of P pixels beforehand aligned $\{(x_i, y_i), i = 1..P \land I(x_i, y_i)=\text{aligned}\}$ is given by:

$$\Psi(x,y) = \sum_{i=1}^{P} \frac{k}{\sqrt{(x - x_i)^2 + (y - y_i)^2}}, k \in R^+ \tag{6}$$

where k is the constant of the electrostatic force, set to 1.

An agent which is able to alter pixels (A_t=true) and situated at position (x_t, y_t) undergoes an attractive force $\overrightarrow{F}$. This force is expressed by the gradient vector of the potential field:

$$\vec{F} = \begin{cases} -\vec{\nabla}\Psi(x_t, y_t) & \text{if } A_t = \text{true} \\ \vec{0} & \text{otherwise} \end{cases}$$

So, the agent movements, which are stochastic in nature, are weighted by the attractive force applied by the potential field. Agents are influenced to head for the pixels of interest, while keeping random moves. The random component of the agent moves allows the exploration of all regions of the image.

A Relaxation mechanism of potential field is also introduced. It allows the agents gathered around pixels of interest to be released and thus to explore other regions of the image. Around a given pixel, the field intensity decreases after every alteration of this pixel. The equation of the relaxation dynamic is expressed as follows:

$$\Psi_{t+1}(x, y) = \mu \times \Psi_t(x, y), \mu < 1 \tag{7}$$

$\Psi_0(x, y)$ corresponds to the created field after the first alteration of the pixel. The constant μ set to 0.9, represents the decrease rate of the field intensity. After several alignments of a given pixel, the field intensity around this pixel decreases, and tends to zero. This situation represents the final state of the process, after which the system can be stopped.

4.3   Edge Detection and Noise Removal

While moving over the image, agents smooth pixels that approximatively belong to their respective planar regions. An agent considers pixels that do not belong to its current region as noise pixels. The agent aligns thus automatically these pixels to its current planar region (Fig. 3b). However, pixels on the boundaries of planar regions are true-edge pixels and thus should not be aligned. Nevertheless, the competition between agents preserves these pixels against an inappropriate smoothing. Indeed, around the edge between two adjacent planar regions, two groups of agents are formed on the two sides of this edge. Each group is formed of agents passing from one region to the other. Agents of each group align the pixels of the boundary to their respective region. So, pixels of the boundary are continuously swapped between the two adjacent regions. This allows these pixels to remain emergent in the image (Fig. 3c). This pattern of competitive actions between agents allows the emergence of image edges. The edge map is not coded in any agent, it results from the collective actions of the agents. Unlike true regions of the image, which remain preserved against erasing, noise regions continuously narrow, and they finally disappear. Borders of these regions are continuously aligned to the true planar regions, that surround them. An agent, having aligned a pixel which belongs to the border of a noise region and having moved inside this region, will not be able to adapt. Consequently, it cannot align any pixel when leaving the noise region. This occurs in two distinct situations: 1) when a region is planar but insufficiently large to allow agents to cross the minimal path-length L necessary to be able to adapt; 2) when a region is sufficiently

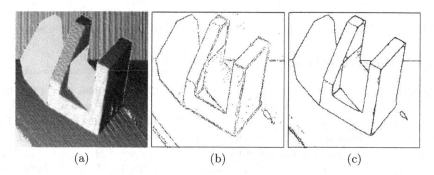

Fig. 3. Underlying edge detection (image abw.test.22): (a) Rendered range image; (b) Aligned pixel at $t=800$; (c) Only edge pixels are emergent at $t=8000$

large but not planar, or made of random depths (noise). In both situations, the agent leaves the noise region and will adapt inside the surrounding planar region. The true regions have large sizes sufficient to allow agent to adapt and then align boundary pixels when leaving these regions. However, noise regions, which are non planar, or having weak size, prevent agents from adapting. Consequently, agents will be unable to align pixels on the boundaries of these regions when leaving them. As a result, boundaries of these regions are continuously aligned from outside by including their pixels in the true surrounding regions. After several execution steps, these regions will be completely erased.

After Several iterations, all image regions are well delimited by the detected boundaries. A simple region growing steered by the detected boundaries allows to extract the regions of the image.

5 Experiments and Analysis

5.1 Evaluation Framework

Hoover et al. have proposed a dedicated framework for the evaluation of range image segmentation algorithms [7], which has has been used in several related works [10,9,13,3,1]. The framework consists of a set of real range images, and a set of objective performance metrics. It allows to compare a machine-generated segmentation (MS) with a manually-generated segmentation, supposed ideal and representing the ground truth (GT). The most important performance metrics are the numbers of instances respectively of correctly detected regions, over-segmented regions, under-segmented regions, missed regions, and noise regions. Region classification is performed according to a compare tool tolerance T; $50\% < T \leq 100\%$ which reflects the strictness of the classification. The 40 real images of ABW database are divided into two subsets: 10 training images, and 30 test images. The training images are used to estimate the parameters of a given segmentation method. Using these parameters, the method is applied to the test images. The Performance metrics are computed and stored in order to be used to compare the involved methods. In our case, four methods, namely USF, WSU, UB and UE, cited in [7] are involved in the result comparison.

5.2   Parameter Selection

Since the evaluation framework provides a set of training images with ground truth segmentation (GT), we have opted to a supervised approach for the selection of parameters. For our System, named 2ARIS for Agent-based Approach for Range Image Segmentation , six parameters should be set: ξ_{min}, ξ_{max}, Tr_θ , Tr_D, N, and L. These parameters are divided into two subsets: 1) ξ_{min}, ξ_{max}, Tr_θ, and Tr_D represent respectively the two alignment strengths, the angle threshold, and the depth threshold. These parameters are used for testing and aligning image pixels, and 2) N and L represent respectively the number of agents, and the adaptation path-length. These two parameters control the dynamic of the multi-agent system. For the first parameter subset, 256 combinations namely (ξ_{min}, ξ_{max}, Tr_θ, Tr_D) $\in$ $\{0.5, 0.3, 0.1, 0.05\} \times \{1.0, 3.0, 5.0, 7.0\} \times \{15, 18, 21, 24\} \times \{12, 16, 20, 24\}$ were run on the training images. The performance criterion for this parameters is the average number of correctly detected regions with the compare tool tolerance T set to 80%. The two alignment strengths ξ_{min} and ξ_{max} are set respectively to 0.3 and 5.0. These values have provided a good edge detection in a reasonable execution time. The threshold Tr_θ was set to 20. We have observed that higher values of this parameter under-differentiate regions regarding their orientations, and lead to an under-segmentation of the image. However, lower values over-differentiate regions, and lead to an over-segmentation. It results in a high number of false and small regions, which should be merged in the true neighboring regions. Finally, the threshold Tr_D is set to 16. Note that values significantly greater than 16 can lead to wrongly merge some parallel overlapped regions. However, if Tr_D is significantly less than 16, highly sloping regions cannot be detected as planar regions [10]. This results in a high rate of missed regions.

The number of employed agents N depends on the size of the image, while the adaptation path-length L depends on the level of detail of the image. These two parameters are critical and must be carefully selected. Inappropriate values of these two parameters can lead to a high rate of segmentation errors. Indeed, an insufficient number of agents lead to an under-processing of the image. So, resulting regions are deprived of a set of pixels which should be included in these regions. A low value of the adaptation path-length L leads to take into account small planar regions which should be considered as noise regions. However, higher values of L can result in missing some true planar regions which are insufficiently large (see section   4.3). In order to set the parameters N and L, 25 combinations of these parameters, namely $(N, L) \in \{1500, 2000, 2500, 3000, 3500\} \times \{3, 5, 7, 9, 11\}$ were run on the training set. In this case, the performance criterion is the average number of noise regions, with the compare tool tolerance set to 80%. Obtained optimal values of N and L are respectively 2500 and 7.

5.3   Experimental Results

Fig. 4 shows an instance of segmentation progression within time. The time t represents the number of steps performed by each agent since the beginning of the process. Displaying a range image by a simple rendering algorithm (Fig. 4a), allows observing the high level of noise in the used images. Figures 4b, 4c, 4d and 4e show the set of pixels of interest (edge or noise pixels) respectively at t=1000, 5000, 9000 and 13000. Regions are progressively smoothed by aligning noise pixels to the surrounding planar regions. Edges between adjacent regions are also progressively thinned. At the end of the process, region borders consist of thin lines of one pixel wide (Fig. 4e). Fig. 4f shows the segmentation result obtained by displaying the borders of the extracted regions.

Fig. 5 shows the segmentation results of the image abw.test.8, with the compare tool tolerance T set to 80%. This image was considered as a typical image to compare the involved methods [7],[3]. Fig. 5a shows the range image, and Fig. 5b shows the ground truth segmentation (GT). Fig. 5c, 5d 5e and 5f are segmentation results obtained respectively by USF, WSU, UB and UE methods. Fig. 5g presents the segmentation result obtained by our method. Metrics in table 1 show that all image regions detected by the best-referenced segmenter

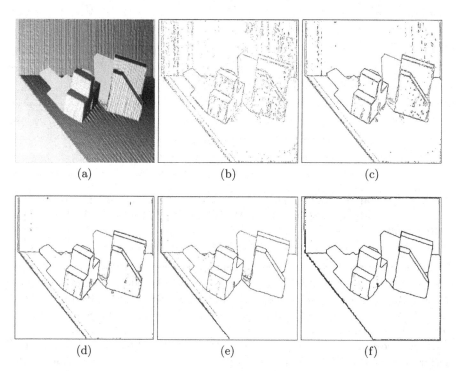

Fig. 4. Segmentation progression. (a) Rendered range image (abw.test.6); (b) at t=1000, (c) at t=5000 ; (d) at t=9000 ; (e) at t=13000 ; (f) Segmentation result (Extracted regions)

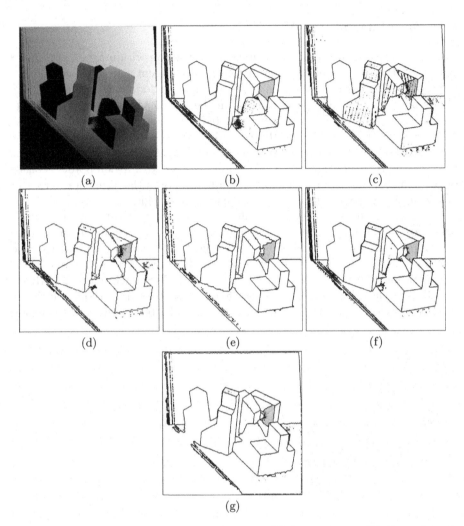

Fig. 5. Segmentation results of abw.test.8 image. (a) Range image; (b) Ground truth segmentation (GT); (c) USF result; (d) WSU result; (e) UB result; (f) UE result; (g) 2ARIS result

(UE) were detected by our method. Except the shadowed region, where all methods fail to detect, all object regions were detected. The incorrectly detected regions are those with small sizes, and situated on the horizontal support. Compared to the other methods, values of incorrect detection metrics are also good. Our method is equivalent to UE, and scored higher that the others.

Table 2 contains the average results obtained with all test images, and for all performance metrics. The compare tool tolerance was set to the typical value 80%. By considering both correct detection and incorrect detection metrics, obtained results show the good efficiency of our method. Fig. 6 shows the average numbers of correctly detected regions for all test images, and according

Table 1. Comparison results with abw.test.8 image for $T=80\%$

Method	GT region	Correct detection	Over- segmentation	Under- segmentation	Missed	Noise
USF	21	17	0	0	4	3
WSU	21	12	1	1	6	4
UB	21	16	2	0	3	6
UE	21	18	1	0	2	2
2ARIS	21	18	2	0	1	1

Table 2. Average results of the different involved methods with $T=80\%$

Method	GT region	Correct detection	Over- segmentation	Under- segmentation	Missed	Noise
USF	15.2	12.7	0.2	0.1	2.1	1.2
WSU	15.2	9.7	0.5	0.2	4.5	2.2
UB	15.2	12.8	0.5	0.1	1.7	2.1
UE	15.2	13.4	0.4	0.2	1.1	0.8
2ARIS	15.2	13.0	0.5	0.1	1.4	0.9

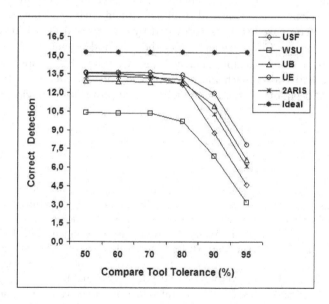

Fig. 6. Average results of correctly detected regions of all methods, according to the compare tool tolerance T ; $0.5 < T \le 1.0$

to the compare tool tolerance T; $T \in \{51\%, 60\%, 70\%, 80\%, 90\%, 95\%\}$. Results show that the number of correctly detected regions by our system is in average better than those of USF, UB and WSU. For instance, our system scored higher than WSU for all the values of the compare tool tolerance T. It scored higher than USF for $T \in \{80\%, 90\%, 95\%\}$, and better than UB for $T \in \{50\%, 60\%, 70\%, 80\%\}$. For all incorrect detection metrics (instances of Over-segmentation, Under-segmentation, Missed Region, Noise Region), our system has equivalent scores to those of UE and USF. The two latter scored higher than UB and WSU.

6   Conclusion

In this paper we have introduced an agent-based approach for range image segmentation. Indirect interaction between autonomous agents moving over the image allows reliable edge detection and efficient noise removal. Competitive actions between agents that are self-gathered around region boundaries have allowed the emergence of image edges. Image edges, for which no explicit detection was coded in any agent, result from the collective action of all the agents. The proposed approach aims to improve efficiency and to deal with the problem of result accuracy. Indeed, obtained results are better than those provided by traditional algorithms, based on region growing techniques. Moreover, employed agents are weakly coupled, and indirectly communicate via the environment (image). This allows parallel or distributed implementations, necessary to obtain a high computational efficiency. Experimental results obtained with real images from ABW database were compared to those provided by four typical algorithms for range image segmentation. Comparison results show a good potential of the proposed method for both segmentation efficiency and accuracy. The proposed approach can be extended to deal with more complex surfaces by defining their specific proprieties, and endowing the agents with the appropriate behavior.

References

1. Hadiashar, A.B., Gheissari, N.: Range image segmentation using surface selection criterion. IEEE Transactions on Image Processing 15(7), 2006–2018 (2006)
2. Bovenkamp, E.G.P., Dijkstra, J., Bosch, J.G., Reiber, J.H.C.: Multi-agent segmentation of IVUS images. Pattern Recognition 37(4), 647–663 (2004)
3. Ding, Y., Ping, X., Hu, M., Wang, D.: Range image segmentation based on randomized hough transform. Pattern Recognition Letters 26(13), 2033–2041 (2005)
4. Fan, T.J., Medioni, G.G., Nevatia, R.: Segmented description of 3-D surfaces. IEEE Journal of Robotics and Automation 3(6), 527–538 (1987)
5. Ferber, J.: Multi-Agent Systems: An Introduction to Distributed Artificial Intelligence. Addison-Wesley Longman Publishing Co., Inc., Boston, MA, USA (1999)
6. Harrouet, F., Tisseau, J., Reignier, P., Chevaillier, P.: oRis: un environnement de simulation interactive multi-agents. Technique et Science Informatiques 21(4), 499–524 (2002)
7. Hoover, A., Jean-Baptiste, G., Jiang, X., Flynn, P.J., Bunke, H., Goldgof, D.B., Bowyer, K.W., Eggert, D.W., Fitzgibbon, A.W., Fisher, R.B.: An experimental comparison of range image segmentation algorithms. IEEE Transactions on Pattern Analysis and Machine Intelligence 18(7), 673–689 (1996)

8. Inokuchi, S., Nita, T., Matsuda, F., Sakurai, Y.: A three dimensional edge-region operator for range pictures. In: 6th International Conference on Pattern Recognition, Munich, pp. 918–920 (1982)
9. Jiang, X., Bowyer, K.W., Morioka, Y., Hiura, S., Sato, K., Inokuchi, S., Bock, M., Guerra, C., Loke, R.E., Hans du Buf, J.M.: Some further results of experimental comparison of range image segmentation algorithms. In: 15th International Conference on Pattern Recognition, Barcelona, Spain, vol. 4, pp. 4877–4882 (2000)
10. Jiang, X., Bunke, H.: Edge detection in range images based on Scan Line approximation. Computer Vision and Image Understanding 73(2), 183–199 (1999)
11. Kang, S.B., Ikeuchi, K.: The complex EGI: A new representation for 3-D pose determination. IEEE Transactions on Pattern Analysis and Machine Intelligence 15(7), 707–721 (1993)
12. Krishnamurthy, E.V., Murthy, V.K.: Distributed agent paradigm for soft and hard computation. Journal of Network and Computer Applications 29(2), 124–146 (2006)
13. Li, S., Zhao, D.: Gradient-based polyhedral segmentation for range images. Pattern Recognition Letters 24(12), 2069–2077 (2003)
14. Li, S.Z.: Roof-edge preserving image smoothing based on MRFs. IEEE Transactions on Image Processing 9(6), 1134–1138 (2000)
15. Li, S.Z.: Markov random field modeling in image analysis. Springer, New York, Inc., Secaucus, NJ, USA (2001)
16. Liu, J., Tang, Y.Y.: Adaptive image segmentation with distributed behavior-based agents. IEEE Transactions on Pattern Analysis and Machine Intelligence 21(6), 544–551 (1999)
17. Newell, A.: Unified theories of cognition. Harvard University Press, Cambridge, MA, USA (1990)
18. Richard, N., Dojat, M., Garbay, C.: Automated segmentation of human brain MR images using a multi-agent approach. Artificial Intelligence in Medicine 30(2), 153–176 (2004)
19. Rodin, V., Benzinou, A., Guillaud, A., Ballet, P., Harrouet, F., Tisseau, J., Le Bihan, J.: An immune oriented multi-agent system for biological image processing. Pattern Recognition 37(4), 631–645 (2004)
20. Simonin, O.: Construction of numerical potential fields with reactive agents. In: AAMAS 2005: Proceedings of the fourth international joint conference on Autonomous agents and multiagent systems, pp. 1351–1352. ACM Press, New York (2005)
21. Tsuji, T., Tanaka, Y., Morasso, P., Sanguineti, V., Kaneko, M.: Bio-mimetic trajectory generation of robots via artificial potential field with time base generator. IEEE Transactions on Systems, Man, and Cybernetics, Part C 32(4), 426–439 (2002)
22. Yang, H.S., Kak, A.C.: Determination of the identity, position and orientation of the topmost object in a pile. Computer Vision, Graphics, and Image Processing 36(2-3), 229–255 (1986)

Coordination in Disaster Management and Response: A Unified Approach

Myriam Abramson, William Chao, Joseph Macker, and Ranjeev Mittu

Naval Research Laboratory
4555 Overlook Ave., Washington DC 20375, USA
{myriam.abramson,william.chao,joseph.macker,ranjeev.mittu}@nrl.navy.mil

Abstract. Natural, technological and man-made disasters are typically followed by chaos that results from an inadequate overall response. Three separate levels of coordination are addressed in the mitigation and preparedness phase of disaster management where environmental conditions are slowly changing: (1) communication and transportation infrastructure, (2) monitoring and assessment tools, (3) collaborative tools and services for information sharing. However, the nature of emergencies is to be unpredictable. Toward that end, a fourth level of coordination – distributed resource/role allocation algorithms of first responders, mobile workers, aid supplies and victims – addresses the dynamic environmental conditions of the response phase during an emergency. A tiered peer-to-peer system architecture could combine those different levels of coordination to address the changing needs of disaster management. We describe in this paper the architecture of such a tiered peer-to-peer agent-based coordination decision support system for disaster management and response and the applicable coordination algorithms including ATF, a novel, self-organized algorithm for adaptive team formation.

1 Introduction

Large scale disasters are characterized by catastrophic destruction of infrastructure (e.g., transportation, supply chain, environmental, communication, etc). The lack of coordination characterizes such disasters. While preparedness is the best response to emergencies [1], a multiagent-based approach to coordination decision support systems (CDSS) can play an important role in disaster management and response (DM&R) in shaping decentralized decision-making on a large scale. However, the diverse aspects of coordination make it difficult to find a unified approach for continuous control. Coordination is at best defined as an emergent property from local interactions, either cooperative or competitive, explicit or implicit, in the pursuit of multiple goals. A taxonomy of coordination is illustrated in Fig. 1. Finding a unified approach is a key problem in disaster management because a cooperative approach in the preparedness phase has to be complemented with a competitive approach in the response phase due to life-threatening situations requiring fast and reactive solutions. For example, satellite-based environmental surveillance requires centralized planning and scheduling in advance due to geo-spatial and atmospheric constraints but needs to be supplemented by unmanned

N. Jamali et al. (Eds.): CCMMS 2007, MMAS 2006, LSMAS 2006, LNAI 5043, pp. 162–175, 2008.

aerial vehicles for timely information requests. It is desirable that planning and pre-paredness decisions in DM&R be relevant in emergency situations to first responders and provide them with guidelines to avoid chaotic situations. A disaster management task is specified by the tuple $\{P, T, A, S\}$ where P is the set of plans, T the set of tasks or incidents, A a set of agents, volunteers, first responders, and coordinators, S the set of sensors, static or mobile, and where $A \subseteq S$. The problem consists of matching the needs of T with the resources of S in a decentralized and concurrent fashion to accomplish goals defined by P.

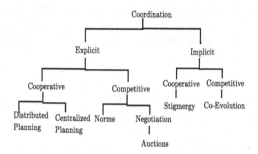

Fig. 1. Coordination Taxonomy and related coordination mechanisms

This paper is organized as follows. First, we explain the agent-based CDSS frame-work in Sect. 2 and motivate a tiered peer-to-peer (P2P) coordination architecture for integrating the different coordination dimensions of DM&R. Then, in Sect. 3, we in-troduce two basic coordination algorithms for heterogeneous agents suitable in disaster management response. In Sect. 4, a self-organized, semi-centralized coordination al-gorithm is introduced in support of the architecture proposed. An empirical evaluation follows in Sect. 5 on a canonical fire/rescue scenario to illlustrate the relative merits of the coordination algorithms. Finally, Sections 6 and 7 conclude with related work.

2 Agent-Based CDSS

Recent technological advances in communication and processing power, enabling sen-sor networks and personal digital assistants, have made possible the self-organization of mobile agents (robots or people) and geo-localized decision support. The complexity of decentralized decision-making is tamed by delegating certain management tasks to proxy agents [2]. Coordination is a pervasive management task that helps reduce inter-ference in role assignments and enhance information sharing. The degree of consensus to obtain before making a decision can be arbitrarily set. The lower the degree of con-sensus, the more flexible the agents are in reacting to outside events and making timely decisions, but more negative interactions can occur. Assuming rational, communicating and trusting agents reduces the degree of consensus overhead required in coordina-tion tasks because the agents are likely to reach the same conclusions given the same information.

Current collaborative web-based tools have essentially a fixed client/server approach because of the relatively stable nature of internet routing. Coordination is achieved through the server as a synchronizing blackboard passively mediating the interactions of intelligent agents (humans or proxies) as clients. P2P approaches, such as JXTA [3], de-emphasize the role of the server as passive synchronizer but the role of mediator is taken up actively by "rendez-vous" peers and "relays." Peers discover each other through advertisements propagated by relays and rendez-vous peers. This suggests a flexible, semi-centralized coordination architecture for complex tasks such as DM&R where the preparedness and information sharing architecture can seamlessly adapt to rapidly changing conditions and communication infrastructure (Fig. 2). In this framework, coordination at the network layer, whereby a host is chosen to act as relay for propagating messages through the network, maps with a coordinator role at the application layer.

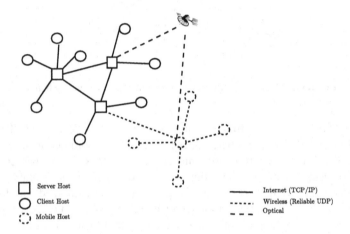

Fig. 2. Semi-Centralized Coordination Architecture

3   Coordination Algorithms for Heterogeneous Agents

One of the key coordination problem in disaster management is the heterogeneity of the players involved. Roles provide a convenient a priori decomposition of a task and are a key coordination tool [4]. Roles can be viewed either as fixed slots in a team structure that are filled by agents or part of an agent's behavior repertoire in its relationships with other agents that can determine the structure of a team. The decision complexity for the role allocation of N agents to p tasks is $O(p^T)$ where T is the number of teams of size t that can be selected from N agents:

$$T = \begin{cases} \binom{N}{t} & case\,1 : homogeneous\,agents \\ \binom{N+t+1}{t} & case\,2 : heterogeneous\,agents \end{cases} \tag{1}$$

Algorithm 1. Basic agent loop for cooperative distributed systems

```
set initial role to explore
active ← true
rounds ← 0
while (no termination condition) do
if (active) then
  sense environment
  act according to role
  broadcast information to neighbors
  active ← false
else
  read neighbors' new information, if any
  deliberate and select role
  active ← true
endif
rounds++
end while
```

t is the number of roles in a team which might not correspond to the number of agents N. In the homogeneous case, $\sum_i^T t_i \leq N$, agents have distinct, mutually-exclusive roles. In the heterogeneous case, agents fill a number of non mutually-exclusive roles (i.e. an agent can perform a number of roles in a team). The complexity of role allocation scales up with heterogeneous agents where the mapping of agents to roles is one-to-many. The basic agent loop for role allocation in distributed cooperative systems is described in Alg. 1. Two basic matching algorithm for generalized role allocation of heterogeneous agents running in polynomial time are described below.

3.1 Hungarian Algorithm

The "Hungarian" algorithm for weighted bipartite matching [5,6] solves constraint optimization problems such as the job assignment problem in polynomial time. An implementation of this algorithm follows Munkres' assignment algorithm [7]. The algorithm consists of transforming a weighted adjacency matrix of *roles × agents* into equivalent matrices until the solution can be read off as independent elements of an auxiliary matrix. While additional rows and columns with maximum value can be added to square the matrix, the optimality is no longer guaranteed if the problem is over-constrained, i.e. there are more roles to be filled than agents. This algorithm can be extended to heterogeneous agents by expanding the original set of agents to virtual homogeneous agents, one for each capability required by the task, ignoring other capabilities. The mapping of agent capabilities to incident needs is illustrated by the bipartite matching graph in Fig. 3. A team preference for a task is proportional to its coverage and the individual preferences of the agents selected for the task, ensuring commitment to mostly completed tasks.

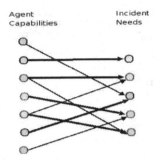

Fig. 3. Weighted Bipartite Matching

3.2   Greedy Set Cover Algorithm

This is an approximate matching algorithm [8] that finds the minimum set cover for a list of resources needed to accomplish a task given the initial capabilities of a set of agents sorted in maximal task coverage order (Fig. 4). In addition, a small penalty is given to capabilities not relevant to the task. Here too, the team preference for a task depends on its coverage of the task and the individual preferences of the agents selected for the task.

This algorithm was found to have a faster performance than the Hungarian algorithm described above and was subsequently used in the experimental evaluation.

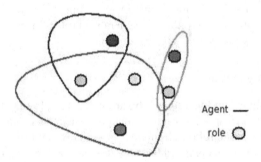

Fig. 4. Greedy Set Cover of a task decomposed into 6 needs (dots) with 3 agents and one over-lapping capability between 2 agents

4   Semi-centralized Coordination Algorithms

Semi-centralized algorithms were found to be both practical and efficient in the large-scale coordination of agents [9] and lend themselves well to the widely used contract net protocol. The level of specificity in the planning of large groups does not extend to individual behaviors. DM&R planning in the National Response Plan [10] provides specific guidelines at the lowest geographical and organizational level but leaves room for self-organization. Semi-centralization with adaptive team formation enables the continuous control of decentralized decision-making to achieve planned objectives and maintain situation awareness through data fusion at the global level. We first describe a cycle-based self-organizing algorithm for the formation of "cluster heads" and then our extension of this algorithm to take into account environmental demands in the form of request for service.

4.1   Low-Energy Adaptive Clustering Hierarchy (LEACH) Algorithm

The LEACH algorithm [11] is a stochastic adaptive algorithm for energy-efficient communication in wireless sensor networks in the task allocation of aggregating and routing messages back to the base station (BS). Because of the limitation on battery power, the task should be fairly distributed among the nodes. In addition, aggregating the data to reduce noise before sending it to the BS is more efficient. Rotating this "cluster head" role among the nodes will (1) minimize the overall energy consumed and (2) allow the battery power to get replenished through solar energy. A round in the algorithm includes a setup phase establishing a transmission schedule to maximize bandwidth utilization and a steady-state phase where data fusion occurs and the aggregated messages are actually transmitted. It is assumed that the percentage of nodes that should take up this role is known a priori by the agents. An algorithm where the agents take turn assuming the "cluster head" role is described in Alg. 2. An agent i assumes the role of "cluster head" if the stochastic probability is below a threshold T, determined as follows:

$$T(i) = \begin{cases} \frac{P}{1-P*(r \bmod \frac{1}{P})} & if\ i \in G \\ 0 & otherwise \end{cases} \qquad (2)$$

where P is the desired percentage of cluster heads known a priori, r is the current round, and G is the set of agents that have not been cluster heads for the past $\frac{1}{P}$ rounds. If below threshold, the agent will advertise its services. Otherwise, the agents elect as their leader the closest agent according to the advertisements received.

4.2   Extension of the LEACH Algorithm

The LEACH algorithm assumes that (1) the activation percentage is given a priori and (2) the activation duration during which a schedule is propagated and messages are transmitted to the base station is fixed. This works well for sensor networks (e.g. unmanned aerial vehicles) where the number of nodes is known in advance and the only mission is to report back to the BS. This algorithm needs to be adapted to act as a relay in a mobile ad hoc network (i.e, transmit messages from any node to any other nodes) and to autonomously adjust to the number of nodes in the network. The time interval allocated to be a "cluster head" need not be limited to a single transmission to the BS and has to adapt to the needs of the network.

Adaptive Team Formation (ATF) algorithm. If an agent i does not assume a network role or "cluster head," it will receive only advertisement messages, and will send only election messages. As long as it receives advertisement messages, it does not have to compete for the network role. However, if everybody assume the same strategy, no service will be provided. The key idea is to predict the correct individual phase to alternate

Algorithm 2. LEACH algorithm

```
active←true
rounds←0
set activation rate
while (no termination condition)
if (active) then
  if (cluster_head) then
    read BS mesgs
    aggregate BS mesgs
    send BS mesgs to BS
    rounds←0
    cluster_head←false
  else
    route BS msgs to elected cluster_head
  endif
  generate a random number r
  T←estimate threshold
  if (r < T) then
    cluster_head←true
    broadcast advertisement messages
  endif
  propagate messages
  active←false
else
  if (cluster_head) then
    read election mesgs
    create transmission schedule
    broadcast transmission schedule
  else
    read advertisement mesgs
    elect cluster_head
    send election mesg to cluster_head
  endif
  active←true
endif
rounds++
end while
```

between roles based not only on internal disposition but also on the state of the environment. A coverage metric as the number of agents reached over the total number of agents looking for service measures the performance of this algorithm. The time-to-live (TTL) parameter, latency and communication range affect the propagation of messages and coverage of a node.

In contrast to other adaptation problems where convergence of an agent to a fixed behavior (or role) is desired, congestion problems like the El Farol Bar problem [12] require learning when to change behavior to resolve conflicts. Response thresholds in swarm intelligence [13] induce a dynamic task allocation depending (1) on the disposition of the agents and (2) the environmental demands. A simple reinforcement learning scheme allocates agents to the task by either raising or lowering their response threshold. In our problem, an increase in connectivity (due to proximity or communication range) should sensitize an agent to be a team leader but a decrease in advertisement messages should also be an incentive to assume the role. The stimulus s_i for an agent i to become a team leader at time t depends on the connectivity of the agents (i.e. the number of other agents within one hop) or degree d_i of the network node, the change in connectivity δ_i, and repulsion factor $\alpha \in (0, 1)$ as follows:

$$s_{i_0} = \frac{d_{i_0}}{d_{i_0} + 1} \tag{3}$$

$$s_{i_{t+1}} = s_{i_t} - \alpha \frac{\#Advertisements}{\#Elections + \#Advertisements + \varepsilon} + \delta_{i_{t+1}} \tag{4}$$

Here $\varepsilon > 0$ is a small constant that prevents division by 0. The agent's response threshold T_i at time t taking into account its internal disposition θ_i and external demands is then as follows:

$$T_{i_t} = \frac{\theta_{i_t}}{1 + e^{-s_{i_t}}} \tag{5}$$

The initial disposition $\theta_{i_o} \in (0, 1)$ of an agent can be a function of its battery power or other hardware capabilities. To avoid specialization and redistribute the manager task fairly among the agents according to their capabilities, θ_t is adjusted based on the "fatigue" of performing the task or the "boredom" of not performing the task measured in cycles as in the LEACH algorithm above (see Subsect. 4.1).

$$\theta_{i_t} = \theta_{i_0} * (r \, mod \, \frac{1}{\theta_{i_0}}) \tag{6}$$

where r is the number of elapsed rounds.

It is assumed that the agents can perform their deliberative task in allocating and/or selecting roles in one round and that roles are noncommittal. The leader determines team compositions with a role allocation algorithm (Sect. 3) by iterating through each task. Roles are allocated to the best ranking team based on coverage of the task and preferences. The process repeats again on the remaining agents and tasks until no team can be formed. Redundancy against message loss occurs when roles are reallocated either by the same manager agent in the next round or another manager agent. Algorithm 3 describes the combined process.

5 Experimental Evaluation

The experiments were conducted with RePast [14], an agent-based simulation and modeling tool where agents act concurrently in a decentralized manner on an $n \times n$ grid. Its powerful scheduling mechanism was used to model the asynchronous behavior of the agents. Communication between agents was implemented by transmitting messages to

---

Algorithm 3. Adaptive Team Formation

```
active ←true
set repulsion rate
rounds ← 0
while (no termination condition) do
if (active) then
  read role allocation mesg
  perform step(s) in role
  generate a random number r
  update stimulus and disposition
  T←estimate threshold
  if (r < T) then
    leader←true
    broadcast advertisement mesg
  else
    leader←false
    elect leader
    send election mesg to leader
  endif
  send role preferences mesgs to leader
  propagate all messages
  active←false
else
  read role preferences mesgs
  read role allocation mesgs
  read election mesgs
  read advertisement mesgs
  if (leader) then
    optimize team allocations
    send role allocation mesgs
  endif
  active←true
endif
rounds++
end while
```

---

agents in a Moore neighborhood of 7 cells, eliminating cycles, and time-to-live parameter set to 6 hops. In addition, a 5% message loss proportional to distance was simulated.

Figure 5 compares the static coverage rates of the LEACH and ATF clustering algorithms for routine messages without task allocation for a varying number of agents in fixed random locations on a 100×100 grid. Only cluster nodes relay messages to other agents. The agents were randomly initialized with a disposition rate varying in the [0,0.1] range. The swarm-based ATF algorithm provides a significantly better coverage albeit with a larger clustering rate for each node. Nodes were cluster nodes at a rate of ~0.5% in the LEACH algorithm while their rate was evaluated at ~0.8% in the ATF algorithm.

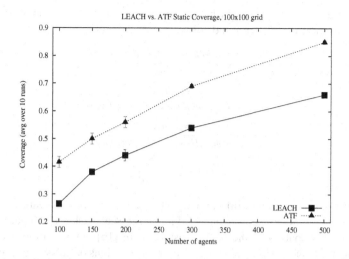

Fig. 5. LEACH vs. ATF static coverage comparison over 100 cycles

5.1 Coordination Metric

Because coordination is an emergent property of interactive systems, it can only be measured indirectly through the performance of the agents in accomplishing a task where a task is decomposed in subgoals. The more complex the task, the higher the number of subgoals needed to be achieved. While performance is ultimately defined in domain-dependent terms, there are some common characteristics. Performance in a task can be measured either as the number of steps taken to reach the goal, i.e. its time complexity, or as the amount of resources required, i.e. its space complexity. An alternative evaluation for coordination is the absence of "failures", for example negative interactions such as collisions or lost messages. Figure 6 illustrates the taxonomy of coordination solution quality in pursuit games. To show the scalability of a solution, the evaluation must linearly increase with the complexity of the task [15].

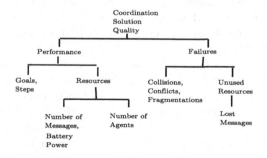

Fig. 6. Taxonomy of coordination solution quality

A combined coordination quality measure is defined as the harmonic mean of goals achieved g, resources expanded r and collisions c as follows :

$$g = \frac{\#Goals\,Achieved}{\#Goals} \tag{7}$$

$$r = \frac{\#agents}{log_2(\#Messages\,Received + 1) + \#agents} \tag{8}$$

$$c = \frac{\#agents}{log_2(\#Collisions + 1) + \#agents} \tag{9}$$

$$coordination = \frac{3grc}{gr + rc + cg} \tag{10}$$

Such a metric combining the different aspects of coordination can evaluate the trade-off of performance and consuming bandwidth in large-scale tasks. The logarithms help normalize the distribution of the data across runs. In [16], coordination is evaluated solely as an effort, such as additional steps to avoid collisions or messages to avoid role conflicts, and do not take into account the indirect effect on performance.

5.2 Fire/Rescue Problem

In our scenario, buildings are randomly created on an $n \times n$ grid with a random probability of being on fire and of spreading fire to adjacent buildings if not extinguished in time. Each fire or incident creates an emergency situation requiring up to k types of resources. In turn, each responder agent can provide up to k matching types of capabilities. There are m capabilities and needs for each agent and incident ($m < k$). The problem consists of dynamically matching capabilities and needs with a team of agents. When a team of agents with the desired capabilities is situated near the incident within proximity range p, the emergency will be removed. There are no scheduling constraints in matching resources but the overall resource requirements might increase over time as the fire spreads leading to a decrease in coordination performance. Each agent has a perception range p and a typically greater communication range h to communicate with its neighbors. There are 5 types of messages in this scenario which are either broadcasted or point-to-point: (1) advertisement messages are broadcasted; (2) election messages are point-to-point; (3) role preferences messages are broadcasted; (4) role allocation messages are point-to-point; and (5) "resource needed" messages are broadcasted upon observation of an incident.

Figure 7 shows the coordination performance (Eq. 10) in this scenario with ATF where the elected leader node performs the network role of relaying messages. In the semi-centralized case, the leader node performs the managerial task of role allocation. In addition, one scout agent broadcast "resource needed" observation messages. In the distributed case, the role allocation task is performed implicitly by each agent. Both cases use the Greedy Set Cover algorithm. Results show that self-organization and semi-centralization of role allocation incurs an overhead with a large number of agents. There is a significance difference under ATF with 50 agents (t-test p-value = 0.002) between fully distributed role allocation and semi-centralized role allocation using the Greedy Set Cover algorithm.

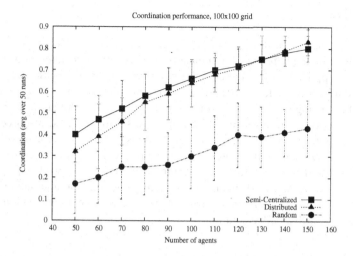

Fig. 7. Comparative coordination performance with ATF ($\alpha = 0.05, m = 4, k = 8$) for 20 incidents and a varying number of agents. Greedy Set Cover was the role allocation algorithm used in the semi-centralized and distributed case.

6   Related Work

Workpad [17] has proposed a 2-layer P2P architecture where the static internet backend provides the information services necessary to first responders in a tethered mobile ad hoc network. The scenarios explored an architecture for a coordination layer on top of the network layer where a team leader would reallocate tasks to solve predicted fragmentation of the network due to the mobility of the agents. In this paper we explored in detail the algorithms for role allocation and for selecting a team leader in a self-organized way.

Cooperative mediation [18] combines distributed role allocation with partial centralization. An agent, acting as mediator, recommends value changes (role assignments) to neighboring agents to optimize local subproblems. If a current solution is different from an optimal solution, the mediator transmits repairs to the relevant agents. Agents are prioritized to act as mediator based on the size of their "social knowledge." If a solution cannot be found, the neighboring agents transmit their constraints which could involve other agents enlarging the context of the subproblem. Cooperative mediation achieves a global optimal solution in a distributed way by exploiting the substructure of the problem. If no local optimal solution can be found, the mediator will progressively enlarge its context until an optimal global solution is found. Similarly, the ATF approach uses the degree of connectivity as a stimulus to influence the tendency of an agent to be a team leader but the election of a leader is explicit. A team leader divides the search space according to the substructure of the problem but does not attempt to reach a more global solution in this paper. The role of the team leader is not only to coordinate other agents in solving a task but also to coordinate the information sharing between agents.

7   Conclusion

We have presented applicable coordination algorithms and introduced a tiered P2P architecture to unify the different communication and coordination dimensions of DM&R with possible applications to other complex environments such as battlespace management. In addition, a novel, self-organized, semi-centralized algorithm, ATF, has been introduced extending the LEACH algorithm to adaptive team formation. Tiered architectures are important to achieve planned objectives with bounded resources and to integrate disparate systems. Experimental evaluations of role allocation algorithms for heterogeneous agents have been presented in the fire/rescue domain along with a coordination metric that takes into account communication costs as well as partial goals achieved. Future work should include (1) dynamic coordination alternating between semi-centralized and fully distributed role allocation and (2) communication between leader nodes to reach a global solution.

References

1. The National Commission on Terrorist Attacks: The 9/11 Commission Report. W. W. Norton & Company (2004)
2. Scerri, P., Pynadath, D., Schurr, N., Farinelli, A., Gandhe, S., Tambe, M.: Team oriented programming and proxy agents: The next generation. In: Workshop on Programming Multi-Agent Systems, AAMAS 2003 (2003)
3. Project JXTA, http://www.jxta.org (last accessed, 02/01/2007)
4. Abramson, M.: Three myths about roles. Technical report, American Association of Artificial Intelligence, Arlington, VA; Fall Symposium Workshop on Roles, an Interdisciplinary Perspective: Ontologies, Programming Languages, and Multiagent Systems (2005)
5. Kuhn, H.W.: The hungarian method for the assignment problem. Naval Research Logistics Quarterly 2(83) (1955)
6. Papadimitriou, C.H., Steiglitz, K.: Combinatorial Optimization: Algorithms and Complexity. Dover Publications (1998)
7. Burgeios, F., Lassalle, J.C.: An extension of the munkres algorithm for the assignment problem to rectangular matrices. Communication of the ACM 14, 802–806 (1971)
8. Cormen, T.H., Leiserson, C.E., Rivest, R.L., Stein, C.: Introduction to Algorithms, 2nd edn. MIT Press, Cambridge (2001)
9. Scerri, P., Liao, E., Lai, J., Sycara, K.: Coordinating Very Large Groups of Wide Area Search Munitions. In: Cooperative Control. Kluwer Publishing, Dordrecht (2004)
10. Department of Homeland Security: National Response Plan, http://dhs.gov/xprepresp/publications (last accessed, 01/23/2007)
11. Heinzelman, W.R., Chandrakasan, A., Balakrishnan, H.: Energy-efficient communication protocol for wireless microsensor networks. In: Proceedings of the 33rd Hawaii IEEE International Conference on System Sciences (2000)
12. Arthur, W.B.: Inductive reasoning and bounded rationality. American Economic Review (1994)
13. Bonabeau, E., Dorigo, M., Theraulaz, G.: Swarm Intelligence: from Natural to Artificial Systems. Oxford University Press, Oxford (1999)
14. North, M.J., Collier, N.T., Vos, J.R.: Experiences creating three implementations of the repast agent modeling toolkit. ACM Transactions on Modeling and Computer Simulation 16(1), 1–25 (2006)

15. Durfee, E.H.: Scaling up agent coordination strategies. IEEE Computer (2001)
16. Rosenfeld, A., Kaminka, G.A., Kraus, S.: Adaptive robotic communication using coordination costs for improved trajectory planning. In: Proceedings of the American Association of Artificial Intelligence (2006)
17. Mecella, M., Catarci, T., Angelaccio, M., Buttarazzi, B., Krek, A., Dustdar, S., Vetere, G.: Workpad: an adaptive peer-to-peer software infrastructure for supporting collaborative work of human operators in emergency/disaster scenarios. In: IEEE International Symposium on Collaborative Technologies and Systems (CTS 2006) (2006)
18. Mailler, R., Lesser, V.: Solving distributed constraint optimization problems using cooperative mediation. In: International Conference on Autonomous Agents and Multiagent Systems (2004)

The Scalability of an Environment for Large-Scale Sensor-Networks

Timothy Middelkoop[1] and Abhijit Deshmukh[2]

[1] University of Florida, Department of Industrial and Systems Engineering, P.O. Box 116595,
Gainesville, FL 32611-6595
t.middelkoop@ufl.edu

[2] University of Massachusetts Amherst, Mechanical and Industrial Engineering,
160 Governors Dr, Amherst, Massachusetts 01003-9265
deshmukh@ecs.umass.edu

Abstract. In this paper we discuss the scalability of an environment for distributed sensor-network resource-allocation. We cover the underlying architecture and demonstrate the scalability of the architecture through a number of experiments and show that different code configurations can have an impact on run-time performance. We conclude with a discussion of some of the challenges in scaling the environment further.

1 Introduction

Coordination in large-scale multi-agents systems is a difficult task. Not only must the problem-solving protocols, algorithms and analysis scale but so must the supporting computational environment. In this paper we discuss one such environment. This environment supports a distributed resource-allocation model for large-scale sensor-network systems[10]. Although the resource-allocation model is an interesting problem the focus of this paper is on the underlying environment. We demonstrate the scalability by a number of experiments and discuss the research challenges in scaling it even further.

Sensor-networks contain a number of interconnected nodes with transducers that sense the environment. Applications for sensor networks are diverse and include battlefield sensor deployment [5,8], homeland security [19], and earthquake and fire monitoring [11]. Modalities range from dynamic sensing with disposable units to expensive fixed-installation units across the country.

The sensor-network model in this paper is similar to the Defense Advanced Research Projects Agency (DARPA) Autonomous Negotiating Teams (ANTs) program challenge problem [8,6] and to the Collaborative Adaptive Sensing of the Atmosphere (CASA) project. A set of fixed sensing stations must coordinate activities to track or detect objects or events in an environment. The issues are linked together by the interdependence of one scheduling problem with another making the coordination process a multi-issue problem. Two key properties of the environment make the problem difficult. The first is that sensing nodes are vulnerable and may only provide intermittent results or even disappear entirely from the system. The second key aspect is that the system may be extremely large and so the resource algorithms must scale with the environment.

N. Jamali et al. (Eds.): CCMMS 2007, MMAS 2006, LSMAS 2006, LNAI 5043, pp. 176–189, 2008.
© Springer-Verlag Berlin Heidelberg 2008

Fortunately, sensor-networks are distributed geographically; it is this property that provides a natural mechanism to distribute the problem. Although the issues (resources under contention) are multi-linked, they do not extend beyond a certain range around the targets and sensors. This key factor is important when constructing the simulations and computations, and will ultimately determine if an implementation will scale or not.

The modeling approach used in this work defines the resource-allocation problem in terms of a collection of *autonomous decision-making entities*, or *agents*, each with its own local and global goals. Bargaining markets provide a natural framework for the analysis of this type of strategic interaction between agents. Bargaining markets combine bargaining theory and markets to provide a description of how local strategic interaction between agents leads to different global outcomes. The agents compute the outcome of the bargaining market and use the results for resource-allocation. The multi-linked bargaining market model used in this paper is described in detail in [10].

The remainder of the paper is structured as follows: In the next section we discuss the construction of the computational environment and its major components. We then discuss the sensor-network system and how it is implemented in the environment. With an understanding of the computational and sensor environment the next section discusses the system performance by presenting a number of experiments to demonstrate scalability. This naturally leads into a discussion about the research challenges in doing science at this scale. Finally, the paper closes with related research and conclusions.

2   Computational Environment

The computational environment plays an important part in both the design and the scalability of the environment. In this section we discuss the high level architecture and the major modules associated with the problem in order to communicate the decision rational in the later sections. We first start with an overview of the architecture of the computational environment.

The architecture is divided in to multiple software layers that are show in Figure 1. Each layer depends on services provided by those above it. This software stack is a result of the architecture, the hardware configuration, and the deployment software, and is discussed in the remainder of this section.

Middleware: The middleware system used in the environment is the Internet Communications Engine [2,1] or ICE. ICE is a lightweight modern alternative to object middleware such as *CORBA* [15]. ICE was designed to be developed for high-performance distributed applications. Currently the platform supports Java, C++, C#, PHP, and Python. The core of the environment was developed with Jython [13] (Python on a JVM). The major strengths of this combined platform is rapid development, stability, small size and ease of use. For an extensive overview of distributed systems and this style of architecture see [18].

World Application: The world application level in the environment is responsible for managing and coordinating the computational resources. The application level provides, and abstracts, information about the hardware to the rest of the system. Changes in hardware configuration are managed from here. Deployment at this level is handled by

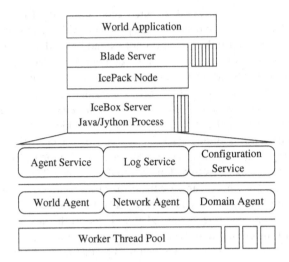

Fig. 1. Software stack

a suite of Ice tools and libraries customized for the hardware and software needs of the environment. After deployment the location abstraction is managed by a name service called the Ice *registry*. This, in conjunction with the application, provides the means for software entities to find and communicate with each other without knowing their physical location.

The relative homogeneity of the simulation environment makes this method of system configuration convenient. The hardware requirements for the simulation are computed at the beginning and remain constant throughout the duration of the run. However, configuration changes are a reality in a commodity cluster environment where hardware failures are a non-zero occurrence and resources must be shared with other users. These changes are made easy by utilizing the centrally deployed world application. After deployment the environment is further customized by the simulation itself by utilizing the location abstracted resources that are deployed by the world application. The runtime utilization of abstracted resources allows the simulation to easily use a large number of nodes and the centralized deployment allows the hardware configuration to be easily changed. This balance is what makes using a cluster easy yet scalable.

Blade Server: The blade server is the actual hardware on which the environment runs. Each blade is managed by an IcePack node that is responsible for controlling processes run on each node; each process is called a *server*. The world application is responsible for assigning *processes* to the hardware. In the case of the hardware used, it was important to run multiple processes on each blade to take advantage of the number of processors and the Hyper-Threading technology. Other servers are responsible for monitoring and keeping the software up to date.

Agent Services: The IceBox server can run multiple modules called *services*. A service is an independent module that can be run with other services in the same virtual machine allowing the Ice library to optimize out some of the communication. Services contain individual instances of objects that are exposed to others via the Ice library. These exposed instances are called *servants* and are spawned in the service by the direction of the *world application*. In the distributed environment there are three main services: (1) an agent service, (2) a logging service, and (3) a configuration service responsible for monitoring and code distribution. This collection of software and hardware collectively represents the support infrastructure for the more interesting *agent servants*.

This structure allows modules and agent to be distributed across process and processors. The number of modules is limited by the address and stack space of the Java Virtual Machine. Running more processes allows better utilization of processors but at the expense of memory and increased communication costs, which we will see later in the experimental section.

Agents: Agent servants are the main software entity in the distributed environment. There are three main classes of agents in the environment: world agents responsible for configuration management, network agents responsible for coordinating the communication and coordination of other agents, and domain agents that the sensors and targets in the sensor-network application. Additionally, these agents use communicating worker-threads, which is a fourth class of servant. For performance reasons worker servants bypass the main agent hierarchy and communication services.

3   Large-Scale Sensor-Network

In this section we describe the construction of the agents in the sensor-network environment. There are three main entities in the sensor-network: the network agent, sensor nodes, and target nodes.

Network agents manage information and communication for sensor and target nodes and manage most of the simulation process. The network agents are deployed by the world application and the simulation is responsible for its configuration. Each network agent is assigned a location and an *effective range* (a circle of control) and informed about neighbors that have overlapping effective ranges. The network agents are then assigned sensor and target nodes that lie within their control area. The nodes use the network agent to discover location and effective range of other entities and to coordinate the simulation. This mechanism eliminates the need for a global location database and centralized synchronization that can become a bottleneck as the environment scales. The network agent also separates the simulation network-protocol from the sensor and target nodes. By reducing the number of network agents in the environment the number of protocol interactions is reduced since domain agents do not directly take part in the protocol.

The number of network agents is a product of the environment configuration. At a minimum there must be at least one network agent per process/blade and at the maximum there is one network agent for each sensor and target node. As the number of nodes per network agent changes so does the total number of network agents along with the size and number of processes run on each blade. With this mechanism the blade configuration can be optimized for performance and increased scalability. Without this optimization faulty configurations are quickly reached.

Figure 2 illustrates an environment with 16 hexagonally packed sensors in a four network configuration. The smaller circles are targets, the medium circles are sensors, and the large circles inscribe the control area of a network agent. In this case each network agent control's four sensors within its effective range. Figure 3 shows an example of a 1512-network and 1512-sensor network. In this case each sensor has a dedicated network agent. The targets/events are randomly placed in the environment and given a constant direction and velocity determined at random. The number of targets is set such that there is a sufficient level of conflict (multiple targets and sensors in the same area) to make the problem interesting: Too small a density and there are insufficient resources to obtain a track (or the problem becomes uninteresting, having only one target per sensor); if there are too many sensors, then there is an excess of resources in the area to track the targets. The target/sensor ratio remains constant throughout the experiments conducted in this paper.

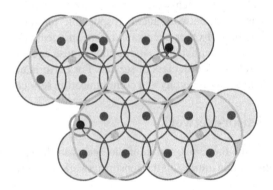

Fig. 2. Example sensor layout (4 networks, 16 sensors, 3 targets)

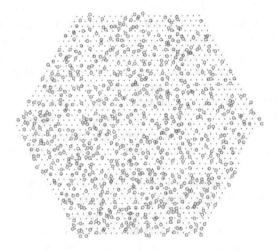

Fig. 3. Example network (1512 sensors, 1512 networks)

With this understanding of the structure of the problem we now present the system performance and scalability in the next section

4   System Performance

The requirements of large-scale simulation and analysis puts extreme demands on hardware and software. This section is the result of a large number of initial experiments designed to increase performance and the maximum problem size that the environment can handle. The end result shows how well the distributed environment scales when adding more hardware and increasing the problem size.

The computational resources in the cluster are arranged in a hierarchical manner, with the calculations performed on the bottom and the entire facility at the top. Fastest computation occurs at the bottom but has limited capacity. As we work up the hierarchy the computation is grouped by various forms of connectivity, thus increasing the total capacity. We now discuss the different groupings, from top to bottom, and their effect on performance.

- **Data Centers** house multiple racks of servers in the same room. Their close proximity allows multiple high-speed links, often in a mesh, that allow high-capacity communication.
- **Blade Centers** usually contain the same type of blades with their own unique capabilities and may span multiple racks. Scheduling resources across blade centers depends on the type of computation being performed.
- **Blade Chassis** contain a number of blades connected by network-switching hardware. Intra-blade-chassis communication is usually at wire speed and limited by the switch bandwidth. Inter-blade-chassis communication is limited by the network connectivity to the blade center switching hardware.
- **Blades** are the fundamental unit of capacity and mark the boundary between network-based communication and communication through memory.
- **Processors** are connected via internal busses and memory. Communication between processors on the same blade is very fast.
- **Hyper-Threading** uses virtual processors that share a single hardware processor. Performance gains can come from reduced pipeline stalling and shared caches.
- **Processes** have their own memory spaces. Communication must be explicit, either using shared memory or a message-passing system. Switching between processes degrades cache performance and has an associated context-switching overhead.
- **Threads** share the same memory space. For Java 32-bit processors this space is limited to less than 2GB. Communication can be done though shared variables.
- **Functions** are the fastest form of computation, as communication can occur at the *register* level. In addition, code and data often occupy the fastest caches.

Since the amount of code and computation are limited at each level, higher levels must be used at the expense of speed induced by the additional communication overhead. Each layer going upwards requires more complex and slower interaction mechanisms. There is a tradeoff when moving computation up the stack. Does the additional

capacity make up for the increased communication? What is the most efficient configuration? To answer these questions for the sensor-network, a series of experiments was
run for a range of problems.

The distributed-environment and sensor-network problem can be configured in a
number of ways. The primary unit of configuration is the network agent and how it
is clustered among the various computational levels. The network agent contains multiple sensors and targets in the same process. The blade server can also contain multiple
network agents in a single process (the Java virtual machine). These mechanisms allow
code to be distributed between threads, processes, and blades. Using the language of
the world application, this breaks down to blades, processes, and agents. Here "agent"
refers to the network agent, the lowest agent visible to the world application. The product of blades, processes, and agents gives the total number of network agents. The target
and sensor agents then must be distributed over the network agents. In the next section
we describe the problem setup and how different configurations are generated to test
the performance of the environment and sensor network problem.

4.1   Experimental Setup

One of the purposes of the experiments conducted in this section was to determine the
best way in which to configure the environment. A number of preliminary experiments
were conducted to determine reasonable bounds on the parameters for the more formal
experiments presented here. The bounds allowed the search space to be restricted, thus
eliminating any configurations that would fail to complete for any number of the following reasons: memory exhaustion, thread exhaustion, exceeding memory address space,
and stack limits, among others. The initial experiments also showed that there are complex performance interactions between the different computational modes. Throughout
the experimentation two factors consistently showed a strong influence: the problem
size (the number of sensors) and the number of blades.

For this experiment three IBM blade servers where used with 14 blades each containing two 2.8GHz Hyper Threaded processors. The blades use gigabit Ethernet and
blade centers are connected via four port gigabit trunks. For experiments 1 and 2 the
problem size is determined by the number of sensors. The environment is then seeded
with one-half the number of targets at random locations and random directions. The
environment is then run for 12 periods. for each period the target location is incremen-
tally updated and the resource-allocation algorithm is run. Experiment 1 tests the main
effects with a large parameter space and Experiment 2 increases the problem size even
further to determine how well the system scales.

4.2   Experiment 1

For experiment 1 a large parameter space was selected for a relatively small number
of sensors. Table 1 shows the range of values for each parameter. Valid configurations
occur when the product of networks and children is equal to the number of sensors. The
term "children" refers to the configuration parameter (a square number) that determines
the maximum number of sensors a network agent will manage. This parameter is also

Table 1. Experiment 1 parameters

Parameter	Range	Comment
sensors	36,60,120, 144,168,216	multiples of 6 with many combinations
targets	sensors/2	
networks	4-216	blades*process*agents
children	1-36	sensors/network
blades	1-42	
processes	1-10	
agents	1-84	
runs	5	times a configuration is run
periods	12	length of simulation

used as an approximation of how many sensors and targets the network agent will manage. Parameter ranges were selected from a known stable and reasonable performing set.

4.2.1 Sensors and Blades

From the initial experiments the main effects on the run-time (the time in seconds it takes for the simulation to complete) was observed to be related to the problem size (number of sensors) and the number of blades used to do the computation. To show that this still holds for the expanded data set, the number of sensors vs. run-time was plotted (log-log) while holding the number of blades constant. The plot for 12 blades is found in Figure 4. This plots show that the number of blades and run-time have a significant log-log relationship. Plots for different number of blades look similar.

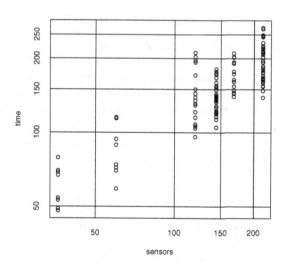

Fig. 4. Experiment 1, blades=12

Likewise, the number of blades vs. run-time was plotted while holding the number of sensors constant. The results for 216 sensors is found in Figure 5. Similarly, we see that blades vs. run-time also have a significant log-log relationship. It should also be noted that the results shown here are for this particular parameter set and problem structure. At the extremes of the parameter space other variables begin to have a non-trivial impact on the run-time.

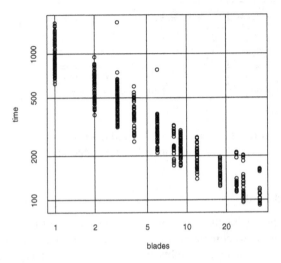

Fig. 5. Experiment 1, sensors=216

Figure 4 and 5 show the log-log relationship between run-time and blades and sensors. Using the software R [9], a multiple linear regression model of

$$log(time) \sim log(sensors) + log(blades)$$

was run on the entire data set. A summary of the model is shown in Table 2 for experiment 1. The low standard error and a multiple R-squared of 0.9156 indicates a good fit. The log-log relationship between problem size and run-time demonstrates that the environment scales well with problem size. The log-log relationship between run-time and the number of blades indicates that adding hardware has a positive impact on the simulation time. These two results indicate that the environment will scale well. In the next section we explore how the number of processes impacts performance, a factor of practical importance when scaling the problem to even larger sizes.

Table 2. Experiment 1 regression

Parameter	Estimate	Standard Error
Intercept	2.57	0.0396
log(sensors)	0.783	0.00796
log(blades)	-0.581	0.00400

4.2.2 Processes

The next contributing factor to run-time is the number of processes used per blade. The number of blades and sensors is fixed and the number of processes vs. run-time is shown in Figure 6.

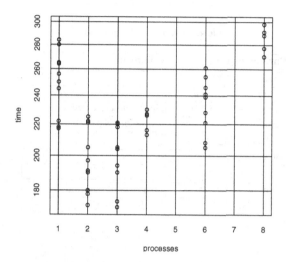

Fig. 6. Experiment 1, sensors=216, blades=9

This experiment shows that a single process performs surprisingly poorly given the multi-threaded nature of Java. This result indicates that the Icebox process must have affinity to a single processor. It is unclear at this time if the middleware architecture or the Java virtual machine itself is a contributing factor. Under the assumption of processor affinity and the combination of dual processors and hyper-threading, a good value should be somewhere between 2 and 4. This observation and informal experimentation for larger problem sizes confirms that we have made a good choice and that the actual number is probably around 3. Finding the exact value is not important for two reasons: (1) the number of processes is an integer value and (2) the exact value in this range does not have a significant impact on performance.

4.3   Experiment 2

Experiment 2 was run with 42 blades and is used to show how well the problem scales to large numbers. The range of parameter values used to construct valid configurations is summarized in Table 4. The log-log plot of the number of sensors and run-time is plotted in Figure 7. The relationship first observed in the first experiment still holds even at this scale. A similar linear-regression model of

$$log(time) \sim log(sensors)$$

was computed again using the statistical package R; the results of this model are summarized in Table 3. The model has a multiple R-squared factor of 0.9901, indicating a

Table 3. Experiment 2 regression

Parameter	Estimate	Standard Error
Intercept	-4.32	0.218
log(sensors)	1.22	0.0207

Table 4. Experiment 2 parameters

Parameter	Range	Comment
sensors	12096-98784	
targets	sensors/2	
networks	84-3360	blades*process*agents
children	5^2-12^2	sensors/network
blades	42	
processes	2	
agents	1-40	
runs	1	times a configuration is run
periods	12	length of simulation

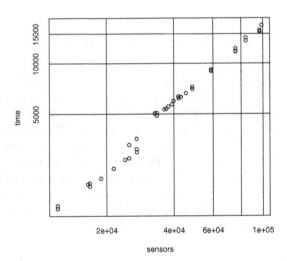

Fig. 7. Experiment 2

good fit. Using this model we can easily estimate how long a problem with a specific sensor count will take to complete. The model also shows that the environment continues to scale well and with a high level of predictably. Although statistically not valid, we could extend the model beyond the problem size explored to estimate even larger problem run-times.

4.4   Experimental Results

The experiments show that the problem run-time scales well with problem size and number of blades. Each experiment is built on the results of the previous in order to raise the number of sensors that could be simulated; in the end there were almost 100,000 of them. Even though at this point the simulation took just over 4 hours, there is no reason to believe that the problem will not continue to scale. Even more interesting would be to run the experiments on a larger computational cluster, thus pushing the problem to even greater sizes.

The experiments also revealed that the threading model of the underlying technology (Java and Ice) does not scale well across processors and merits further research. This result demonstrates the importance of using experimental techniques to detect performance issues and the necessity of finding good computational configurations to maximize performance. In the next section we discuss some of the research challenges that this work revealed.

5   Research Challenges

The distributed environment has two methods of managing the simulation, ad-hoc and monolithic. The first can be thought of as a loose collection of computational resources. As the resources are activated they first discover their neighbors and then join the simulation. In this case, clocks need to be coordinated and synchronized between agents. It is also possible that entire simulation domains (independently running simulations) must be joined. The join protocol must coordinate this joining activity, all in a distributed manner, without a centralized clock mechanism. The approach taken for the experiments done in this paper was to use a simple monolithic protocol designed to take advantage of the homogeneous layout and the simultaneous startup of the agents in order to avoid the problems of a distributed startup. The ad-hoc method is more applicable to a real deployment of a distributed environment, whereas the monolithic protocol is more applicable to an experimental simulation scenario.

Although the current ad-hoc method worked in the majority of cases presented in this paper, more dynamic and larger environments induce conditions where the protocol fails more often. When analyzed, the conditions needed to cause the problem seemed obscure, but the size of the problem ensured that even the most remote scenario where covered. Adding to the difficulty, failures in a distributed asynchronous environment are non-obvious and non-trivial to debug. These issues emphasize the need to develop and use rigorous protocols that are theoretically sound.

At the current scale the monolithic protocol was adequate. However, at this scale most parts of the configuration environment that rely on centralized mechanisms are beginning to approach failure at the upper bounds of the experiments. The shear size of the problem makes it difficult for single node to cope at even the operating-system and hardware levels. If the configuration environment, and by extension the problem, is going to scale to the next level the configuration environment must also be distributed. This challenge must be overcome before the environment can scale even further.

6 Related Literature

The development and execution of large scientific problems is not a trivial task. There is a wide range of approaches from distributed algorithms [7,18] to distributed artificial intelligence[12] and multi-agent systems [20]. What distinguishes this work is the combination of a distributed philosophy and the use of loosely coupled clusters.

Although the hardware used in this work is a collection of commodity based computers the environment does not subscribe to the job-based architecture that typifies a *Beowulf* style cluster [17]. Commodity gigabit networking and heterogeneous environments do not make traditional parallel computing, such as MPI[16], an obvious choice either. The result is a style of computation that is highly coupled but loosely synchronized using commodity hardware and middleware.

The "Farm Distributed Simulation Environment" [4,3] is an environment that uses a similar style of computation. It is also constructed of loosely coupled agents (*meta-agents*) distributed over workstations that are analogous to the *network agent* in this paper. The difference is in how time is managed. A system that uses a similar notion of time to the work in this paper is the System for Parallel Agent Discrete Event Simulation (SPADES) [14]. Unfortunately SPADES uses a centralized event and synchronization system, an important issue when considering scalability.

7 Conclusions

In this paper the performance and scalability of a cyberinfrastructure for distributed sensor-networks was evaluated. It was shown, for the multi-linked bargaining market model, that the problem size and the number of blades have a log-log relationship with the problem run-time for the range of problems run on the hardware. The experiments also showed that the distributed environment can handle very large sensor-network problems – on the scale of hundreds of thousands. However, for even larger scales, it was observed that even the environments configuration needs to be distributed.

Acknowledgements. The research presented in this paper was supported in part by NSF Grants # DMI-9978923, # DMI-0122173, # DMI-0330171, # IIS-0325168; NASA Ames Research Center Grants # NAG 2-1114, NCC 2-1180, NCC 2-1265, NCC 2-1348; and DARPA/AFRL Contract #F30602-99-2-0525. The two blade centers on which the experiments were run was provided by generous hardware grants from IBM and Sun Microsystems.

References

1. Henning, M.: Massively multiplayer middleware. ACM Queue Magazine 1(10) (2004)
2. Henning, M.: A new approach to object-oriented middleware. IEEE Internet Computing 8(1), 66–75 (2004)
3. Horling, B., Mailler, R., Lesser, V.: Farm: A Scalable Environment for Multi-Agent Development and Evaluation. In: Advances in Software Engineering for Multi-Agent Systems, pp. 220–237. Springer, Berlin (2004)

4. Horling, B., Mailler, R., Lesser, V.: The Farm Distributed Simulation Environment. Computer Science Technical Report 2004-12, University of Massachusetts (2004)
5. Horling, B., Vincent, R., Mailler, R., Shen, J., Becker, R., Rawlins, K., Lesser, V.: Distributed Sensor Network for Real Time Tracking. In: Proceedings of the 5th International Conference on Autonomous Agents, pp. 417–424. ACM Press, Montreal (2001)
6. Lesser, V., Ortiz, C.L., Tambe, M.: Distributed Sensor Networks: A Multiagent Perspective. Kluwer Academic Publishers, Dordrecht (2003)
7. Lynch, N.A.: Distributed Algorithms. Elsevier Science & Technology Books, Amsterdam (1996)
8. Mailler, R., Vincent, R., Lesser, V., Middelkoop, T., Shen, J.: Soft-real time, cooperative negotiation for distributed resource allocation. In: Proceedings of the AAAI Fall Symposium on Negotiation Methods for Autonomous Cooperative Systems, Falmouth, MA, pp. 63–69, FS-01-03 (2001)
9. Maindonald, J.H., Braun, J.A.: Data Analysis and Graphics Using R: An Example-Based Approach. Cambridge University Press, Cambridge (2002)
10. Middelkoop, T.: Distributed resource allocation using multi-linked bargaining markets. Ph.D. thesis, University of Massachusetts Amherst (2006)
11. Moehlman, T., Lesser, V.: Cooperative planning and decentralized negotiation in multi-fireboss phoenix. In: Proc. of the Workshop on Innovative Approaches to Planning, Scheduling and Control, San Diego, CA, pp. 144–159 (1990)
12. O'Hare, G.M., Jennings, N.R. (eds.): Foundations of Distributed Artificial Intelligence. John Wiley & Sons Inc., Chichester (1996)
13. Pedroni, S., Rappin, N.: Jython Essentials: Rapid Scripting in Java. O'Reilly Media, Sebastopol (incorporated, 2002)
14. Riley, P., Riley, G.: SPADES — a distributed agent simulation environment with software-in-the-loop execution. In: Chick, S., Sánchez, P.J., Ferrin, D., Morrice, D.J. (eds.) Winter Simulation Conference Proceedings, vol. 1, pp. 817–825 (2003)
15. Siegel, J., Klein, A., Thomas, A., Frantz, D., Mirsky, H.: CORBA Fundamentals and Programming. Wiley, John & Sons, Chichester (1996)
16. Snir, M., Otto, S., Huss-Lederman, S., Walker, D., Dongarra, J.: MPI–The Complete Reference, 2nd edn. The MPI-1 Core, vol. 1. The MIT Press, Cambridge (1998)
17. Sterling, T.L. (ed.): Beowulf Cluster Computing with Linux. MIT Press, Cambridge (2001)
18. Tanenbaum, A.S., Steen, M.V.: Distributed Systems: Principles and Paradigms. Prentice Hall, Englewood Cliffs (2001)
19. U.S. Department of Homeland Security: The national strategy for the physical protection of critical infrastructures and key assets. U.S. GPO, PR43.14:P56 (2003)
20. Weiss, G. (ed.): Multiagent Systems: A Modern Approach to Distributed Artificial Intelligence. MIT Press, Cambridge (1999)

Author Index

Lecture Notes in Artificial Intelligence (LNAI)